COMMUNICATIONS
AND NETWORKING
FOR THE IBM PC

Executive Editor: Terrell Anderson
Production Editor/Text Designer: Donna M. Griffin
Art Director/Cover Designer: Don Sellers
Assistant Art Director: Bernard Vervin

Typesetter: Harper Graphics, Inc., Waldorf, MD
Printer: R. R. Donnelley & Sons, Harrisonburg, VA
Typefaces: Times Roman (text), Souvenir Demi-Bold (display)
Index by: Frances Kianka

Note to Authors

Do you have a manuscript or a software program related to personal computers? Do you have an idea for developing such a project? If so, we would like to hear from you. The Brady Co. produces a complete range of books and applications software for the personal computer market. We invite you to write to David Culverwell, Editor-in-Chief, Robert J. Brady Co., Bowie, Maryland 20715.

COMMUNICATIONS
AND NETWORKING
FOR THE IBM PC

Larry E. Jordan
Bruce Churchill

Robert J. Brady Company
A Prentice-Hall Publishing and Communications Company
Bowie, Maryland 20715

Communications and Networking for the IBM PC

Library of Congress Cataloging in Publication Data

Jordan, Larry E., 1947–
  Communications and networking for the IBM PC.

  Includes Index.
  1. Data transmission systems.   2. IBM Personal Computer.
I. Churchill, Bruce, 1939– .   II. Title
TK5105.J67   1983   001.64′404   83-12250
ISBN 0-89303-385-5

Prentice-Hall International, Inc., London
Prentice-Hall Canada, Inc., Scarborough, Ontario
Prentice-Hall of Australia, Pty., Ltd., Sydney
Prentice-Hall of India Private Limited, New Delhi
Prentice-Hall of Japan, Inc., Tokyo
Prentice-Hall of Southeast Asia Pte. Ltd., Singapore
Whitehall Books, Limited, Petone, New Zealand
Editora Prentice-Hall Do Brasil LTDA., Rio de Janeiro

Printed in the United States of America

83 84 85 86 87 88 89 90 91 92 93 10 9 8 7 6 5 4 3 2 1

CONTENTS

PREFACE

This book is designed to introduce the communications novice to the data communications capabilities of the IBM Personal Computer. The development of the IBM Personal Computer is a significant event in the short history of microcomputers and the communications capabilities of the machine will make a major contribution to the revolution that is taking place in computer communications.

The purpose of this book is to introduce the reader to both the fundamentals and the applications of data communications on the IBM Personal Computer. The reasons for selecting data communications over other forms of data transfer are explored. The mechanics of data communications are discussed in sufficient detail to prepare the reader for discussions on communications hardware and software. Hardware and software discussions are included to give the reader a good background for the purchase and installation of both. These two topics are covered in general with explanations of capabilities and characteristics provided. Discussions of specific products available on the market are limited because they would become quickly outdated. The information presented should prepare the reader for the evaluation, selection, and use of both hardware and software as these products change and improve over the next few years.

Local area networks are also becoming popular with personal computers. Expensive hardware such as hard disks and letter quality printers can be shared by several microcomputers, thereby reducing the effective cost per work station for network configurations. This topic as it applies to the IBM Personal Computer is explored in both fundamental concept and practical application. This information should prove useful for the small business that needs network power but not the computing power of a mainframe system.

The future of communications is exciting and new. Applications of the technique are developing that will allow the user to reach out to information banks and to services never before available. Information that improves business performance and provides individual entertainment is available now and new horizons are developing rapidly. Some of these new horizons are presented.

On the practical side, problems sometimes arise during the initial stages of setting up data communications. Some typical problems and solutions to those problems are presented as questions and answers at the close of the book.

This material bridges the gap between the fundamentals of communications and the practical aspects of making it work for you. The material was derived from the authors' experience in teaching communications to IBM Personal Computer novices and provides a good starting point for other communication novices.

Larry E. Jordan
Gaithersburg, Md.

Bruce Churchill
Fairfax, Va.

ACKNOWLEDGMENTS

This book, like most other books, owes its existence to the efforts of many people. Our wives, Betsy and Kathy, showed great patience during its development. The reviews of Richard Bowers and others provided fresh ideas and helped clarify concepts. The typing assistance of Mary Crook was also instrumental in getting the book off to a good start and keeping the momentum going during its development. Our thanks go to Harry Gaines, President of the Brady Company, and David Culverwell, Editor-in-Chief of the Brady Company for their confidence and support. Thanks also go to Terry Anderson and Jessie Katz of the Brady Company for their coordination and assistance during the review of the book.

LIMITS OF LIABILITY AND DISCLAIMER OF WARRANTY

The author and publisher of this book have used their best efforts in preparing this book and the programs contained in it. These efforts include the development, research, and testing of the programs to determine their effectiveness. The author and the publisher make no warranty of any kind, expressed or implied, with regard to these programs, the text, or the documentation contained in this book. The author and the publisher shall not be liable in any event for claims of incidental or consequential damages in connection with, or arising out of, the furnishing, performance, or use of the text or the programs. The programs contained in this book and on any diskettes are intended for use of the original purchaser-user. The diskettes may be copied by the original purchaser-user for backup purposes without requiring express permission of the copyholder.

TRADEMARKS

IBM Personal Computer, IBM-BASIC, VM/370, MVS/TSO, Time Manager, and PC-DOS are trademarks of IBM.

Word Plus is a trademark of Oasis Software.

CP/M, CP/M-86, MP/M-86, CP/NET, and Concurrent CP/M-86 are trademarks of Digital Research, Inc.

WordStar is a trademark of MicroPro International Corporation.

Omninet, CONSTELLATION, CONSTELLATION I, CONSTELLATION II, Mirror, and Multiplexer are trademarks of Corvus Systems.

Ethernet is a trademark of Xerox Corporation.

SuperCalc is a trademark of Sorcim Corporation.

COMPAQ is a trademark of COMPAQ Computer Corporation.

PCnet is a trademark of Orchid Technology.

WANGNET is a trademark of Wang Laboratories.

Localnet 20 is a trademark of Sytek.

EtherLink, EtherShare, EtherPrint, and EtherMail, are trademarks of 3Com Corporation.

dBASE II is a trademark of Ashton-Tate.

PC-TALK is a trademark of FREEWARE.

PCMODEM is a trademark of Solution Software Systems.

HOSTCOMM is a trademark of JANADON, Inc.

Hayes Stack Smartmodem is a trademark of Hayes Microcomputer Products Inc.

TELENET is a trademark of GTE Telenet Communications Corporation.

TYMNET is a trademark of Tymshare.

OASIS-16 is a trademark of Phase One System.

VisiCalc, VisiFile, VisiDex, VisiTrend/Plot, Visi Desktop Plan, and VisiSchedule are trademarks of VisiCorp.

XENIX and Multiplan are trademarks of Microsoft Corporation.

1-2-3 is a trademark of Lotus Development Corporation.

Remote Access is a trademark of Custom Software.

Lync is a trademark of Midnight Software.

THE SOURCE, CSTORE, BARTER, MUSICSOURCE, RADIOSOURCE, PROFES-SIONAL BOOK CENTER, Participate, and SourceMail are trademarks of Source Telecomputing Corporation.

CompuServe is a trademark of the H&R Block Company.

PCcrayon is a trademark of PCsoftware.

TELIgraph is a trademark of MicroTaure Inc.

EasyWriter is a trademark of Information Unlimited Software, Inc.

Volkswriter is a trademark of LifeTree Software.

VIDTEX and EMAIL are trademarks of CompuServe Information Service.

QUBE is a trademark of Warner Communications.

Dow Jones News Retrieval Service is a trademark of Dow Jones & Company, Inc.

Pfs:Graph, Pfs:File, and Pfs:Report are trademarks of Software Publishing.

Colby is a trademark of Colby Computers.

Eagle 1600 is a trademark of Eagle.

ULCnet is a trademark of Orange Compu Company.

Columbia MPC is a trademark of Columbia Data Products, Inc.

Comp-U-Store is a trademark of Compu-U-Card.

1

Introduction to Data Communications

The introduction of the IBM Personal Computer has produced a great deal of excitement in the microcomputer world. One of the PC's most useful capabilities is data communications. To take advantage of that capability, however, requires that the user have some understanding of the techniques of communications. To help pave the way for an easy transition into the world of Personal Computer communications, this book provides facts and information on the subject. After a discussion of the roles and current applications of data communications, the book guides you through the technical aspects of communications, the hardware required to support communications, and the software required to make your PC communicate. This information has been designed to take the mystery out of IBM Personal Computer communications and to help you make educated decisions on the purchase and use of both communications hardware and software.

I. CURRENT ROLES OF COMMUNICATIONS

The two major categories of communications usage are business and personal, but there are many gray areas between these two major categories. Big businesses with mainframe computers are interested in communications because it allows them remote access to their centralized data bases, mainframe computing and information handling centers. Small businesses are interested in communications because it allows them to share expensive hardware between small computers and to access time-sharing information and business systems. Home-users are interested in communications because it allows them to obtain information, shop from home, and reach forms of computer entertainment not otherwise available to them.

There are also many communications buffs who are simply thrilled by the aspect of conversing or communicating with another computer or service system and will frequently do so whether or not they achieve anything worthwhile. This type of com-

1

munication often results in useful facts and information moving from one part of the country to another. For example, a Personal Computer programmer in Dallas, Texas may produce a new sorting program and communicate the utility to a friend who in turn communicates it to a national electronic bulletin board where it is then communicated to thousands of Personal Computer users, all within a period of days. It would take two or three months for this same information to reach users through computer magazines and journals. Thus, a harmless pastime becomes a useful service in the business of communications.

II. ADVANTAGES OF ELECTRONIC DATA TRANSFER

The three primary advantages of electronic information transfer are that it can be done at any time of the day or night, it can be done at a rapid rate of speed, and because of the standardization of communication codes, it can be done between equipment made by different vendors. Complete transmission error checking is also possible. Text can be transmitted at 120 characters per second over most standard telephone lines which means that an entire 200 page book can be transmitted in approximately 40 minutes. This may sound like a great deal of transmission time, but when you stop to consider that the book can be completely reformatted or printed in a variety of styles on the receiving end without rekeying the text in, it may be well worth the time.

Business situations often require rapid, accurate information transmission across town or country to stay one step ahead of the competition, and data communications helps make that possible. Express delivery and facsimile (telecopy) services are two other options available for information transfer, but these services have limitations. The express delivery services usually take at least 24 hours for delivery coast-to-coast and packages usually have to be sent on a scheduled basis. Telecopy is an immediate transfer of information, but the quality of the end product is not always satisfactory for business use and the process is time consuming. Sending large volumes of information by telecopy is impractical on both a cost and time consumption basis. There is also the option of transporting information physically on electronic disk or tape so that further processing can take place on the receiving end. Physical transfer of information, however, requires transport time and the transport medium is subject to electromagnetic, environmental, and physical handling damage. Incompatibility between disk storage formats used by the computers on the sending and receiving ends may also make physical transfer of information impractical.

Hobbyists and home-users of microcomputers sometimes want or need up-to-the-minute information on stock prices, news on events that are taking place in the world, or information pertaining to their computers. Access through communications to time-sharing information sources or local electronic bulletin boards allows these users to obtain that information. This same category of users is also often interested in obtaining public domain software. Data communications allows them to transfer programs from time-sharing systems and personal computer host systems to their own disk storage units. Access to these public domain programs might not otherwise be possible unless there is an active user group in the area willing to make the data communications transfers and then distribute the programs on public domain diskettes.

Electronic transfer is not, however, always the best method of getting data from one place to another. If time is not a critical constraint or if the information will not require further development on the receiving end, other methods of transfer may be more cost efficient. Also, physical transport of electronic media may be required due to copy protection provided with software.

There are many other considerations that must be made before you decide to go with electronic transfer of information. All those considerations are not presented in this text. Some common uses of Personal Computer communications are presented, however, to give your imagination a good starting point. The pros and cons of electronic transfer can be better assessed with a good understanding of data communications.

III. BUSINESS APPLICATIONS

One prevalent business application of computer communications is the collection of data from several sources during the compilation of a single larger set of data. For example, a host computer can be set up to receive portions of software from several authors; then those portions can be linked together to form a volume of text or a computer program. The development of this book is a good example of that kind of communication. As each section was completed by one author, it was transmitted to the other author for review. Each segment was preprocessed by an author, reviewed and modified by both authors, then post-processed for delivery to the publisher. Thus, portions of the book were created in an interactive off-line mode, then transmitted to another author for further off-line development. This procedure took advantage of the highly efficient interactive method of creating text using word processing and met the time constraints of getting copy to another author on a tight schedule.

Aside from the development of text and software using a team approach, there are many other advantages in the electronic transfer of data via the Personal Computer. The technique can also be used to put together expertise from different parts of the country and can allow work to be performed at home. Businesses are always looking for ways to reduce overhead costs, and combining remotely produced portions of a project as well as portions produced by participants who work at home could produce a deciding competitive edge for some companies. There are problems associated with this kind of development work, such as quality control of contributions, elimination of duplicated efforts, and the remote scheduling of tasks which will require special project management talents; but the offsetting advantages may make such development attractive.

IV. INFORMATION SERVICE APPLICATIONS

You probably receive at least one Personal Computer magazine or publication each month and find that some, if not all the information presented, is already out of date.

Because of the lead time required to compile and publish these periodicals, publishers are unable to provide you with up-to-the-minute changes that are taking place in the industry. To get this kind of information, you have to rely on word-of-mouth transfer of facts or tune in to a medium that changes as rapidly as the Personal Computer world changes. Other than local users groups, the best sources of such information are the electronic information services, sometimes called *information utilities*.

Electronic information sources take many forms, but they can be generally categorized as either profit-making businesses information systems or private non-profit *bulletin boards*. Some examples of business information services are *THE SOURCE, CompuServe*, the *Dow Jones News Retrieval Service*, and *NewsNet*. These services provide individuals and businesses with a wealth of information ranging from stock quotations to current news, and they can be accessed by dialing local telephone numbers in most major metropolitan areas. The new low cost long distance rates offered by *MCI* and *Sprint* also make these services attractive for users located outside major metropolitan areas.

The information utilities currently available actually function as *information brokers*. These services buy information from a variety of sources, store the information, and provide user access to the stored data. The sources of information are responsible for updating the data, and the information utilities are responsible for maintaining the storage and access hardware and software. Because of this division of responsibility, the user is assured of getting reliable access to well-maintained information. Summaries of the services provided by the major information utilities and the current costs of those services are provided in Tables 1-1, 1-2, 1-3, and 1-4.

The major advantage offered by these electronic information services is the *timeliness of the information* they provide. Stock quotations can be updated continuously as can other items such as the news and local area activities. Magazines and published periodicals cannot match such timeliness although television, radio, and newspapers can come close. These sources of information do not, however, allow you to do selective searching for information based on subject matter or key words, which is possible using the electronic alternatives.

For the IBM Personal Computer owner, both THE SOURCE and CompuServe have special areas set aside for IBM PC information exchange. By gaining access to these areas, you are apprised of the latest news and developments associated with the PC. You will also have access to tips and utilities provided by other PC owners. In addition, you will have access to public domain software, some of which is actually better than some of the commercially available packages that purportedly perform the same tasks. Because of the lack of quality control of the software placed in the files of these services, however, you may also find software there that does not perform as advertised by the authors. You or someone you know who has the expertise will have to test the software you obtain from these services to be sure it performs properly.

Finally, the major advantage these services provide is access to thousands of other Personal Computer owners, one of whom may have a solution to your most pressing problem. An uncanny phenomenon of the microcomputer world is the abundance of users who are more than happy to share solutions to problems just for the sake of

Table 1-1. THE SOURCE.

Current Usage Costs:	300 Baud	1200 Baud
Prime Time (7am–6pm)	$20.75/hr	$25.75/hr
Evenings/Weekends/Holidays	$ 7.75/hr	$10.75/hr
After Midnight	$ 5.75/hr	$ 8.75/hr

Minimum Cost of Service:	
Initial Fee	$100.00
Monthly Fee	$ 10.00

Sample of Services:

- UPI News Service—Keyword search capability lets you locate specific news or sports stories within minutes after UPI release.
- Electronic Mail—Messages or reports can be transmitted immediately to other subscribers anywhere in the country.
- Electronic Travel Service—Allows you to make airline and hotel reservations and charge them to a major credit card.
- The New York Times Consumer Library—Allows you access to the New York Times Consumer Data bases containing timely articles on a variety of current issues.
- Computer Search International—Allows a company to search for employees using the services of a network of executive recruitment firms located in major cities across the nation.
- Financial Services—Provides timely information on stocks, bonds, commodities, precious metals, futures, etc.
- Information on Demand—A reach organization which will send you hard copy reports on any available article throughout the free world with language translations when required.
- Business Programming Power—BASIC, Fortran, Cobol, RPG11 and assembly language are available for you to write and run your own programs.
- Chat—Allows you to interact with other users who are on-line when you are.
- Consumer Aids—Information to help you solve energy problems or improve your health.

How To Start: Purchase the package from a local microcomputer dealer or call THE SOURCE at 800-336-3366.

helping a desperate soul. If you have a problem and ask for suggested solutions in an open request (unprotected message to anyone who calls in) you are likely to get several suggested solutions within a short period of time. If your problem is legitimate and no one can come up with a suggested solution, the problem may become a major issue among IBM PC owners simply because of the visibility of the complaint. In any event, you are more likely to get sound suggestions from the myriad of service users than you are from some local retailers who do not maintain technical staffs to handle owner problems.

Table 1-2. CompuServe Information Service.

Current Usage Costs:	300 Baud	1200 Baud
Prime Time (8am–6pm)	$22.50/hr	$35.00/hr
Evenings and Weekends	$ 5.00/hr	$17.50/hr

Minimum Cost of Service:		
Initial Fee	$19.95	
Minimum Monthly Fee	None	

Sample of Services:

- News, weather, and sports from major newspaper and international news services
- Financial information with updates and historical information on stocks, bonds, and mutual funds
- Entertainment—theater, book, movie, and restaurant reviews plus information on opera, symphony, ballet, dance, museums, and galleries
- Electronic Mail—you can create, edit, send, and receive messages from other users
- Home Information—government publications and articles from home magazines
- Personal Computing Services:

Software exchange	Line printer art gallery
Word processing	Programming languages
Business software	Educational software
Computer games	IBM Personal Computer area

- Citizens Band radio simulation
- National Bulletin Board system and special interest bulletin boards
- Feedback to CompuServe—comments, suggestions, and questions
- CompuServe System News on new or modified services

How To Start: Purchase a Videotex package (Catalog number 26-2224) from your local Radio Shack store.

V. LOCAL AREA INFORMATION EXCHANGE

Another category of communication that is proving to be popular with the IBM Personal Computer is *local area information exchange*. This includes both *public bulletin boards* and private personal computer *host systems* which are set up by individuals and users groups just for exchanging tips, software, and information about the Personal Computer.

To give you some perspective on the demand for this type of service, the Washington, D.C. area's Capital PC User Group bulletin board logged over 6400 calls during its

Table 1-3. Dow Jones News Retrieval Service.

Current Usage Costs*:	300 and 1200 Baud
Prime Time (6am–6pm)	$0.60/min–$1.20/min
Evenings/Weekends	$0.20/min–$0.90/min
Minimum Costs of Services:	
Initial Fee	$19.95–$95.00
Minimum Monthly Fee	None

Sample of Services:

- Financial News—as recent as 90 seconds or as old as 90 days; from the pages of the Wall Street Journal, Barron's, and the Dow Jones News Service.
- Current Market Quotes:
    1. Stocks and warrants, corporate bonds, and options updated continuously.
    2. Nasdag OTC stocks updated hourly.
    3. Selected U.S. Treasury Notes, bonds, and mutual funds updated daily.

- Detailed financial statistics including stock price, volume, and financial indicators are available for all New York and American Stock Exchange traded companies plus 800 over-the-counter traded companies.
- Wall Street Week—transcripts of the PBS television program discussing the latest economic developments.

How To Start: 1. Purchase a Videotex package (Catalog number 26-2224) from your local Radio Shack store.

2. Purchase the IBM Dow Jones Reporter package from any IBM Product Center or other IBM Personal Computer retail store.

*Each service shown in the sample of services has a different cost schedule.

first seven months of operation. The average call resulted in a connect time of 40 minutes during which the caller read messages and tips on various operational characteristics and anomalies associated with the PC or its peripherals. Programs and software patches were also downloaded. Of the 6400 calls received by the bulletin board, 45% were long distance calls from outside the Washington, D.C. area. Because of the lack of timely information available on the PC, people were willing to pay long distance telephone tolls to get such information.

Local area bulletin boards can be entertaining as well as informative. Some offer games that can be played by either single individuals or by simultaneous correspondence with other users. Some bulletin boards also provoke controversy by offering a forum for the discussion of such issues as morality, religion, and abortion. Others allow local users groups to post notices for upcoming meetings and products that will be available for purchase at the meeting. Many bulletin boards also allow callers to leave messages for other individual callers or to leave general nature messages such as comments on

Table 1-4. NewsNet.

Current Usage Costs:	300 Baud	1200 Baud
Prime Time	$24.00/hr	$48.00/hr
Evenings (8pm–8am)	$18.00/hr	$36.00/hr

Cost of Service:	
Initial Fee	None
Minimum Monthly Fee	$15.00

Sample of Services:

NewsNet offers electronic newsletter editions of many national newsletters. The service provides keyword searches, archival indexing, and publisher contact covering the following topics:

Advertising and Marketing	Publishing and Broadcasting
Aerospace	Government and Regulatory
Automotive	Health and Hospitals
Building and Construction	International
Chemical	Investment
Education	Management
Electronics and Computer	Office
Energy	Politics
Entertainment and Leisure	Telecommunications
Environment	Real Estate
Farming and Food	Research and Development
Finance and Accounting	Social Sciences Taxation
General Business	

How to Start: Telephone NewsNet at (800) 257-5114 or (609) 452-1511 (in New Jersey) and request a contract package.

---

products for all callers to read. A summary of these characteristics plus others associated with local bulletin boards are shown in Table 1-5.

The recent introduction of software that allows you to turn your Personal Computer into an unattended host is also initiating a revolutionary use of communications for the PC. The introduction of PC operating systems that allows the operation of such software while the Personal Computer owner simultaneously does other work on the machine will also advance the use of host software.

A detailed list of the capabilities of a private host communications system is shown in Table 1-6. As you can see from this array of capabilities, host software allows individuals, users groups, and companies to set up IBM Personal Computers to do a great deal of work for them. Messages and software can be exchanged between friends, exchanged among the members of a users group, or exchanged among the employees of a company. This type of software also allows companies to advertise their wares and take electronic orders for hardware and software on a 24-hour-a-day basis. Other

Table 1-5. Typical bulletin board features.

Leave Message—Allows you to leave a private message to one individual or a public message for anyone who calls in (directed to "ALL").

Scan Messages—Allows you to scan brief summaries of all messages and mark ones of interest for later retrieval.

Retrieve Message—Allows you to retrieve either marked or specified message numbers.

Kill Message—Allows you to delete a message you left earlier.

Userlog—Allows you to see a list of recent callers' names and locations.

Bulletins—Gives you a series of messages left by the system operator.

Information—Gives you information on the bulletin board hardware and software.

Help—Gives novice users help in using the bulletin board.

Download—Allows you to obtain public domain software directly over the telephone.

Upload—Allows you to place public domain software on the bulletin board for other users to later download.

Chat—Allows you to page the system operator for an on-line electronic chat session.

Expert Mode—Allows you to change the detailed menu to a brief abbreviated menu or allows you to eliminate menus completely.

Format Screen—Allows you to change the screen display from 80 to 40 columns.

Alter Baud—Allows you to switch data transfer rate while on-line.

Merchandise—Allows you to order equipment or software while on-line.

Terminate—Allows you to terminate the communication session and log-off the bulletin board.

---

applications of host systems will also develop as use of the IBM Personal Computer continues to advance.

These local area information exchange items are presented to illustrate two points. First, communication with local area information services is an important and vital part of IBM Personal Computer communications. And, second, the hobbyist and home user is also going to be a significant user of the Personal Computer's communication capabilities. As private host and public bulletin board software for the Personal Computer becomes more readily available, more users are going to be "coming on-line" with communications.

VI. COMMUNICATION NETWORK SYSTEMS

After a discussion of all the reasons for using Personal Computer communications and the various applications of communications, it is appropriate to discuss communication network systems. Network systems, as they are discussed here, pertain to the services available to the public for communicating between an IBM Personal Computer and the various information sources discussed earlier in the chapter. *Local area networking* of Personal Computers will be covered in Chapter 6.

Table 1-6. Example of personal host communications.

Software Name: HOSTCOMM
Version: 1.1
Description: IBM Personal Computer Host Communications System
Published by: N F Systems, Ltd., P.O. Box 76363, Atlanta, Ga. 30358
Written by: JANADON, Inc.
Software Capabilities:

- Automatically answers incoming calls
- Greets callers (computers or terminals) with general messages
- Delivers special messages to designated callers at log-on
- Allows callers to leave the HOSTCOMM operator messages:
    1. Up to 16 lines of text from all callers
    2. Up to 50 lines of text from selected callers
    3. Messages may be directed to the Personal Computer printer or disk
- Screens callers based on tri-level password system:
    1. Terminates unauthorized callers
    2. Allows access to one of two main menus
    3. Allows access to one of nine file receive/transmit directories

- Allows selected callers to execute programs from remote locations
- Allows unattended operations for long periods of time
- Allows operation with printer on or off
- Allows selection of communication baud rate, parity, number of data bits, and number of stop bits
- Allows HOSTCOMM system operator to "chat" with callers in on-line conversation mode
- Allows callers to receive text files from or transmit text files to the HOSTCOMM system

The oldest and most commonly used network is the public telephone system. Because of the widespread availability of this system, it is frequently used for microcomputer communications. For local area communication or infrequent long distance communication, this network is a good choice for Personal Computer owners. For frequent long distance communication, however, the user should consider other *common carrier services*. Recent Federal Communication Commission deregulation actions have resulted in the development of several new *public networks*.

The two most commonly used alternatives to the public telephone system are *value-added networks* and *private telephone systems*. The value-added systems such as *Tymnet* and *Telenet* use special hardware and software to perform the routing (called *packet-switching*) of data between connections in a network. The network is made up of leased public telephone circuits and hardware, and the service rates are less than those charged for public telephone services. Besides packet-switching of data, these services provide *backup equipment*, *alternate data routing*, and *error-checking* of transmitted data. Because of the redundancy of equipment used and the error-checking performed, these services provide more reliable and accurate data transfer than that achieved using the public telephone system. During certain periods of the day, however, these attributes may be offset somewhat by *degraded response time* caused by heavy user loading. Degraded response time results in longer connect-times for batch file transfers and annoying delays for interactive communication.

The other major category of common carrier is the *private telephone networks*. Two of the major competitors in this category are *MCI* and *Sprint*. Both of these services require you to dial a local access code plus an authorization code before dialing a long distance number, but the savings in long distance toll charges can be substantial if you do much long distance communicating. Generally, the longer the distance, the greater the savings compared to Bell System charges. The rates, number of cities served, and the quality of these services are constantly changing, however, so a potential user would be well advised to thoroughly investigate all aspects of each service before deciding to go with a particular one for data communications. Other new private networks are also being introduced that will provide competition for MCI and Sprint, and these services should also be investigated. Some users may find that a combination of two or more of these services may be needed in order for all their needs to be met.

VII. GROWING EXCITEMENT

With all the data communications applications currently in use, it is easy to see why people are getting interested in this application of the IBM Personal Computer. To take advantage of all these opportunities, however, it is necessary to have some understanding of the mechanics of data communications. Much that you will learn about communications will come from trial and error on the PC, but having a good background in the subject will make that learning process progress much faster. The following chapters are designed to give you the background you need to get into this exciting field of microcomputer application.

2

Taking the Mystery Out of Communications

There are many buzz words associated with microcomputer data communications, and this chapter takes some of the mystery out of these terms. In addition, the following paragraphs will provide a good background for the discussion of IBM Personal Computer hardware and software contained in later chapters. This chapter is a good reference to use when terms and concepts in communications articles are not clear.

I. DATA COMMUNICATIONS OVERVIEW

The phrase *data communications* is broad in scope and covers everything from the transfer of data between disk drives and memory to the transfer of data from the IBM Personal Computer to a mainframe system in another country via satellite. That broad a scope is much too large to be adequately covered in a single book. Since there are many good books available that explain the concepts and details of microcomputer input/output communications with peripherals, this book concentrates on the aspect of data communications between the IBM Personal Computer and other computers. Some aspects of internal communication and communication with peripherals are discussed, but only as background for the discussion of external communications.

The IBM Personal Computer, like all other digital computers, stores and processes data as signals that represent 1's and 0's. Each of these 1's and 0's represent a *binary digit (bit)* of information. The IBM PC stores these bits in groups of eight called *bytes*. The PC also stores pairs of bytes (16 total bits) as *words*. Although information may occupy two bytes of total storage space in the PC's memory, it can only be communicated one byte at a time because the PC's *internal data bus* is eight data lines wide. Thus, one byte of data at a time can be transferred between internal PC devices or transferred between the PC and a device that allows the PC to connect with the rest of the world. A simplified diagram of the major data communication flow paths used by the IBM PC is shown in Figure 2-1.

Although all IBM PC data are stored and communicated as bits, rules must be followed during storage and transfer of data. The *central processing unit (CPU)* and all its peripherals must "speak the same language" or data transferred and stored will not be useful. *Rules* and *conventions* must be followed or devices provided for use in the PC will be incompatible. Rules and conventions must also be followed in the design and implementation of devices used for external communications between the Personal Computer and other computer systems. These data communication rules and conventions are primarily developed by the standards organizations shown in Table 2-1.

The ISO seven layer model referred to in Table 2-1 was developed for large computer networks, but its rules apply to the IBM Personal Computer as well when its communications extend to other remote computer systems. The model is shown graphically in Figure 2-2 and each layer is described briefly in Table 2-2.

This model is presented to give the reader a feel for the standardization in communications. The existence of these layers is seldom a concern for communication users. The layers are designed to make communication functions more manageable

Table 2-1. Standards organizations.

IEEE

The Institute of Electrical and Electronic Engineers (IEEE) is an American professional group that establishes electrical standards. The organization has a microprocessor standards committee that sets electrical and electronic standards for the design of microcomputer components and systems.

EIA

The Electronics Industries Association (EIA) is an organization that represents American manufacturers. The EIA publishes standards such as RS-232-C and RS-449 that govern the electrical characteristics of connections between the personal computer and external peripherals such as printers and modems.

CCITT

The Consultative Committee in International Telegraphy and Telephony (CCITT) is an International Telecommunications Union (ITU) committee. Two study groups within the CCITT develop data communications standards. The standards produced by the CCITT study groups are international versions of the standards produced by the EIA.

ISO

The International Standards Organization (ISO) is a worldwide group composed of standards organization representatives from member nations. The American National Standards Institute (ANSI) represents the United States. The ISO develops international standards for data communications. A seven layer model was developed by this organization to define a universal architecture for interconnecting heterogeneous computer systems.

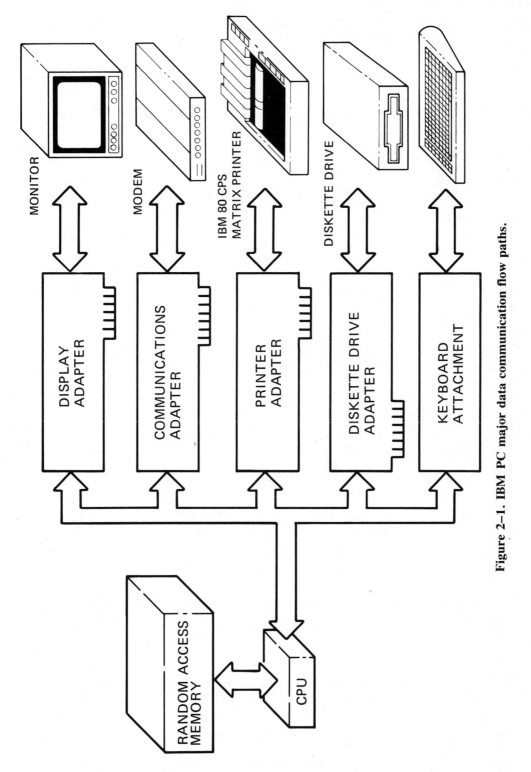

Figure 2–1. IBM PC major data communication flow paths.

COMMUNICATIONS LINE

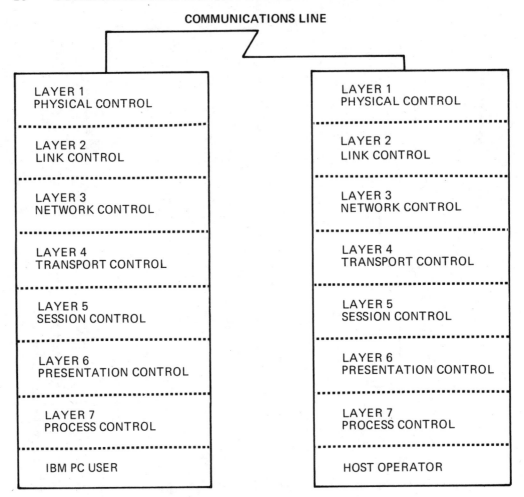

Figure 2–2. ISO seven layer model.

and useful and the existence of the layered design actually aids in hiding the complexity of communications from the user.

The layered or modular design of communication systems also helps to prevent significant system redesigns when parts of a system change—as they always do in the rapidly changing world of computers. By isolating functions into layers and standardizing each layer, the design and implementation of systems can be performed within each layer independently of the other layers. This concept is not very different from other common forms of communication. Take voice communication by telephone as an example. For two people to effectively communicate by telephone, they must be able to convey a concept by using a language and a physical means of transporting the verbalization of that language. The concept, such as the solution to an engineering problem, has rules that govern its implementation that are independent of the rules that govern the language used to convey that concept. The rules that govern the language

Table 2-2. ISO seven layer model.

Layer 1: Physical Control

Rules that apply to the physical hardware used to transfer data bits. Interface cables and connectors covered by the EIA RS-232-C and RS-449 standards fall into this category.

Layer 2: Link Control

Rules that apply to the transfer of blocks of data over a physical link. This layer governs the information that must precede and follow blocks of data and defines a protocol for the data transfers. The synchronous data link control (SDLC) used by some mainframe networks fall into this category.

Layer 3: Network Control

Rules that apply to computers that are communicating but not connected to the same physical line. This layer governs the use of multiple lines and circuits used during communications and ensures that discrete packets of information are delivered to remote computers in the same sequence as they were transmitted.

Layer 4: Transport End-to-End Control

Governs the end-to-end integrity of transmissions between two users to prevent lost transactions, prevents double processing of transactions, controls the flow of transactions, and ensures proper addressing of user machines. This layer provides a standard user interface with a transport service regardless of the type of network used.

Layer 5: Session Control

Governs the process of setting up or terminating a communication session. This layer checks to determine if proper communication is taking place. If proper communication is not taking place, this layer must restore the session without data loss or terminate the session in accordance with specified rules if the session cannot be properly restored.

Layer 6: Presentation Layer

Governs the character set and data code used for communication. Printer and screen displays are also governed by this layer. The conversion of one character set to another and the compacting of a character stream into a smaller bit stream is also controlled by this layer. Communication software design that involves character code translation and terminal features fall into this category.

Layer 7: Process Control

Governs applications of communications that interface with other high level functions such as distributed data base activities and file transfers. This layer prevents data transfer integrity problems or data transfer speed mismatches with receiving devices.

---

used to communicate are also independent of the rules that govern the design of the telephone communications equipment. More than one concept can be discussed without the necessity to switch to other languages, or another language can be used to convey the same concept without the necessity to change the design of the telephone system. The independence of each of these layers reduces the total complexity of communications by allowing one layer to change without another layer having to necessarily change. This same concept applies to data communications and is implemented through the seven layer ISO model.

The remainder of this chapter discusses the implementation of the rules and standards developed by the communication standards organizations. A thorough understanding of these concepts is not necessary to perform data communications, but the information provides a good background for the solution to communication problems that may arise. It also provides a foundation for the hardware and software discussions provided in later chapters.

II. DATA TRANSFER MODES

The IBM Personal Computer uses two modes of data transfer depending on the computer's proximity to the device with which it is communicating. For distances less than 100 feet, data can be transferred using *parallel communications*, whereas data transfers over distances greater than 100 feet generally are done using *serial communications*. Although both methods fall under the heading of *input/output (I/O)*, there are many differences in the way they are performed. The following paragraphs explore both modes of communication, but serial communication is explored in more detail because of its relevance to other data communications topics contained in this book.

PARALLEL I/O

In parallel data transfer, eight data bits are simultaneously moved from one device to another. As illustrated in Figure 2-3, the sending device transmits eight data bits through eight separate data lines called a *data bus*. The data are received by the destination device over those same eight data lines, and the data are used without modification or translation. After all the publicity indicating that the Personal Computer is a 16-bit microcomputer, this explanation of 8-bit data transfer may seem inappropriate, but it does apply to the PC. The Personal Computer does use the *16-bit Intel 8088 microprocessor*, but it communicates internally through an *eight-bit data bus*. The 16-bit data words or instructions used by the 16-bit CPU are simply transmitted in sets of eight bits.

Parallel data buses used in the transfer of parallel data may take several physical forms, but each form accomplishes the same result. Most of the Personal Computer internal data buses are printed circuit boards and tracing the path of the flow of data may prove difficult for a hardware novice. Other internal buses, such as the cable connecting the disk drive controller board to the disk drive, are flat ribbon cables and can be easily traced. External data buses, on the other hand, are often round shielded cables with the shield material grounded to the chassis of the Personal Computer. This latter form of cable is used with most dot matrix parallel printers and serves to trap extraneous radio frequency signals.

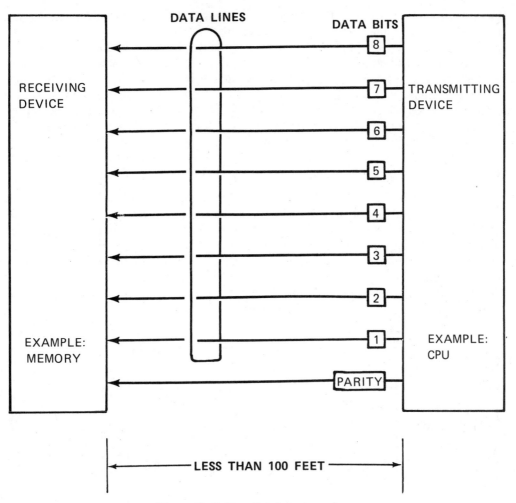

Figure 2–3. Parallel data transfer.

SERIAL I/O

In serial data transfer, one data bit at a time is transmitted between the source and the destination. Compared to the simultaneous transfer of groups of eight data bits that takes place in parallel communication, this type of communication does not appear to be a fast technique of moving data, and in actual practice it is not as fast as parallel transfer. Why then, you might ask, does anyone choose that alternative over parallel transfer? The answer to that question is the same as the answer to many other hardware design questions—serial data transfer is chosen when the economics and practicality of hardware implementation dictate that it must be chosen.

Parallel data transfer requires that a cable containing at least eight data lines be installed between two communicating computers. At short distances (less than 100 feet) that can be done at a reasonable cost. For long distance data transfers, however, it becomes more economical to use existing telephone equipment than to install expensive parallel signal amplifiers and parallel cable. Because of the design of the telephone lines and equipment, it is necessary to go to serial data transfer to use this equipment. If computers and data communications had been invented before voice communications, it would probably be possible to use long distance parallel data communications today, but technology did not evolve in that sequence. Voice communications came first and long distance voice communications did not require eight parallel signal paths. Now that tremendous sums of money have been invested in voice communications equipment, it makes good sense to convert data communications into signals that are compatible with that equipment.

As illustrated in Figure 2-4, the sending device in the Personal Computer transmits eight simultaneous bits of data to the serial conversion hardware, but data bits move sequentially one bit at a time from that equipment to the receiving station. The parallel data bit stream must go through a transformation to a serial bit stream at the transmit end and then go through a transformation back to a parallel bit stream at the receiving end. The process is not, however, as easy as it looks in Figure 2-4. The device that does the data transformation at each end of the communications link must do a great deal of work to make the transferred data usable at the receiving end.

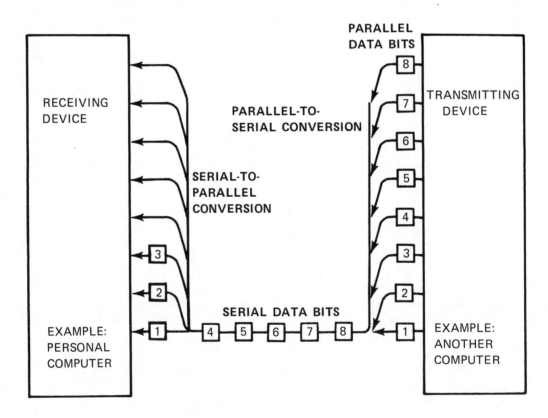

Figure 2–4. Serial data transfer.

Serial Duplex Configurations

Figure 2-5 shows the three commonly used conventions for serial data lines. The *simplex configuration* only allows data flow in one direction and is sometimes called a *unidirectional data bus*. The *half-duplex configuration*, on the other hand, allows data flow in either direction and is called a *bidirectional data bus*. The half-duplex

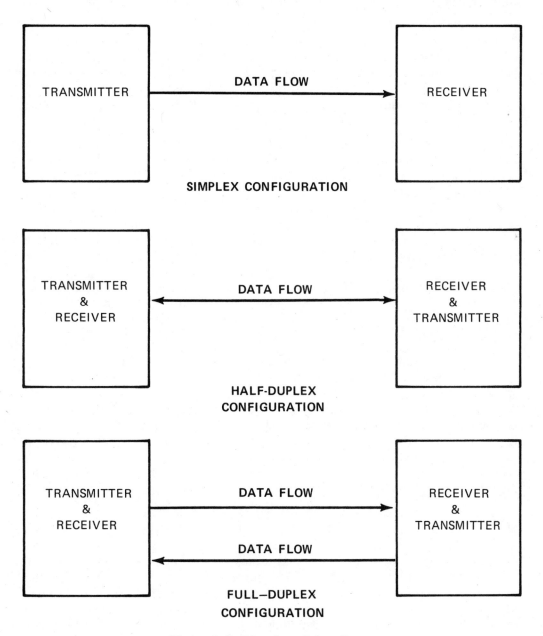

Figure 2–5. Direction of data flow.

configuration surpasses the simplex mode in that data can flow both ways, but the half-duplex design is such that data can only flow in one direction at a time. So, as a result, half-duplex is really simplex that switches directions. The third configuration shown in Figure 2-5 is the *full-duplex interface* (sometimes just called *duplex*), and it offers the advantage of allowing data to be transmitted in both directions simultaneously. Thus, full-duplex is a dual simplex configuration that requires that both communicating devices have full and independent transmit and receive capabilities.

Half-duplex and full-duplex operations are independent of the number of wires in the communication line. The terms *two-wire* and *four-wire* used to describe the design of a communications line are sometimes confused with half-duplex and full-duplex, but this description is incorrect. The public telephone system uses two wires—one for voice transmit and one for voice receive. Leased telephone lines, on the other hand, may have a pair of lines for receiving and a pair of lines for transmitting. Either communications system will support both half- and full-duplex.

The term *local echo* is also often confused with duplex mode. The confusion arises from the capability of most communication software to produce a local echo of characters when a *duplex mode mismatch* exists between the host's modem and the modem used with the PC. If the host computer is communicating in full-duplex, it will echo characters back to the PC immediately after receiving them. This immediate echo, referred to as *echo-plex*, allows the PC user to verify that transmitted characters were properly received by the host. When the host computer is operating in half-duplex, it will not echo received characters back to the PC so another technique is required. The PC user can switch the local modem to the half-duplex mode, which will cause the modem to echo transmitted characters to the PC's monitor, or he or she can instruct the communications software to print transmitted characters on the screen. The term to describe the latter of these two options is local echo. Thus, the local software echo is a substitute for switching the local modem to half-duplex.

Another important factor in serial data transfer is the timing of data transmission and the timing of data receipt. In parallel data transfer, eight data bits are transferred simultaneously leaving no doubt about which byte each bit is associated with. In serial data transfer, on the other hand, each data bit is sent sequentially and *synchronization* is required between the data source and data destination to segregate bits, characters (bytes), and messages. Without synchronization the receiving device will receive a series of signals that have no meaning. Synchronization that signals the start of data transmission is necessary for the received signals to be interpreted as meaningful information.

Synchronization between two communicating stations is governed by the rules and conventions contained in the Data Link Control layer of the seven layer ISO model discussed earlier. Data link control is accomplished by transmitting bits, characters, or messages along with data as the data go from one station to another. This data link control information is added and deleted by communication hardware or software and is transparent to the user. The information is used to synchronize the clocks contained in the hardware of both the sending and receiving stations so that the receiving station recognizes the bits sent by the transmitting station in the same pattern in which they were sent. The two methods used to synchronize and control data communications between stations are *asynchronous* (also called *start-stop*) and *synchronous*. The asynchronous method of data link control is used in several protocols including the *teletypewriter (TTY) protocol* used by the PC's asynchronous communications adapter. The synchronous method of data link control is used in three protocols that define the rules for message exchange; those protocols are *binary synchronous* (also called *BSC* or *bisync*), *synchronous data link control (SDLC)*, and *high-level data link control (HDLC)*.

Asynchronous data transmission, as its name implies, is not transmitted as a continuous bit stream and is characterized by the presence of synchronizing bits added to every byte that is transmitted. As illustrated in Figure 2-6, each asynchronous byte is preceded by a *start bit* which tells the receiving device to begin measuring the subsequent data for the presence of 1's and 0's. The start bit is always preceded by a low voltage signal on the data line called a *marking line* or *marking state* which provides a clear contrast for the detection of the beginning of a new start bit. At the end of every "train" of eight data bits is a "caboose" called a *stop bit*. (There may actually be one, one and one-half, or two stop bits at the end of each character, but one stop bit is used for most IBM Personal Computer communications.) The stop bit is a low voltage marker that tells the receiving device that one entire byte has been transmitted; it also returns the data line to the marking state. These start and stop bits *frame* each transmitted byte so that the 1's and 0's in that byte are clearly segregated from subsequent 1's and 0's that come down the line.

In contrast with the individually framed asynchronous bytes, synchronous data are transmitted in *blocks* and synchronization information is either provided within the blocks for long distance transmission or provided on a separate data line for local transmission. Figure 2-7 shows the SDLC protocol data structure in which blocks of data are marked at the beginning and end to tell the receiving device where the blocks of data start and end. The individual eight bit groups of 1's and 0's are not framed by synchronizing bits as they are in the asynchronous communication mode. In fact, synchronous data transfer may not be character-oriented at all. The data link control of synchronous protocols may be either character-oriented or bit-oriented. *Character-*

DATA START FLAG	8–BIT ADDRESS FIELD	8–BIT CONTROL FIELD	DATA FIELD	CYCLIC REDUNDANCY CHECK	CYCLIC REDUNDANCY CHECK	DATA END FLAG

INFORMATION FLOW

←

Figure 2–6. Asynchronous data structure.

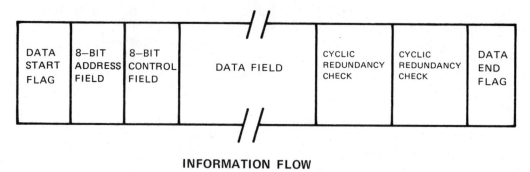

Figure 2–7. Synchronous data structure.

oriented protocols recognize bytes of data as specific characters, whereas *bit-oriented protocols* do not impose character assignments to transmitted data bits.

The synchronous communication method offers three advantages over the asynchronous method. The elimination of synchronizing bits with each character results in a greater ratio of data bits to total bits transferred with the synchronous mode compared to the asynchronous mode. The synchronous method also allows a user to transmit data that are not made up of eight bit characters. The greatest advantage in using the synchronous method, however, is that it allows the IBM PC user to communicate with *mainframe networks* that use synchronous mode communication.

Although synchronous data transfer offers several advantages to the IBM PC user, it is normally limited to business applications. The hardware and software required to support this method of data link control is prohibitively expensive for personal use. A business that already has a synchronous network installed can justify the cost of synchronous support for the PC, but many hobbyists will have difficulty justifying the difference in cost. Synchronous hardware and software combinations can cost 8–12 times the cost of asynchronous hardware and software combinations.

Serial Data Transfer Speed

In serial data transfer the *data transfer rate* is measured in *bits per second (bps)*. The term used to describe the total number of *binary signal events* occurring per second is *baud rate*. Baud rate is directly related to the duration of the voltage signal used to represent a binary digit. The following formula is an exact mathematical definition of the term:

$$\text{Baud Rate} = \frac{1}{\text{Bit Signal Duration}}$$

By decreasing the duration of the bit signal (*bit time*), you can increase the baud rate, and, conversely, by increasing the duration of the bit signal you can decrease the baud rate. Baud rates available for communications are normally discrete values that are determined by communications hardware and selected through communications software. For most Personal Computer communications applications, the baud rate used will also equal the bps data transfer rate. Business applications that require rapid data transfers may require the use of devices that superimpose several binary data signals on each binary signal event, thereby making the data transfer rate greater than the baud rate.

III. DETAILS OF SERIAL DATA TRANSFER

Although most of the IBM Personal Computer internal communications are in the parallel mode, most of the communications with which the user interacts are in the serial mode. Communication of data between the Personal Computer and other computer systems is typically done over distances greater than 100 feet, making serial communication the only economically feasible technique to use; it is less expensive to use existing telephone lines and equipment that support serial communication than to install parallel communication cables and parallel signal amplifying equipment. Because of this heavy dependence on serial data communication, the remainder of this chapter concentrates on the details of serial data transfer.

ASYNCHRONOUS COMMUNICATION

The term *asynchronous communication* will be used throughout the remainder of this book to describe the *TTY data communications protocol* used by the IBM Personal Computer asynchronous adapter. This ''plain vanilla'' protocol duplicates most of the characteristics of a hard-copy teletypewriter terminal and can be used to access any computer or word processor that has a communications port configured for TTY data communications. To communicate properly with host computers or word processors that do not support the TTY protocol, the IBM PC must communicate through a *protocol translator* or a *protocol and code translator*. These translators eliminate the compatibility problems associated with *vendor specific protocols* that are typical of most word processors. Protocol translators may also be used to connect an asynchronous device to a synchronous network such as the BSC and SDLC networks described later in this chapter.

Asynchronous communications, as explained earlier, refers to serial data transfer characterized by irregular transmission of data segments. This form of data link control is character-oriented—each set of data bits transmitted constitutes one character and each character is provided with its own *framing data*. A start bit and a stop bit frame the character's data bits and act as *synchronizing flags* for the receiving device. After receiving a start bit, the receiving device must be able to accurately measure a total of nine bits (eight data bits and a stop bit) to determine whether each is a logical 1 or 0. Because of this *character-by-character resynchronization*, asynchronous communication allows some tolerance for inaccuracies between the clocks of the transmitter and receiver, which, as you might expect, helps to keep the cost of this synchronizing method low. The following paragraphs provide more details on the framing, parity, and data bits used in asynchronous data transfer.

Start Bit

As shown in Figure 2-6, an idle asynchronous data line is maintained in a *marking status* until data are transmitted. This marking signal is represented by a logical 1 data line voltage. A change in data line voltage to a logical 0 for one bit time period is called a *start bit* and that signal tells the receiver to ''wake up'' and starting measuring data bits. This signal simply signifies the start of a character; it contains no information on the length or type of data to follow. All the receiver knows is that it should keep counting bits until told to stop by another signal.

A potential problem with the start bit concept is *data line noise*. Line noise caused by electrical storms or faulty telephone equipment could be interpreted by a receiver as a logical 0 and the start of a character. An occurrence of this type would result in an error because no data bits would follow. Asynchronous communications hardware eliminates this type of error by trapping faulty start bits. The data line voltage is checked frequently during the marking state so that the duration of a start bit can be accurately measured. Signals that appear to be start bits but do not meet the start bit duration requirements are ignored.

Data Bits

After a start bit is transmitted, the actual information to be transferred is transmitted as *data bits*. Figure 2-8 shows the five, six, seven, and eight *data bit configurations* supported by asynchronous data link control. The maximum number of characters that can be represented using each configuration is also shown. Almost all the asynchronous

Number of Data Bits	Serial Data Configuration*	Maximum No. Bit Patterns	Maximum No. Characters	8-bit ASCII Supported
5	ØxxxxxP1	2^5	32	No
6	ØxxxxxxP1	2^6	64	No
7	ØxxxxxxxP1	2^7	128	No
8	ØxxxxxxxxP1	2^8	256	Yes

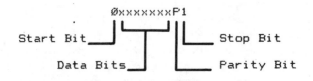

```
                    * Data configuration legend:

                          ØxxxxxxxP1

            Start Bit____|  |   |   |  |____Stop Bit

                Data Bits____|       |____Parity Bit
```

Figure 2–8. Data bit alternatives.

communications performed using the IBM Personal Computer will use either seven or eight data bits, principally because of the larger number of characters that can be represented with these combinations. It should also be noted that the use of eight data bits eliminates use of a parity bit with the IBM PC.

The number of data bits to be used in transmitting data may be dictated either by the receiver or by the type of data to be transmitted. The *American Standard Code for Information Interchange (ASCII)* discussed briefly in the following paragraph and in detail in Chapter 3 is by far the most commonly used character code for computers, and most information services use this code. When transmitting certain types of files, however, the data will not transmit properly unless eight data bits are used (sometimes called *8-bit or high-bit ASCII*). Examples of these files are word processing documents and computer programs containing *special text graphics* (characters whose ASCII value exceeds 127). To transmit these files, the Personal Computer has to be set up to operate with eight data bits and no parity.

ASCII Data

ASCII is the character code format chosen by IBM for the Personal Computer. All files produced by Personal Computer text editors are stored in ASCII and only files stored in that format can be edited using IBM PC text editors. BASIC files are not stored in ASCII by the Personal Computer unless they are saved using the following save command format:

save "Filename.ext",a

BASIC files stored without the A option are in a *tokenized (compressed)* format and cannot be edited with a text editor, listed using the Personal Computer TYPE command, or transmitted using the 7-bit ASCII data bit format. The tokenized format is used as the default storage method for BASIC files because files stored in that format are approximately 20% smaller and load much faster than the same files stored in the ASCII format.

Caution should be taken when transferring Personal Computer files using the ASCII format because the ASCII code contained in the Personal Computer BASIC Manual is not necessarily the same as the ASCII code used by other computers. The ASCII characters with values from 0 to 127 are the same as those used by most other computers, but characters with ASCII values above 127 are not. The first 128 IBM Personal Computer ASCII characters are *standard 7-bit ASCII code* and files which contain only those characters will transmit properly using seven data bits. Files containing the IBM Personal Computer *special extension characters* with ASCII values greater than 127 will contain errors when transmitted using seven data bits. The ASCII values of these characters will be reduced to values in the range 0–127 and a great deal of editing may be required before the received files can be used. BASIC ASCII files containing special characters can be transmitted using seven data bits by editing the file before transmission; all special characters have to be changed to string equivalents using the BASIC CHR$(n) function. This modification can be done quickly using a text editor that supports global search and replace.

Binary Data

ASCII files containing special 8-bit ASCII characters are sometimes called *binary files*, a term which causes confusion among data communications novices. Binary files are not word processing files that contain special ASCII control characters—they are files produced by assemblers or compilers, and transferring these files is more complicated than transferring word processing files. You may use communications programs written in Personal Computer BASIC to transmit and receive word processor files by using eight data bits, but you may not be able to use the same programs to transmit and receive binary files. A communications program will not properly transmit or receive binary files if it uses the ASCII *end of file marker* (a *control-Z*) to identify the end of a file transfer. Some binary data bit patterns duplicate the control-Z causing files to be prematurely closed before all data are either transmitted or received.

To properly transfer binary files (for example, files with EXE and COM extensions), the Personal Computer user should either use a communications software package designed to transfer files by blocks of bits or preprocess the data file before it is transmitted. Binary files may be transferred between certain software packages using special protocols that ensure error-free transfer or they can be converted into a *hexadecimal ASCII equivalent* before transmission and then converted back to binary data after receipt. Several public domain BASIC programs are also available that will convert binary files into ASCII BASIC programs which will recreate the binary files when run on the receiving end.

Parity Bit

Errors invariably occur during serial data transmission regardless of the type of data line used, and a method of detecting errors is required. The asynchronous data link control allows the use of a *parity bit* to perform this *error detection*. Since asynchronous communication is based on the premise that data are transmitted intermittently and transmission of a single character at a time is supported, it then follows that asynchronous error detection should be performed on a character-by-character basis. The parity bit, *when activated*, does exactly that.

Instead of sending the same character twice to detect transmission errors, the parity bit provides information in a single bit which describes the character sent. This is achieved by counting the total number of logical 1's in the character's data bits, then determining the value of the parity bit based on whether that total is even or odd. When *even parity* is chosen, the parity bit is set at 0 if the number of 1's in the character data bits is even, or it is set at 1 if the number of 1's in the character data bits is odd. When *odd parity* is chosen, the parity bit is set at 1 if the number of 1's in the character data bits is even, or it is set at 0 if the number of 1's in the data bits is odd.

Examples of parity bit determinations are as follows:

ASCII Character	Character Data Bits	Parity Bit for Even Parity	Parity Bit for Odd Parity
A	1000001	0	1
D	1000100	0	1
F	1000110	1	0
DEL	1111111	1	0

This single bit error detection method is an easy way to check for errors, but it is also subject to failure. Single bit errors are flagged, but multi-bit errors—the type of noise generated errors most often found on data communication lines—may not be detected. For example, an "A" may be transmitted, but noise on the telephone line may result in a "D" being received. As seen from the aforementioned examples of parity bit calculation, this error will not be detected because the resulting number of logical 1's is still even for even parity or odd for odd parity. The error detection limitations of the parity bit can be overcome in asynchronous communications, however, by using a *protocol file transfer* that contains a more sophisticated error detection scheme. Protocol transfer is discussed later in this chapter.

Parity error detection also fails to detect *data bit truncation* when transmitting 8-bit ASCII characters. If seven data bits are selected for data transmission, all characters with ASCII values higher than 127 (the DEL character shown in the previous example) will be transmitted as other characters, but the transmitted and received parity will be the same. Examples of this type of transmission are as follows:

IBM PC Character	IBM PC Character Code	7-bit Code Transmitted	Character Received	Error Detected
⌐	10110011	0110011	3	No
=	11001101	1001101	M	No
Σ	11100100	1100100	d	No
β	11100001	1100001	a	No

The only way to avoid this type of error is to always use eight data bits for data transfer, but this may not always be practical. Many information services and bulletin boards operate with seven data bits and even parity detection, but some services, particularly personal host systems, do not actually check for parity errors. Communicating with this latter type of system still requires that you use seven data bits and parity, or communications will not take place properly.

The parity bit can also be set to off, space, or mark by some communications systems. *Off* or *no parity* simply means that the parity bit will not be checked for transmission errors. No parity is required when using eight data bits with the PC communications adapter. *Mark parity* means that the parity bit will always be set at 1, and *space parity* means that the parity bit will always be set at 0. Some mainframe systems that use the mark or space parity will not communicate properly with another computer or a terminal unless the same parity bit mode is used on both ends of the communication link. Other systems transmit in the mark or space parity mode but do not check received parity; these systems can be accessed by the IBM PC using a communications package that transmits either even or odd parity but does not perform received parity error-checking. This applies to many IBM PC communications packages—very few of them check received parity.

Stop Bits

The final binary signals associated with asynchronous communication are *stop bits*. Stop bits follow the data bits and the parity bit (if parity is used) and constitute the end of transmission of a character. The start bit constitutes the *starting frame* of a character and stop bits constitute the *ending frame* for that same character. Stop bits are software selectable and are either 1-, 1.5-, or 2-bit times in length. They are simply logical 1's and are used to ensure that the data line is at the marking state before another start bit (logical 0) is received. This marking state precursor to new character start bits is necessary for accurate detection of the start of characters. Without accurate detection of start bits, *false start bits* could not be detected and eliminated and synchronization of *bit measurements* could not be achieved.

Although the number of stop bits is *software selectable*, a value of 1 will be used for most Personal Computer communications. Stop bits do not contain useful data, so their duration should be set at the minimum allowable value to maximize the data transfer rate. The following is a good guideline for stop bit selection:

Baud Rate Range	Stop Bits Required
Less than 110	2
110	2
300	1
Above 300	1

Putting It All Together

Now that you understand the meaning of start, data, parity, and stop bits, you may wonder how you are ever going to keep track of when to use which combination. Fortunately, the selection and use of these parameters is not as confusing as it sounds.

The two most common sets of default communication parameters used in communication software available for the Personal Computer are shown next. (The two sets are arbitrarily numbered for reference purposes only.)

Parameter Set	Data Bits	Parity	Stop Bits
1	7	Even	1
2	8	None	1

The first parameter set will work with most information services and bulletin boards, some of which are listed in Table 2-3, but you may find the second set to be the most commonly used by other microcomputers. The second set will also allow you to transfer the special IBM Personal Computer ASCII characters if the receiving computer is also using eight data bits. The key to proper communication for any of these applications is to use the same selection of parameters for both the sending and receiving computers. If you do not know the communication parameters of a host system with which you wish to communicate, you may have to call the host and experiment until you make a parameter selection that works. Until you find the right combination, you will probably receive characters from the host that look like a tokenized BASIC file listed using the Personal Computer DOS TYPE command. An example of parameter-mismatch screen display is shown in Figure 2-9.

Table 2-3. Information utility communication parameters.

Parameter	THE SOURCE	CompuServe	NewsNet	Dow Jones
Baud	300/1200	300/1200	300/1200	300/1200
Data Bits	8	7/8	8	8
Parity	None	Even/None	None	None
Stop Bits	1	1	1	1
Duplex	Full	Full	Full	Full

For clarification regarding error checking, the Personal Computer does use even parity for memory chip communication error detection, but asynchronous communication with the Personal Computer is software controlled and parity may be selected even or odd or it may be turned off entirely. Internal error detection will not be affected by the parity error detection mode selected for asynchronous communication. Parity error detection is a good method of testing for internal communication errors because random access memory tends to *drop single bits* when a memory chip starts to fail, but parity error detection is not as useful in external communication error detection because telephone line noise is bursty in nature resulting in *multi-bit errors*.

Figure 2–9. Communication parameter mismatch screen display.

SYNCHRONOUS COMMUNICATION

As stated earlier in this chapter, a major difference between asynchronous and synchronous serial data transfer is the continuity of data transmitted. Asynchronous transfer is characterized by discontinuity in data transmission, whereas synchronous transfer is characterized by continuous data transmission. Because of the differences between the protocols necessary to support asynchronous transfer and synchronous transfer, however, there are few similarities between these two categories of serial transfer. Synchronous communication protocols are more complex than asynchronous communication protocols. The most prevalent of the synchronous protocols are reviewed in the following paragraphs.

Bisync Protocol

Bisync is an acronym for *Binary Synchronous Communication* and is a product of IBM Corporation. Bisync protocol is character-oriented, meaning that each character has a specified boundary. Each character is not provided with synchronizing bits as is the case with asynchronous data. Instead, bisync synchronization is performed at the beginning of each data message. The transmitting station sends two or more *leading pad characters* to the receiving station before data are transmitted. The leading pad character is an alternating 1 and 0 bit pattern that allows the receiving station clock to *synchronize with the transmitting station clock*. The bisync protocol requires that a data bit be transmitted during every bit interval, but before data transmission can begin, *character synchronization* must take place. A signal is required to provide the receiver with the length of individual data units and a mark that identifies the start of a data unit boundary. The *synchronous idle character (SYN)* is used to perform this *handshaking* and two or more of these characters are provided at the start of all bisync data streams.

The bisync protocol SYN character is similar to the asynchronous start bit in that it is the "wake up" signal for the receiver. While waiting for a data stream to start arriving, the receiver is in a "hunt" mode. All incoming bits are searched for the presence of the SYN character. After the receiver detects a SYN character, the device starts to count incoming bits so that it can identify the first bit of a character. To reduce the probability of erroneous data interpretation, most applications of the bisync protocol use the *SYN pair* instead of a single SYN character at the start of a data message. The data link control characters used in the bisync protocol are shown in Table 2-4. Typical bisync data streams employing these control characters are shown in Figure 2-10.

There is no limit to the number of *blocks of data* that may be contained in a stream of bisync data, and a block of data called a *heading* may also be included. The heading describes the data to be transmitted but is not retained as useful data by the receiver.

The data units in a bisync data stream follow the same rules as asynchronous data. Each character may contain five, six, seven, or eight data bits and each character may be followed by an optional even or odd parity bit. The 7-bit ASCII code is normally transmitted with seven data bits and a parity bit, but it can also be transmitted using

Table 2-4. Bisync control characters.

Bisync Character	Hex Value	ASCII Value*	Character Description
SYN	32	22	Synchronous idle
PAD	55	85	Start of frame pad
PAD	FF	255	End of frame pad
DLE	10	16	Data link escape
ENQ	2D	5	Enquiry
SOH	01	1	Start of heading
STX	02	2	Start of text
ITB	1F	15	End of intermediate block
ETB	26	23	End of transmission (block)
ETX	03	3	End of text

*ASCII decimal as described in Appendix G of the IBM Personal Computer BASIC Manual.

eight data bits and a parity bit. The *EBCDIC communication code* (used with large IBM computers) described in Chapter 3 is also supported and is normally transmitted using eight data bits.

When using bisync protocol, data can be sent in either the *transparent* or *non-transparent mode*, but data headings are always sent in the non-transparent mode. The transparent mode allows the user to transmit all characters, including *data link control characters*, as text. In this mode, a data link control character only becomes effective when it is preceded by a data link escape (DLE) character. All other data link control characters are assumed to be text. The transparent mode is initiated by a DLE STX character sequence as shown in Figure 2-10. A DLE followed by an ETB, ETX, or ITB character ends the transparent mode; all subsequent data link control characters will perform their assigned control functions.

When data bits are not being transmitted, the bisync protocol requires some form of continuous signal transmission to maintain transmission synchronization. During these pauses, which typically occur in terminal conversation between blocks of data transfer, the transmitting device sends a stream of SYN characters while in the non-transparent mode or a stream of DLE SYN characters while in the transparent mode. These "padding characters" are ignored by the receiving device as it waits for meaningful data.

Bisync data headings vary with applications, but typical information contained in a heading is as follows:

- Identification of originating device
- Identification of receiving device
- Priority of data
- Data security class
- Destination routing for data
- Control or information nature of data

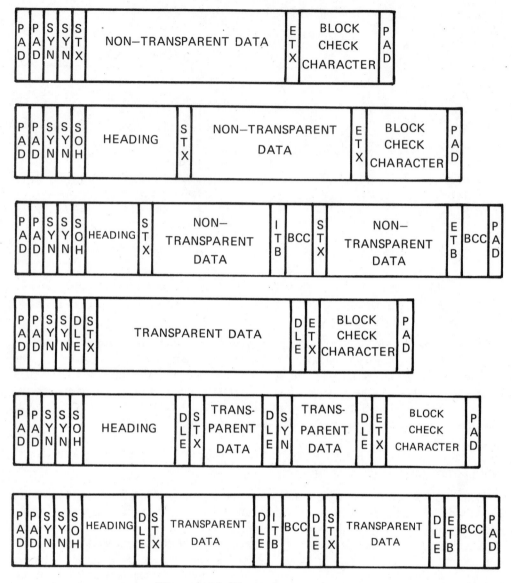

Figure 2–10. Bisync data structure.

Each block of bisync data transmitted is checked for errors on the receiving end in one of three ways, depending on the functions or code used. These error-checking techniques are *vertical redundancy checking (VRC)*, *longitudinal redundancy checking (LRC)*, or *cyclic redundancy checking (CRC)*. The VRC is an odd parity error-check and is the same as odd parity error checking described for asynchronous communications. The LRC uses all character bits to form a check character at both the transmitting and receiving ends of the communication link called a *block check character (BCC)*. At the completion of a transmission, the receiving station sends its BCC to the transmitting station to check the accuracy of received data.

The CRC is a more accurate error detection method than the LRC and may take two forms. The *CRC-12* was used with older 6-bit transmission codes, and the *CRC-16* is used with modern 8-bit transmission codes. The CRC uses a mathematical algorithm to divide a constant (derived from a polynomial) into the numeric binary value of all character bits contained in a block of data. The resulting quotient is discarded and the remainder is retained as a block check character (BCC). A receiving station compares the transmitted BCC to its own computed BCC and accepts the data if the two BCCs are equal. Both the LRC and CRC methods of error detection are more accurate than the VRC because they are just as effective at detecting multi-bit errors as they are at detecting single-bit errors.

Both the non-transparent and transparent modes of bisync communication are shown in Figure 2-10. From these examples it becomes obvious that the longer the blocks of data, the faster the transfer of data because the ratio of data characters to control characters is higher. This observation is only valid, however, for good data line connections. When the probability of noise on a data line is high, smaller data blocks should be transmitted to reduce the need to retransmit large blocks of data when transmission errors are detected.

The bisync protocol provides a significant advantage over asynchronous protocols because of the ratio of data information to control information. Large blocks of data can be transmitted with few start, stop, and error test characters in the bisync protocol, whereas the ratio of start, stop, and error test characters is always the same in asynchronous communication. This translates into a greater bit per second transfer rate for bisync data when large volumes of data are involved.

Many business mainframe networks use the bisync protocol and adding bisync to an IBM PC will allow the PC to communicate in such a network without having to communicate through a protocol converter. Several bisync hardware/software packages are available for the PC that will allow it to emulate (perform almost exactly as) an IBM bisync terminal. By implementing a bisync emulation package, the PC can access mainframe data bases and computing power otherwise not available.

SDLC and HDLC Protocols

The *Synchronous Data Link Control (SDLC)* and *High-Level Data Link Control (HDLC)* synchronous data transfer protocols are not used by hobbyists because of their initial cost, but they are becoming world standards for business communications. IBM is supporting the SDLC protocol for the Personal Computer with the *SNA 3270 Emulation and RJE Support* package which will advance the use of the protocol with the PC. Because of the business interest in SDLC and HDLC protocols, they will be reviewed briefly in this text. Also, because of the common elements of SDLC and HDLC, they will be discussed together in the following paragraphs. The two protocols will only be discussed individually when there are differences between them.

The actual data transmitted under SDLC/HDLC is called an *information field* and that field is simply a serial stream of binary numbers. The field may be any length from zero data bits up to a maximum that is determined by memory size or the protocol implemented. The data stream is bit-oriented, meaning that no character boundaries are provided with the data. If the data do contain characters, the receiving device must segregate them after receipt of the data.

The continuity of data for SDLC/HDLC is different from that allowed under the bisync protocol. Pauses in data transmission are allowed in bisync but not in SDLC/HDLC. There is no SDLC/HDLC equivalent of the bisync SYN character. Both SDLC and HDLC require continuous data transmission until the entire information field is transmitted. If a pause or break occurs in the data transmission before the entire information field is transmitted, the transmitting device assumes an error has occurred and aborts the transmission.

SDLC and HDLC information fields are serial data streams that are created by SDLC/HDLC adapter hardware from parallel data. A parallel data stream is converted into a serial data stream in much the same way as the asynchronous conversion described earlier. SDLC/HDLC data, like bisync data, are provided with only one set of framing data for the entire stream—compared to the framing provided with each character in asynchronous communication. As shown in Figures 2-11a and 2-11b, the SDLC and HDLC information fields are framed by several data fields. Each information unit begins with a *beginning flag* and ends with an *ending flag*. These flags are 01111110 bit patterns and serve as the outside boundaries of each frame of data. The beginning flag is followed by two fields called the *address field* and the *control field*. Both of these fields are eight bits long for SDLC and HDLC. The HDLC frame has one additional address field called a *packet header* that routes the frame through a *packet-switched network* to its proper destination.

The SDLC/HDLC information fields end with a *frame check* that is similar to a block check character. The cyclic redundancy check error detection bit pattern is calculated from the bit patterns of the address, control, and information fields and is used to check for data transmission errors. All SDLC/HDLC fields are required to fulfill the requirements of an SDLC/HDLC frame of data or a *framing error* is assumed and the data are retransmitted. Between frame transmissions, a transmitter may send either a sequence of *flag characters* or a *continuous high idle signal* to maintain communication contact with the receiver.

The structure of SDLC/HDLC data frames allows the use of this protocol in mainframe network systems, which is the basis for the popularity of this protocol in business applications. A Personal Computer with the proper SDLC hardware and software can be used to emulate an IBM 3270 terminal in a network configuration in addition to being used as a local stand alone microcomputer to support spreadsheet and data base applications. Combining these two capabilities in one set of hardware makes the Personal Computer a powerful tool for business applications. Typical Personal Computer SDLC networks are shown in Figure 2-12.

As shown in Figure 2-12, the SDLC/HDLC protocols allow only one primary station, but one or more secondary stations are supported. The address field in an SDLC/HDLC frame identifies the primary and secondary stations as either intended recipients

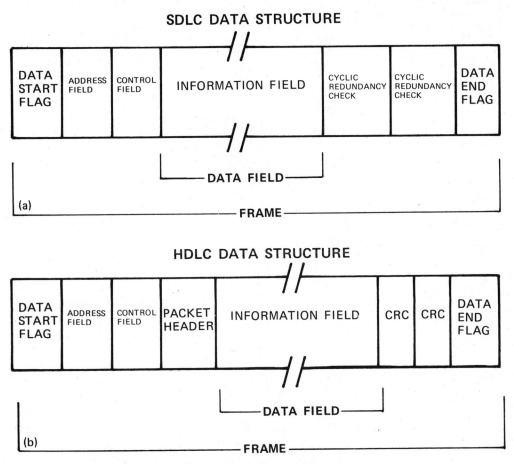

Figure 2–11. SDLC and HDLC protocols.

of data or sources of data. The address field of the primary station's frame contains a secondary station's address, whereas the address field of a secondary station contains its own source address because a secondary station can only communicate with one destination device—the primary station. For additional information on the SDLC/ HDLC protocols, please refer to the following references: *IBM Synchronous Data Link Control—General Information*, IBM publication GA27-3093 and *Binary Synchronous Communication—General Information*, IBM publication GA27-3004.

Systems Network Architecture

Systems Network Architecture (SNA) is an IBM standard for the design and fabrication of communication products. SNA also controls the protocol used in IBM communication networks, which is a form of the SDLC protocol described in the previous paragraphs.

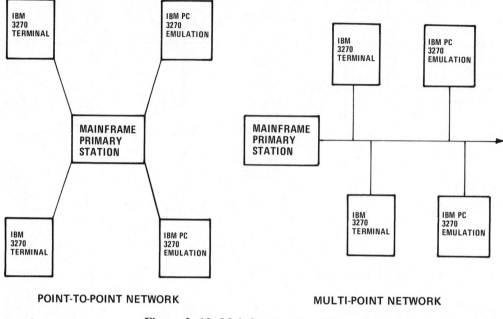

POINT-TO-POINT NETWORK   MULTI-POINT NETWORK

Figure 2–12. Mainframe networks.

The SNA concept uses six layers as shown in Figure 2-13. These layers are used for the same reasons that seven layers are used in the ISO model discussed earlier in this chapter. Applications programmers do not have to worry about network configurations and programs do not have to be recoded to reflect changes in specific equipment used in a network because of the specifications for equipment and software provided by the model. Programmers and equipment designers can be more productive because they can concentrate on the details of their work without concern for the overall network. SNA makes this possible by defining the functional responsibilities of each network component and the rules for communication between components.

Communication in an SNA network is done between logical units. Users access the network through these logical units to send and to receive data from the network. A logical unit is made up of both hardware components and program code and is implemented in the IBM PC through the purchase of an expansion board and a software package.

The data structure used in an SNA network is SDLC. As shown in Figure 2-14, Request/Response Units (RU) format the data. Request/Response Headers (RH) are added to the RUs to indicate whether or not the SDLC information field is a request, a response, or data. Transmission Headers (TH) are added to indicate the origin or destination address of the RU. The combination of TH, RH, and RU is called a Path Information Unit (PIU). A Link Header and a Link Trailer are also added to the PIU to complete an SDLC frame called a Basic Link Unit (BLU). This BLU is transmitted and received by the PC when it is properly equipped with SNA terminal emulation

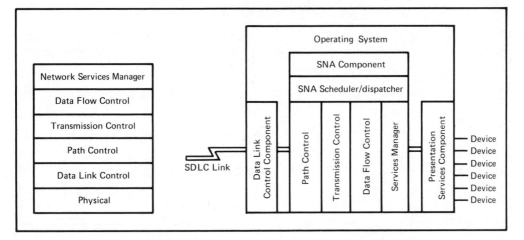

Figure 2–13. Structure and function of SNA.

hardware and software. This capability allows the PC to communicate in an IBM mainframe network and allows the PC user to establish "sessions" with applications programs that reside on a host computer within the network.

ASYNCHRONOUS COMMUNICATION SPEED-MATCHING

The previous discussions of serial data transfer were based on the assumption that data are transmitted from one computer directly to another device or computer and immediately put to use on the receiving end, but this is often not true. If transmitted data could be converted from a parallel stream to a serial stream, routed to another device, then converted back to a parallel stream and printed, displayed, or saved with each operation taking place at the same speed, there would be no delays or interruption in the serial transfer of data. Differences in the speed of some of these operations, however, result in the need for *data transfer flow controls*. These data flow *speed-matching techniques* come in a variety of forms, but most of them can be categorized as either *on-off data flow toggles* or *temporary data storage mechanisms*. IBM Personal Computer asynchronous communication applications of both of these techniques are discussed next.

Communication Buffers

A *communication buffer* is random access memory that is set aside to temporarily store data to compensate for differences in data transfer and receipt rates. In data communications, buffers are often provided on both the transmitting and receiving end of a communication link, but the term communication buffer is normally used when re-

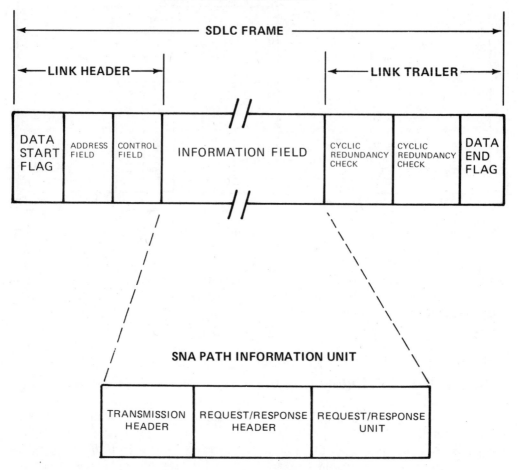

Figure 2–14. SNA data structure.

ferring to the buffer on the receiving end. The following paragraphs describe the flow of data, starting from a disk file in one microcomputer and ending with that disk file being saved in a disk file on a remote microcomputer to provide insight into the operation of transmit and receive buffers.

Information being transmitted to a remote computer is often read from a *stored disk file*. During the transfer, data are moved in blocks from the file into a *transmit buffer*. Each block read operation continues until the buffer is full, then reading is temporarily halted until the contents of the transmit buffer have been sent to the remote computer. Data are transferred from the transmit buffer on a *first-in first-out* basis so that they are transmitted in the same sequence in which they were received. When the transmit buffer has been emptied, more data are loaded into it from the disk file. A typical transmit buffer holds 255 characters of text (approximately three 80-column lines), which results in many disk file read operations during the transmission of a large file.

The transmit buffer size is ordinarily determined by the microcomputer operating system, and changing the buffer size is not normally a communications package option. Some IBM Personal Computer communication software packages allow the user to select a transmit block size, but block size does not pertain to the size of the transmit buffer. Block size selection in that context determines the number of characters to be transmitted between transmission error checks.

Of the two types of communication buffers, the *receive buffer* size is by far the more crucial and the one with which most IBM Personal Computer users will be concerned when performing data communications. Receive buffers act in the same manner as transmit buffers, but the direction of data flow is reversed. A receive buffer accepts data coming in from the communication line and stores it until the communication program can display, print, or store the data in a disk file or memory space. Displaying and storing the data are fast operations and may not result in a heavy loading of the receive buffer, but simultaneous display and printing of received data can result in a *receive buffer overflow*. Such an overflow causes data to be missed by the receiving computer, and the lost data are said to have gone "into the bit bucket" or "onto the floor."

Assembly language programs are capable of handling data quickly and may not need a communication buffer, but communication programs written in the BASIC language operate at slower speeds and require 1024 bytes or more of receive buffer, or data may be lost during file transfers. Even after compiling a BASIC communication program you may find that it still has to have a receive buffer, but the faster operation of the compiled code may allow you to reduce the size of the buffer.

The receive buffer size of IBM Personal Computer BASIC communication programs may be set using the /C: option when Disk or Advanced BASIC is loaded into memory. This option is placed on the command line with the word BASIC or BASICA and follows the name of the BASIC communication program to be loaded and run. The BASIC default communication buffer size is 256 bytes (256 text characters), but the /C: option can be used to change that value to any size from 0 to 32,767 bytes. IBM recommends 1024 for normal high speed communication line use, but you may find that a value of 4096 or higher is required to prevent communication buffer overflow during large file transfers. If the BASIC program does much control character filtering, a value of 1024 will almost always be too small. The following is the IBM Personal Computer DOS command used to set up a receive buffer with 4096 bytes:

A> BASIC PC-TALK /C:4096

The available random access memory in an IBM Personal Computer can also limit communication buffer size when using a BASIC communications program. A 64K system will often be pushed to the limit by a good BASIC package. After loading DOS, the BASIC interpreter, and the communications program, there may only be enough memory space left for a 1024 byte receive buffer. Performing an available free memory test by breaking the execution of the program (pressing the Ctrl and the Scroll Lock keys simultaneously) and executing the direct statement PRINT FRE(0) will tell you the remaining free memory, but increasing the communication buffer size based on that figure could cause problems unless the program is designed to frequently force *housecleaning*. The BASIC interpreter requires a certain amount of memory for the storage of strings during the execution of a program, and the program will fail if sufficient memory is not available for that storage. The required *string space* can be minimized by forcing the interpreter to frequently clear that portion of memory with a statement such as N = FRE(''''), but the software has to be designed to force that housecleaning operation more frequently than would normally occur. A one-time check of free memory space could occur just following a housecleaning operation, and increasing communication buffer size based on that single check could result in insufficient free memory for string handling; hence the communications program would fail during a communication session or file transfer.

Because practical limits such as the one just described often prevent communications users from setting the buffer size large enough to handle all speed-mismatch situations, other data flow throttling techniques are required. These techniques are employed to keep data from arriving faster than they can be processed instead of providing temporary storage space for the data after they arrive. The most frequently used flow throttle is the XON/XOFF transmission protocol.

XON/XOFF Control

The *XON/XOFF data flow control protocol* is a more positive mechanism of controlling the flow of data than the communications buffer because it is an *active* rather than a *passive* technique. The capacity of a communications buffer can be exceeded if the mismatch in flow of data is significant and the data file being transmitted is large, but the XON/XOFF flow control toggles the flow of data on and off to prevent buffer overflow.

If the XON/XOFF protocol is properly implemented at both the host and the Personal Computer ends of a communications link, proper data flow speed-matching is handled entirely by the Personal Computer communications software. When the volume of data being held in the communications receive buffer begins to reach the capacity limit of the buffer, the software sends an XOFF to the host. (The XOFF character is ASCII Device Control 3 and is equivalent to Control S.) On receipt of the XOFF, the host temporarily halts data transmission, allowing the Personal Computer to process the data contained in its communication buffer. When the buffer has been emptied to a predetermined low level, the Personal Computer software sends the host an XON character. This character is ASCII Device Control 1 (equivalent to Control Q) and signals the host to resume data transmission. This cycle may be repeated many times during the transfer of a data file without user knowledge or involvement.

Most mainframe host computer systems support the XON/XOFF speed-matching technique, but not all communication software for the IBM Personal Computer or other microcomputers have that capability. Almost all assembly language Personal Computer communications software use XON/XOFF control, but some software written in the BASIC language do not support the protocol. Assembly language software operates fast enough to watch for and react to XOFF characters, but BASIC language software may not operate fast enough to search received characters for the presence of an XOFF.

The BASIC interpreter does operate fast enough to send XOFF and XON characters when a file is being received, but a communication software package user should read the package documentation carefully to be sure the protocol is supported during the file transmission mode.

Protocol Transfer

Another data flow control technique is the *protocol transfer*. This method requires that the communication software being used on both ends of the communication link recognize the same set of *ASCII control characters* to facilitate transfer of *fixed length blocks of data*. A lack of standardization of control characters used in the implementation of this technique often requires that two microcomputers use communication software from the same vendor to perform protocol file transfers. Most of the software vendors that offer this transfer option for use with the IBM Personal Computer also have the software available for other types of microcomputers.

The protocol file transfer technique may use the End of Transmission Block (ETB), the End of Text (ETX), or the Enquiry (ENQ) along with the Acknowledge (ACK) and Negative Acknowledge (NAK) ASCII characters to perform flow control (see Chapter 3 for a detailed review of the use of these characters). The receiving device must be able to recognize one of the first three characters as the end of block transfer signal, and the transmitting device must be able to recognize the ACK as the acknowledgment of block receipt signal. The transmitting device must also recognize the NAK as a signal indicating improper transfer of a block of data.

The *Ward Christensen XMODEM protocol* is a public domain protocol used in several IBM PC communication software packages and serves as a good example of the *handshaking* these file transfer techniques provide. The protocol is illustrated in Figure 2-15. As you can see from that figure, XMODEM does not begin the transfer of data until the receiving computer signals the transmitting computer that it is ready to receive data. The Negative Acknowledge (NAK) character is used for this signal.

After the NAK is received, XMODEM sends a Start of Header (SOH) character, followed by two characters that represent the block number and a "one's complement" of the block number to be transferred next. The "one's complement" block number is calculated by subtracting the block number from 255. After these numbers are transmitted, a 128-byte block of data is transmitted followed by an *error-checking checksum*. The checksum is calculated by adding the ASCII values of each character in the 128-byte block; the sum is then divided by 255 and the remainder is retained as the checksum. After each block of data is transferred, the receiving computer computes its own checksum and compares the result to the checksum received from the transmitting computer. If the two values are the same, the receiving computer sends an Acknowledge (ACK) character to tell the receiver to send the next sequential block. If the two values are not the same, the receiving computer sends the transmitter an NAK to request a retransmission of the last block. This retransmission process is repeated until the block of data is properly received or until nine attempts have been made to transmit the block. If the communications link is noisy, resulting in improper

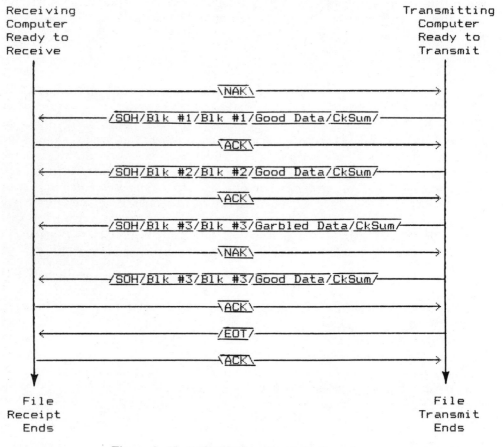

Figure 2–15. XMODEM protocol file transfer.

block transmission after nine attempts, the file transfer is aborted and has to be manually restarted.

The XMODEM protocol uses the two block numbers at the start of each block transfer to be sure the same block is not transmitted twice because of a handshake character loss during the transfer; the receiving computer checks the transmitted block to be sure that it is the one requested. Blocks that are retransmitted by mistake are thrown away by the receiving computer. When all data have been successfully transmitted, the transmitting computer sends the receiver an End of Transmission (EOT) character to indicate the end of file.

The XMODEM protocol offers the IBM PC three advantages over other protocols. First, the protocol is in the public domain which makes it readily available for software designers to incorporate into a communications package. Second, the protocol is easy to implement using high level languages such as BASIC or Pascal. Third, the protocol only requires a 256-byte communication receive buffer which makes it attractive for IBM PC owners who only have 64K systems. Finally, the protocol is used by many bulletin boards and having the protocol in a communications package allows the IBM PC user to receive error-checked files from these bulletin boards.

Protocol file transfer in general offers three advantages over other asynchronous file transfer methods. First, some protocols allow the user to select transfer block size. By selecting the block size smaller than the receive buffer on the receiving end of the communication link, the transmitter can ensure that a receive buffer overflow will not occur regardless of the speed-mismatch between the transmitter and receiver. Second, protocol transfer allows the user to transfer non-ASCII data files between microcomputers because it calculates the end of a file based on file size and uses handshake signals to indicate the end of a file instead of relying on an end of file marker character to terminate a file transfer. Finally, protocol transfer error-checking is superior to normal asynchronous parity error checking. The parity method of error-checking is 95% effective if the software on the receiving end checks for parity errors. Protocol error-checking is 99.5 to 99.9% effective, and the software on the receiving end must check for errors. Parity errors detected also do not result in automatic retransmission of the bad data; protocol detected errors result in *data retransmission* until no errors are detected or until a specified number of retransmissions have been attempted.

Print Spoolers

Another data transfer speed-matching technique is the print spooler. A *print spooler* is nothing more than a *buffer* between the IBM Personal Computer and a printer which allows files to be printed while other tasks are being performed simultaneously. This mechanism facilitates data communication speed-matching because incoming data may be printed without slowing down operation of the communications program. A large portion of unused random access memory is set up as a print spooler and incoming data that are to be printed are routed to this area of memory and held there until they are eventually sent to the printer on a first-in first-out basis . Without such a device, the communications program has to wait to process each newly received block of data until each old block of data has been printed. A typical IBM PC default printer buffer is only 80 bytes (equivalent of one 80-character line of text), whereas software or hardware implemented print spoolers can add 64K bytes or more to that buffer. Printing of received data may go on for long periods of time after a communications session is completed with the application of these spoolers, particularly when communicating at 120 characters per second and printing at less than 80 characters per second.

Creating large print buffers may not always solve speed-matching problems. When very large files or multiple files are being transferred, even the largest print spoolers can be overloaded. These instances will require the use of an active speed-matching technique such as the XON/XOFF method described earlier.

Disk Emulators

A *disk emulator* is a portion of unused random access memory that is set up to operate as an *electronic disk*. The transferring of data from a communications port to an electronic disk file can be done ten times faster than the transfer of the same data to a floppy disk file because of the shorter access time required for the electronic disk. This faster transfer of data results in a faster emptying of the receive buffer, thereby reducing the chances of receive buffer overflow.

The disadvantages of disk emulators are the volatility of stored files and the extra steps required to transfer files from the emulator to a floppy disk. Files stored on an electronic disk will be lost if a power outage occurs before they are transferred to a floppy disk. Some disk emulators are also destroyed if a system reset (warm boot) has to be performed to recover from a software crash. Disk emulators that require reconfiguration of the memory switches on the Personal Computer mother board (to show less random access memory than the PC actually contains) generally stay intact during system warm boot and allow the user to retain electronically stored files for later transfer to a floppy disk.

Some Personal Computer software packages offer both an electronic disk and a print spooler combination that can be used with systems configured with more than 128K of random access memory. This capability can be combined with a communications package in such a way that files can be captured in an electronic disk file and spooled to a printer at the same time. A 320K random access memory system can be configured with a 32K print spooler and a 160K electronic disk leaving 128K for active memory use with DOS and the communication software.

Hard Disks

The *fixed* or *hard disk* is the final speed-matching technique used with the IBM PC. With the announcement of DOS 2.0, IBM began supporting the hard disk and made this a viable option for users who insist on using only IBM distributed equipment and operating systems. The data transfer rate from memory to a hard disk is greater than the data transfer rate to a floppy disk, which makes the hard disk a better device for data communications speed-matching when files are being captured to disk. The data transfer rate to a hard disk is less than the transfer rate to an electronic disk, but the hard disk can typically store more data than an electronic disk. Data stored on a hard disk are also *non-volatile*—a power outage immediately following the receipt of a file will not result in a loss of transferred data unless the hard disk is damaged by the event; data stored in an electronic disk will be lost during a power outage or surge unless the PC is equipped with backup power or power surge protection.

There are several other data flow control mechanisms used on other microcomputers that have not been implemented on the IBM Personal Computer. The reverse channel is one of these techniques. This method requires a modem interface signal that is not likely to be used with the Personal Computer, so the method will be not be discussed here.

A subject that does deserve complete coverage is the communication character set used by the IBM Personal Computer. Without a standard set of signals for communication, many of the capabilities discussed in this chapter would not be possible. The following chapter covers the character codes and controls used with the Personal Computer.

3

Communication Codes and Controls

Computer communication codes are to the IBM Personal Computer what Morse Code was to the telegraph operator. It is a standard sequence of signals that can be translated into meaningful information by a recipient. Without standardization of these signals, however, significant incompatibilites between equipment made by different vendors would probably develop. Fortunately for the IBM Personal Computer owner, there are standards for communication character representations which have kept many of these potential problems from developing.

There are two predominant character codes presently in use in the United States. The *American Standard Code for Information Interchange or ASCII* (pronounced ass-key) is by far the most widely used character code throughout the world. The IBM-developed *Extended Binary Coded Decimal Interchange Code or EBCDIC* (pronounced ebb-see-dick) is the other major code and is used for communication between almost all IBM computer equipment. There is also a third code in use on older communications equipment called the *Baudot code*. The characteristics and applications of each of these codes are discussed in the following paragraphs. Because of the predominant use of the ASCII code in communications, that code is explored in detail. The other two codes are only briefly discussed at the end of the chapter.

I. THE ASCII CHARACTER SET

The ASCII character set is the most universally used convention for the encoding of alphanumeric characters and is a new twist for IBM equipment. Before the introduction of the Personal Computer, all IBM equipment except the System/34 used the IBM-developed EBCDIC character set as a standard interchange code.

The first 128 characters of the Personal Computer's ASCII character set are defined by the ANSI X3.4 1977 *standard ASCII character set*. Almost all American computer hardware companies and many foreign hardware producers support this ASCII code, which places the Personal Computer in an excellent community of standardized communications hardware and software. Participation in communication networks using commercially available hardware is assured because of this use of standardized code.

A translation table showing the binary coding of the standard 7-bit ASCII character set is shown in Figure 3-1. The characters included in this set are 26 uppercase letters, 26 lowercase letters, 10 numbers, and other special text characters found on most typewriter keyboards. A set of standard communication control codes is also provided and is discussed in detail later in this chapter. A complete listing of all ASCII characters supported by the IBM Personal Computer is provided in Appendix A.

The standard ASCII characters shown in Figure 3-1 can be represented by seven data bits, but the *IBM Personal Computer special ASCII extension characters* require eight data bits. Seven data bits give you the ability to combine two things (either a 1 or a 0) seven at a time, resulting in a total possible unique combinations of 2 to the 7th power. If you perform that computation, you will find that the result is 128. This value equals the number of standard ASCII characters (0–127). If you do the same computation by taking two things eight at a time, you will find that the result is 256, which equals the total number of ASCII characters shown in Appendix A. This simply means that Personal Computer ASCII characters with values greater than 127 can only be represented with eight data bits. This is the case whether the character is being stored in an ASCII file or transmitted long distance to another microcomputer.

Data Bits →							0	0	0	0	1	1	1	1
							0	0	1	1	0	0	1	1
							0	1	0	1	0	1	0	1
7	6	5	4	3	2	1								
x	x	x	0	0	0	0	NUL	DLE	SP	0	@	P	`	p
x	x	x	0	0	0	1	SOH	DC1	!	1	A	Q	a	q
x	x	x	0	0	1	0	STX	DC2	"	2	B	R	b	r
x	x	x	0	0	1	1	ETX	DC3	#	3	C	S	c	s
x	x	x	0	1	0	0	EOT	DC4	$	4	D	T	d	t
x	x	x	0	1	0	1	ENQ	NAK	%	5	E	U	e	u
x	x	x	0	1	1	0	ACK	SYN	&	6	F	V	f	v
x	x	x	0	1	1	1	BEL	ETB	'	7	G	W	g	w
x	x	x	1	0	0	0	BS	CAN	(	8	H	X	h	x
x	x	x	1	0	0	1	HT	EM	)	9	I	Y	i	y
x	x	x	1	0	1	0	LF	SUB	*	:	J	Z	j	z
x	x	x	1	0	1	1	VT	ESC	+	;	K	[	k	{
x	x	x	1	1	0	0	FF	FS	,	<	L	\	l	|
x	x	x	1	1	0	1	CR	GS	-	=	M	]	m	}
x	x	x	1	1	1	0	SO	RS	.	>	N	^	n	~
x	x	x	1	1	1	1	SI	US	/	?	O	_	o	DEL

Figure 3–1. Standard ASCII character set.

The ANSI standard for ASCII characters divides them into two major categories according to their function. Characters that are used to generate readable text are labeled *graphic characters* and characters that are used to achieve action are labeled *control characters*. The former of these categories is somewhat misleading because the standard ASCII graphic characters are actually normal text characters. The term graphic would better apply to the *special extension characters* provided in the Personal Computer character set. The special characters and symbols with values of 176 through 223 are useful in the creation of graphic images on a Personal Computer monochrome display.

The ANSI standard for ASCII control characters breaks the group down into functional subgroups of *communication controls*, *format effectors*, and *information separators*. There is a fourth group not categorized by the ANSI standard which performs special functions; these characters are called *special control characters* for later reference. A diagram of the hierarchy of ASCII characters is shown in Figure 3-2 to give you a feel for the relationship between the different categories. The entire group of ASCII control characters is sometimes called *non-printing control characters*, but the

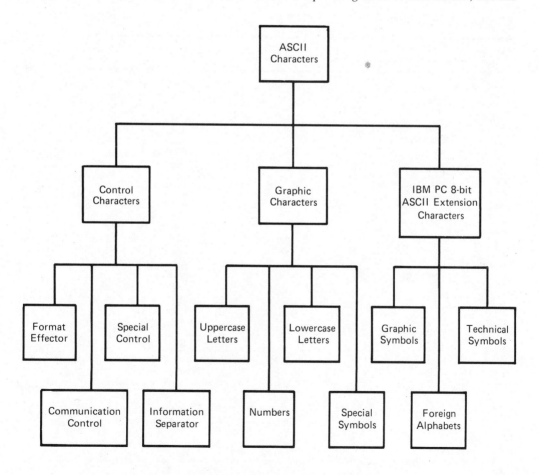

Figure 3–2. Hierarchy of ASCII characters.

label does not apply for the Personal Computer. Some of these characters have been assigned a graphic representation as you can see in Table 3-1. This table also provides a brief description of each control character and the control group that it falls within.

The ANSI definition of a communication control (CC) character is a character that controls or facilitates data transmission over a communications network. Several of these characters, including SYN, SOH, STX, ETX, and DLE, are illustrated in the discussion of bisync protocol in Chapter 2. These characters are typically used in synchronous serial protocols for data transfer handshaking. They tell the receiving device what to expect in the way of data, they indicate a transition in type of data being transmitted, or they are used to verify proper transmission and receipt.

The format effector (FE) characters are used to control the position of characters being printed or displayed. Sending these characters to the IBM printer either directly

Table 3-1.   ASCII   control   characters.

ASCII value	IBM-PC Character	Control Character	ASCII Character	Group	Communication Usage
000	(null)	^@	NUL	CC	Null character — filler
001	☺	^A	SOH	CC	Start of heading
002	●	^B	STX	CC	Start of text
003	♥	^C	ETX	CC	End of text
004	♦	^D	EOT	CC	End of transmission
005	♣	^E	ENQ	CC	Enquiry
006	♠	^F	ACK	CC	Acknowledge affirmative
007	(beep)	^G	BEL	SC	Audible alarm
008	(backspace)	^H	BS	FE	Backspace one position
009	(tab)	^I	HT	FE	Physical horizontal tab
010	(line feed)	^J	LF	FE	Line feed
011	(home)	^K	VT	FE	Physical vertical tab
012	(form feed)	^L	FF	FE	Form feed
013	(enter)	^M	CR	FE	Carriage return
014	♫	^N	SO	SC	Shift out
015	☼	^O	SI	SC	Shift in
016	►	^P	DLE	CC	Data link escape
017	◄	^Q	DC1	SC	XON or resume
018	↕	^R	DC2	SC	Device control 2
019	!!	^S	DC3	SC	XOFF or pause
020	¶	^T	DC4	SC	Device control 4
021	§	^U	NAK	CC	Negative acknowledgment
022	▬	^V	SYN	CC	Synchronous Idle
023	↨	^W	ETB	CC	End of transmission block
024	↑	^X	CAN	SC	Cancel
025	↓	^Y	EM	SC	End of medium
026	→	^Z	SUB	SC	Substitute
027	←	^[	ESC	SC	Escape
028	(cursor right)	^/	FS	IS	File separator
029	(cursor left)	^]	GS	IS	Group separator
030	(cursor up)	^^	RS	IS	Record separator
031	(cursor down)	^_	US	IS	Unit separator
127	⌂		DEL	SC	Delete

or as a BASIC CHR$(N) string allows you to produce text formatting. Word processing packages use these control characters in the control of text layout.

The information separator (IS) characters are used to control the separation of logical divisions of information as it is transmitted over communication channels. These characters are not generally used in Personal Computer communications and will not be reviewed in detail in this text.

The special control (SC) characters are used for printer control, data transmission speed-matching, or special data transmission error signaling. Some of these characters such as ESC and EM perform communication control functions, but they are not included in that category by the ANSI standard. More detailed information on the use of the ASCII control characters will be provided in the following paragraphs.

II. COMMUNICATION CONTROL CHARACTERS

To eliminate ambiguity and establish specific guidelines for the use of communication control characters, the ANSI has given each character a unique definition. These definitions and the specific IBM Personal Computer utilization of these characters are discussed next.

NUL

The Null character is, as its name implies, a null entity. The character is a non-printing time delay or filler character. The NUL may be inserted in or removed from a sequence of ASCII characters without affecting the meaning of the character sequence. Removal or addition of NUL characters may be performed, however, to produce desired information layout or equipment control. These characters are especially useful for communicating with printing devices that need a finite amount of time for print head positioning. Hard copy printing communication terminals often require at least two NUL characters following each carriage return to give the print head sufficient time to return to the left margin before receiving the next character. Some host system software packages allow you to specify a certain number of NULs to be transmitted to your computer after each carriage return.

SOH

The Start of Heading (SOH) is a communication control character used in bisync data streams to denote the start of a message heading data-block. Stations in a network check the data that follow this character to determine whether they are to be recipients of the data that will follow the heading. In essence, it is a "listen to see if your name is called" signal for stations in a network.

The SOH character is sometimes used in asynchronous communications to transfer a series of files without handling each file as a separate communication. The SOH character is used during multiple file transfers to signal the beginning of the filename of each file before transfer of the file begins. In asynchronous communications, there is only one receiver monitoring the communication line, so there is no need for a destination device address to follow the SOH character; only the filename of each file is needed. This type of file transfer is often limited to communications between microcomputers that are using the same communications software because it is not a standardized file transfer protocol.

The SOH is also used with the XMODEM file transfer protocol to signal the start of a 128-byte data block transfer. This character is followed by two block number bytes that are used to ensure proper block transfers.

STX

The Start of Text (STX) communication control character is also used in the bisync protocol. It signals the end of heading data and the beginning of information data.

ETX

The End of Text (ETX) communication control character is a bisync protocol signal that tells a receiver that all information data have been transmitted. This character can also be used to signal the beginning of block check characters that are used to detect communication errors.

EOT

The End of Transmission (EOT) communication control character is used to indicate the end of transmission of all data associated with a message sent to a particular device. This character also tells other devices in a network to check further transmissions for the presence of messages directed to them. The EOT character is the end frame for a message that is initiated by an SOH character. It is also used in the XMODEM protocol to indicate the end of a file transfer.

ETB

The End of Transmission Block (ETB) communication control character indicates the end of a particular block of transmitted data. The bisync protocol uses this character instead of an ETX character when data are transmitted in two or more blocks instead of a single continuous block.

ENQ

The Enquiry (ENQ) communication control character is used to request a response from a communication receiving station. It may be used to obtain the identification of a device or it may be used to determine data transmission status. Some IBM Personal Computer asynchronous communication packages use this character in protocol file transfers. In response to the receipt of the ENQ character, a receiving device may be required to respond with the number of the last block successfully received. This non-standard application of ENQ facilitates the retransmission of data blocks that were not properly received by the destination device.

ACK

The Acknowledge (ACK) communication control character is used to verify proper communication between a transmitter and receiver. One application of ACK is in data transmission error detection. After receipt of a block of data, a receiver may be required to send the transmitter an ACK character indicating that the error check character or characters show no transmission error. The transmitter may be required to receive the ACK before more data can be transmitted.

NAK

The Negative Acknowledge (NAK) communication control character is used to indicate improper communication between a transmitter and a receiver. This character is generally transmitted by a receiver to initiate a retransmission of data when an error-check indicates the presence of data transmission errors. The ENQ, ACK, and NAK characters are often used together for protocol data transmission that does not involve user interaction. These signals take place between two communication software packages and, when they are being properly executed, are transparent to the user. The NAK is also used in the XMODEM protocol to tell the transmitting computer that the receiving computer is ready to start a file transfer.

BEL

The Bell is a special ASCII control character that performs a function in keeping with its name. This character may be included in a text file or it may be transmitted between devices to signal the need for human attention. When transmitted in the conversation mode, which can be done by pressing the CTRL and G keys simultaneously, the character will cause the IBM Personal Computer speaker to emit an attention-getting beep. This same character can be transmitted to the IBM Personal Computer printer by using the BASIC command LPRINT CHR$(7).

BS

The Backspace (BS) control character is a format effector used to control the active print position for both the visual display monitor and the printer. This character moves the IBM Personal Computer cursor to the left one position, assuming the cursor is not in column one when the character is executed, and removes any character displayed in the position vacated. The key that produces this character is sometimes called the backspace delete key because of the action it produces. This character can be transmitted as data just as any other character is transmitted, but it is normally used only in conversation mode data transmission. Properly designed communication software will perform a backspace when the character is received instead of printing a new character. The backspace is used by the IBM printer to clear the print buffer and move the print head one position to the left.

HT

The Horizontal Tabulation (HT) format effector causes the active printing device to move to the next predetermined position before printing the next character. The HT character is executed on the Personal Computer keyboard by using special tab stop keys and can be executed on the IBM printer by performing a BASIC LPRINT CHR$(9).

LF

The Line Feed (LF) control character causes the active printing position to advance to the same column position in the next line. The results produced by this character are often confused with that of the carriage return (CR) discussed next. The line feed does not advance the cursor or print head to the first column of the next line unless it is preceded by a CR. Most business-oriented communications packages do not send line feeds with CRs unless specifically instructed to do so, and a file received without line feeds cannot be properly listed on an IBM Personal Computer Monitor until they are added. Using the DOS TYPE command to display such a file results in a stream of text that moves rapidly across the screen in a single line. Appendix B contains a listing of a BASIC program that will add line feeds after each CR contained in a file so that a user can list or edit the file.

VT

The Vertical Tabulation (VT) character is a format effector which causes the active printing or display position to advance to the same column a predetermined number of lines down from the present line being printed or displayed. Some conventions use the VT to move the cursor or print head to the first column of the new line. Transmitting a VT character to the IBM printer produces the same result as a single line feed—the print head moves down one line, but the column position remains the same.

FF

The Form Feed (FF) format effector is used to advance a print head to the next logical top of form or to a predetermined line of the next form or page. If the print head is at the top of a page when the printer is turned on, transmitting a FF character to the IBM printer while in the "On Line" mode (or depressing the FF push button on the printer while in the "Off Line" mode) will cause the printer to advance the print form to the top of a new page, regardless of the number of lines already printed on the page. If the print head is not at the top of a page when it is turned on, a FF will cause the paper to advance but not to the top of a new page. The logical top of form that will be advanced to on receipt of a FF is the line position on a new page that matches the line position of the print head when the printer was powered up.

A FF character will also clear the IBM PC display and place the cursor at the upper left-hand corner of the screen. This is often used by bulletin board and host systems to clear the display before starting a new function.

CR

The Carriage Return (CR) format effector advances the active print or display position to the first column of the same line. Unless the carriage return is followed by a line feed, the characters that follow the carriage return will over strike characters already printed on the line. This will often be the case when printing or displaying files that were received electronically from host or bulletin board systems because those systems normally do not send line feeds after each carriage return. The carriage return is also used to initiate the printing of a line when used with the IBM Personal Computer Printer. The printer captures all characters it receives in an area of its memory called a print buffer, then sends those characters to the print head when it receives a carriage return.

SO

The Shift Out (SO) is a special ASCII control character that serves to extend the standard graphics character set. The receipt of this character turns on the IBM Personal Computer Printer double width printing mode for the remainder of the line of text or until a DC4 control character is received. This same character is used by other printers to extend the character set to special graphic symbols used in math and engineering.

SI

The Shift In (SI) control character may be used to reset the receiving device to the Standard ASCII character set. It is also used by some printers to reset the print mode initialized by the Shift Out character. The IBM Personal Computer printer does not use this convention, however. It uses the DC4 character to frame or terminate the printing of double wide characters and uses the SI character to initiate compressed mode printing. The compressed mode is retained until the printer receives a DC2 character.

DLE

The Data Link Escape (DLE) communication control character is used to modify the meaning of a limited number of subsequent characters. It is used in the bisync protocol along with other control characters to signal the start and end of transparent mode data field transmission.

DC1

The Device Control 1 (DC1) character is an electronic toggle switch. Its function may be different for different vendor-supplied equipment, but it is generally used to control ancillary devices. For local display of files, this character (a Ctrl-Q) will reinitiate the listing of a file that was temporarily halted by a DC3 character (a Ctrl-S). In data communications, this character is often designated as XON and is used to reinitiate the transfer of data that was temporarily halted by the transmission of an XOFF character. The IBM Personal Computer may or may not use this handshake convention, depending on the communication software being used. Many communication programs written in the BASIC language are capable of transmitting the XON to a host but are incapable of recognizing the receipt of either XON or XOFF characters because of the limited data handling speed of the BASIC interpreter.

DC2

The Device Control 2 (DC2) character is also a toggle switch control character, and its role varies with vendor applications. The DC2 character is used with the IBM Personal Computer printer to turn off the compressed printing mode and empty the print buffer.

DC3

The Device Control 3 (DC3) character is another ASCII toggle switch, and it is often used with the DC1 character for data transfer speed-matching. The DC3 character is an XOFF, and it is used to temporarily halt the transmission of data. When a receiving device has received all the data it can handle, it may send the host an XOFF to stop the flow of data. When the device has printed or saved all the data received before the XOFF was transmitted, it will send an XON character to the host to reinitiate data transmission.

As indicated with the DC1 character, many BASIC communication programs are capable of sending XOFFs but cannot recognize XOFFs received from other microcomputer or host systems. To recognize and act on received XOFF characters, a BASIC program would have to compare every character bit pattern received to the XOFF bit pattern as other characters are being received and displayed, printed, or saved. This comparison technique would slow down data handling and result in long duration file transfers. Assembly language communication programs, on the other hand, often use an interrupt design that reacts quickly to XOFF characters, thereby making them excellent programs for large file transfers. This character is also temporarily used to halt the local listing of a file. It can be invoked by holding down the Ctrl key then pressing either the S key or Num Lock key.

DC4

The Device Control 4 (DC4) character is the fourth and last electronic toggle switch used in the ASCII character code, and like the other three toggle characters, its role is often vendor specific. The IBM Personal Computer uses this character to turn off its dot matrix printer double wide print mode that is initiated by the Shift Out character.

SYN

The Synchronous Idle (SYN) communication control character is used in the bisync protocol to initiate or maintain communication synchronization when no data are being transmitted. This character performs a function similar to the stop bit in asynchronous communication—it maintains a known signal on the data line when no data are being transferred. The interruption of a series of SYN characters is an indication of heading or data information to follow.

CAN

Cancel (CAN) is a special ASCII control character that has many different applications that are vendor specific, but it is generally used to denote an error in data transfer. The character is an indication that the data received should be disregarded.

EM

The End of Medium (EM) is another special ASCII control character, and it is used to indicate either the physical end of a data medium (data storage, representation of communication material) or the end of a portion of data medium containing desired data.

SUB

The Substitute (SUB) character is used for data communication accuracy control. It replaces a character that is determined to be in error, invalid, or impossible for the receiving device to display or print.

ESC

The Escape (ESC) control character is used extensively for communications with printers. It is normally transmitted just before the transmission of other characters or numbers to provide character code extensions or control code extensions. The sets of characters vary from one printer design to another. The IBM Personal Computer dot matrix printer is capable of accepting escape code sequences to perform such functions as turning emphasized print on and off and predetermining the values for horizontal and vertical tabs. Other dot matrix printers are designed to accept over 30 escape codes to perform these same functions plus many other advanced features such as dot addressable graphics control. The key to proper utilization of this character is the compatibility of software and hardware combinations.

FS

The File Separator (FS) is an information separator control character that is used to mark a logical boundary between files being transferred.

GS

The Group Separator (GS) is an information separator character used to mark logical boundaries between groups of transmitted data.

RS

The Record Separator (RS) is the third information separator character, and it is used to mark the boundaries between records in data transmission.

US

The Unit Separator (US) is the final information separator character, and it is used to mark the logical boundaries between distinct units of data.

DEL

The Delete (DEL) character is not actually a character but is used to erase or obliterate characters. The IBM Personal Computer BASIC editor uses this signal to remove characters positioned above the cursor. The character also causes the IBM dot matrix printer to delete the last received character. Other applications of the DEL character are comparable to the time delay application of the NUL character. The DEL can affect information layout or equipment control, however, which necessitates careful placement of the character.

III. OTHER COMMUNICATION CODES

As discussed earlier in the chapter, the other two data communication codes are the EBCDIC and Baudot. The EBCDIC code is used exclusively for communication between IBM equipment and is presently only supported on the IBM Personal Computer with the synchronous protocol. To replace an IBM 3270 terminal with an IBM Personal Computer, the 3270 terminal emulator packages must be able to communicate using the EBCDIC code. All other applications of IBM Personal Computer communications and the one used by most hobbyists is the ASCII character code.

The EBCDIC character set is based on an eight data bit binary signal standard that supports a wide array of characters. The ASCII and EBCDIC codes are listed in Appendix C, and from that listing you can see that most of the 7-bit ASCII characters are duplicated by 8-bit EBCDIC characters. This is not, however, an exhaustive listing of all characters supported by these two codes. The listing is only provided to show contrast in the two codes.

The Baudot code is an old five-data-bit code that is still used in some networks, but the code will see little application on the Personal Computer. The complete Baudot character set is listed in Appendix D, and from that listing you can see that the code does not support a large array of characters. The 5-bit code can only support 32 characters (2 to the 5th power), but two of the characters are used to shift between upper and lowercase, resulting in a full alphabet of uppercase letters and a limited set of numbers and figures.

The communication codes discussed in this chapter fall within the Data Link, Applications, and Presentation Layers of the seven layer ISO communications model discussed in Chapter 2, but the capabilities of these layers cannot be implemented to allow the Personal Computer to "talk" to other systems without the elements of the Physical Layer. Chapter 4 discusses the hardware required to implement this layer on the Personal Computer.

4

Communications Hardware

In the implementation of the Physical Layer of communications, the Personal Computer user will have to become familiar with several pieces of equipment. The selection of that equipment will depend on the serial communications protocol chosen. The communications adapter that is installed inside the Personal Computer system unit, the modem that connects to a telephone line, and the cable that connects the modem to the back of the communications adapter will be different for asynchronous and synchronous communications. This chapter concentrates on the equipment used in asynchronous communications since most Personal Computer communication is done in this mode; however, the last section of the chapter provides some information on synchronous terminal emulation hardware. Some typical hardware problems experienced by communications novices are also presented in Chapter 8.

I. THE ASYNCHRONOUS COMMUNICATIONS ADAPTER

The expression *communications adapter* is often used to describe the circuit board that permits the Personal Computer to communicate externally, but this label is only one of many used to describe this device. Other names for this board are serial port, serial board, asynchronous communications interface adapter, and Universal Asynchronous Receiver/Transmitter or UART (pronounced you-art). All these descriptions refer to a circuit board or a part of a circuit board that is designed to fit into an internal expansion slot and perform parallel-to-serial or serial-to-parallel conversions of binary data and other functions described in the following paragraphs.

As explained in Chapter 2, the IBM Personal Computer communicates internally with an 8-bit data bus, which is eight parallel wires. By using this technique, an 8-bit character can be transferred by sending all eight bits to a device simultaneously, resulting in rapid internal communications. When data have to be transferred over long distances, however, routing cable containing eight parallel wires becomes costly. Rather than route dedicated computer cables, most computer communications arrangements use ordinary public telephone equipment instead. Thus, the eight parallel bits that are transmitted by the computer must be funneled into a stream of sequential serial bits that can be sent over ordinary telephone lines. The communications adapter performs this electronic traffic cop chore. A graphic representation of the process is shown in Figure 2-2, page 16. At the receiving end, the communications adapter converts the serial flow of data bits back into a parallel flow so the receiving computer can process the information on its internal parallel buses.

Because of the serial nature of telephone communications and because of the potential for the introduction of communications errors from the telephone system, the communications adapter performs more than just parallel-to-serial and serial-to-parallel bit stream conversion. Some of the other functions performed by this device are listed in Table 4-1. To perform these diverse functions, the communications adapter is supplied with a small microprocessor, a separate clock and random access memory. The adapter is actually a self-contained microcomputer and its sophistication allows many of the functions described in Table 4-1 to be performed without the need for user involvement.

One communications adapter vital function is the control of data transmission speed. As explained in Chapter 2, data transmission is measured in bits per second, which is called bit rate or baud rate for asynchronous communications. The communications adapter supplied by IBM supports baud rates of 75, 110, 150, 300, 600, 1200, 1800, 2400, 4800, and 9600, which are selected and initiated by the software package used

Table 4-1. Asynchronous communications adapter functions.

- Monitors the communications link with the modem to prepare the communications line for data transmission.
- Allows software control of communications parameters.
- Regulates the speed of data transmission and reception to a predetermined fixed rate from 50 to 9600 baud.
- Adds start bits to character bit strings being transmitted.
- Adds error checking parity bits to the end of transmitted characters if instructed to do so by the communications software.
- Adds stop bits to character bit strings being transmitted.
- Buffers data waiting to be transmitted or waiting to be received by the computer.
- Detects and ignores false start bits.
- Deletes start bits from received character bit strings.
- Checks for errors between characters received and their associated parity bits if parity is being used.
- Sends parity error indication to the communications software.
- Deletes stop bits from character bit strings received.

to perform the communications. The important thing to remember regarding baud rate selection is that the baud rate being used by the Personal Computer during transmission has to match the baud rate of the receiving computer for data to be communicated properly. Otherwise, the data being received will appear to contain many transmission errors. Some sophisticated (and expensive) modems will detect the incoming baud rate being used at the start of a communications session and switch rates to match that of the incoming call if the incoming call is operating at a different baud rate. Some communications software will perform this switching function also. Usually neither the modem nor the software you use for communications is capable of automatically performing the switch to the proper baud rate, and you must manually switch the communications baud rate with your communications software.

Since asynchronous communications is, by definition, not continuous, a computer system receiving this type of data must know when data transmission is starting so the receiving computer's timing device can synchronize with that of the transmitting device. As discussed earlier, this is accomplished with a start bit. The communications adapter adds a start bit to each string of data bits (an alphanumeric character when transmitting ASCII) as it passes through the adapter to tell the receiving computer to prepare itself for the receipt of data. The communications adapter on the receiving end, after synchronizing with the incoming signal, must strip the start bit from the data because it serves no further purpose; it would only occupy valuable space when stored with the transmitted data.

The communications adapter may also be used to add a parity bit to each character transmitted. By adding the parity bit to each string of data bits, the adapter can make the total number of bits per character even or odd. The receiving computer's communications adapter can then check each set of data bits received to be sure it contains either an odd or even number of 1 bits. If the receiving adapter detects an error, it can signal the user, through communications software, that a transmission error has occurred.

Following the transmission of a character, the communications adapter must signal the receiving computer that transmission is finished. This is accomplished by adding stop bits (equivalent to binary 1's) between transmitted characters. This "test period" allows the receiving adapter to translate the last transmitted serial data into parallel data and to transmit that data to the receiving memory buffer or disk file. It also allows accurate measurement of the start point for the next character start bit. Stop bits may be 1-, 1.5-, or 2-bit times in length. Normal use requires 2 with 110 baud and 1 with baud rates of 300 and higher.

Other functions performed by the communications adapter will not be discussed here because they are normally transparent to the user and beyond the scope of this book. It is worth noting, however, that the functions provided by the communications adapter can be combined with that of parallel printer circuitry and additional memory capacity on a *single combination expansion board* to conserve expansion slots in the IBM Personal Computer. Many of the vendors marketing these combination boards have duplicated the functions of single-function IBM boards, and the user cannot detect the difference between the operation of the single function boards and a combination board.

II. THE RS-232-C STANDARD

When shopping for data communications equipment, you will frequently see the phrases "standard RS-232-C" and "RS-232-C compatible." These statements usually mean the device or cable uses a *DB-25 connector*, but it does not guarantee that all the signals defined by the *RS-232-C standard* are supported by the device. Many standard RS-232-C cables have been purchased to connect modems and serial printers to Personal Computers but were returned when the user found that some of the modem or printer features could not be activated because of signals that were not being transmitted by the cable. Because of a lack of conformity in the implementation of the RS-232-C standard, some serial printers will not work at all without special cables designed specifically for the make and model being used.

The RS-232-C is a standard that was published in 1969 by the *Electronic Industries Association (EIA)*. The RS is an acronym for Recommended Standard and the 232 is the identification number for that particular standard. The C designates the last revision made to the RS-232 standard. The purpose of this standard is to define the electrical characteristics for the interfacing of *data terminal equipment (DTE)* and *data communications equipment (DCE)*. For the IBM Personal Computer user, these terms refer to the Personal Computer and a modem respectively. Other devices such as serial printers may be configured as DCE or DTE devices, depending on the manufacturer. The differences between these configurations are discussed in the following paragraphs. Figure 4-1 is a diagram of the application of the RS-232-C interfacing cable with the Personal Computer. From this figure you can see that the RS-232-C interface performs a critical role in Personal Computer communications. It is the link that facilitates the transfer of data to and from another computer via the telephone system.

Other pertinent facts regarding the application of the RS-232-C standard to the Personal Computer is the baud rate and cable lengths supported. The standard applies to serial data transfer rates in the range from 0 to 20,000 bits per second which adequately covers the 50 to 9600 baud range available for the Personal Computer. The

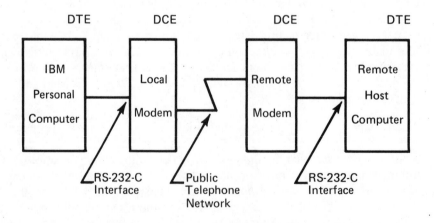

Figure 4–1. RS-232-C interface application.

cable length limitation specified by the standard is 50 feet, which should also cover most Personal Computer communications hardware configurations. Cable lengths greater than 50 feet can be used (and are often used on mainframe systems), but such applications should be thoroughly tested to ensure signal quality before being relied upon.

RS-232-C SIGNAL CHARACTERISTICS

To ensure that binary data are transmitted properly and that equipment controls are properly performed, it is necessary to agree on the signals that will be used. The RS-232-C standard provides voltage ranges for data and control signals to satisfy this requirement. These ranges are shown in Table 4-2 and Figure 4-2.

Table 4-2. Interchange voltage standard.

Interchange Voltage	Binary Logic State	Signal Condition	Interface Control Function
Positive	0	Space	On
Negative	1	Mark	Off

The IBM Personal Computer user is not normally concerned with the voltage ranges and signals associated with those ranges as they pertain to communications. These signals are of concern to hardware vendors and are used during the design of asynchronous communications adapters and modems, but when properly implemented, the operation of these signals will not require Personal Computer user interaction.

RS-232-C PIN ASSIGNMENTS

The physical implementation of the RS-232-C standard is shown in Figure 4-3. This figure illustrates the *pin assignments* used in the design of the DB-25 connector normally

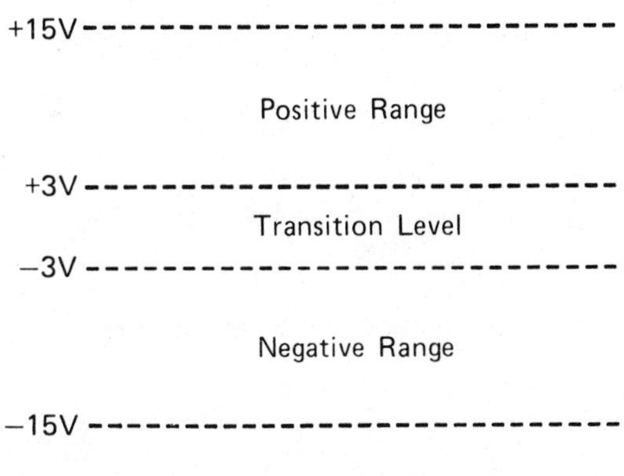

```
+15V -----------------------------

             Positive Range

 +3V --------------------------------
             Transition Level
 -3V ---------------------------

             Negative Range

-15V ---------------------------
```

Figure 4-2. Interchange voltage ranges.

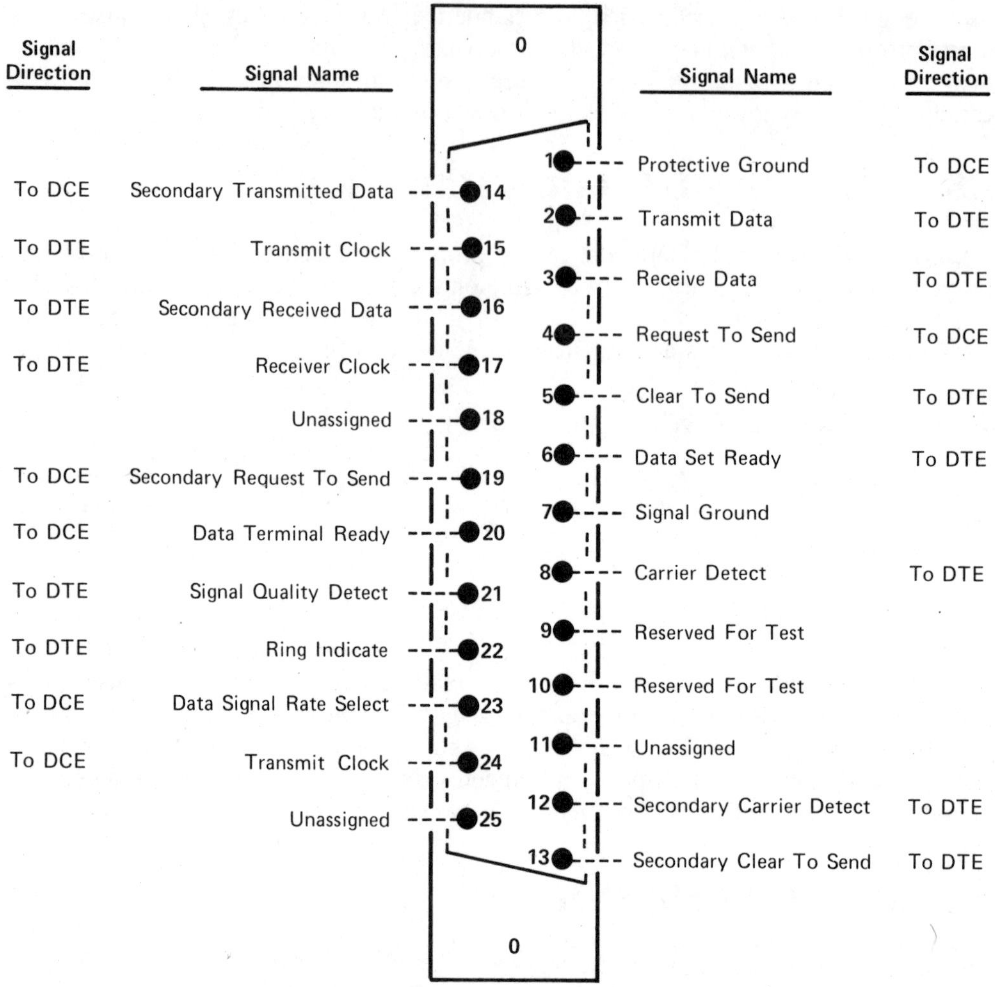

Signal Direction	Signal Name			Signal Name	Signal Direction
		0			
		1		Protective Ground	To DCE
To DCE	Secondary Transmitted Data	14	2	Transmit Data	To DTE
To DTE	Transmit Clock	15	3	Receive Data	To DTE
To DTE	Secondary Received Data	16	4	Request To Send	To DCE
To DTE	Receiver Clock	17	5	Clear To Send	To DTE
	Unassigned	18	6	Data Set Ready	To DTE
To DCE	Secondary Request To Send	19	7	Signal Ground	
To DCE	Data Terminal Ready	20	8	Carrier Detect	To DTE
To DTE	Signal Quality Detect	21	9	Reserved For Test	
To DTE	Ring Indicate	22	10	Reserved For Test	
To DCE	Data Signal Rate Select	23	11	Unassigned	
To DCE	Transmit Clock	24	12	Secondary Carrier Detect	To DTE
	Unassigned	25	13	Secondary Clear To Send	To DTE
		0			

DTE=Data Terminal Equipment (Personal Computer)
DCE=Data Communications Equipment (Modem)

Figure 4–3. RS-232-C pin assignments.

used on each end of an asynchronous communications cable. Although these pin assignments are defined under the RS-232-C standard, the actual design of the connector is controlled by the International Standards Organization document ISO 2113. Also, the female version of this connector is supposed to be used on modems and the male on communications adapters, but equipment vendors do not always follow that standard.

The pin assignments shown in Figure 4-3 would lead you to believe that data are always transmitted on the wire assigned to pin 2 and that data are always received on pin 3. Both the computer and a modem or printer cannot, however, transmit and receive over the same wire, which makes the pin assignments somewhat confusing. A discussion of each pin that is implemented with the IBM Personal Computer asynchronous adapter is provided next to eliminate some of the confusion. Also, the pin labels assigned by the RS-232-C standard are from the perspective of the DTE (Personal Computer, in this case), which should help clarify some of the confusion.

Transmit Data (TD, Pin 2)

The signals on this pin are transmitted from the Personal Computer to a modem or printer. The asynchronous adapter maintains this circuit in the marking condition (logic condition 1 equivalent to a stop bit) when no data are being transmitted.   ~ie 'Idle'

Receive Data (RD, Pin 3)

The signals on this pin are transmitted from a modem or printer to the Personal Computer asynchronous adapter. This circuit is also maintained in a marking condition when no data are being transmitted.

Request to Send (RTS, Pin 4)

This circuit is used to send a signal to a modem or printer requesting clearance to send data over circuit 2. This signal is used with the Clear to Send circuit to control the flow of data from the Personal Computer to a modem or to a serial printer.

Clear to Send (CTS, Pin 5)

This circuit is used by a modem or serial printer to indicate to the Personal Computer that it is ready to receive data. When this circuit is OFF (negative voltage or logic 1 state), the receiving device is telling the Personal Computer that it is not ready to receive data.

Data Set Ready (DSR, Pin 6)

When this circuit is ON (logic 0), it is a signal to the Personal Computer that a modem is properly connected to the telephone line and in the data transmission mode. Auto-dial modems send this signal to the Personal Computer after successfully dialing a host computer.

Signal Ground (SG, Pin 7)

This circuit serves as a signal reference for all other circuits used in communications. It is at zero voltage relative to all other signals.

Carrier Detect (CD, PIN 8)

A modem sends the Personal Computer an ON signal on this circuit when a proper carrier signal is being received from a remote modem. This signal is used to illuminate the CD (carrier detect) LED indicator located on the front of a modem.

Data Terminal Ready (DTR, Pin 20)

The Personal Computer turns this circuit ON when it is ready to communicate with a modem. Most modems cannot signal the Personal Computer that a proper telephone connection has been made with a host system until this circuit is turned ON. If the Personal Computer turns this signal OFF during communications with a host system, this type of modem will drop the telephone connection. The function of the DTR signal as well as the CTS, DSR, and RTS in communications with a modem are shown on the flow chart in Figure 4-4.

Ring Indicate (RI, Pin 22)

This circuit is used by an auto-answer modem to indicate a telephone ring signal. The circuit is maintained ON during each ring and OFF between rings.

All the aforementioned signals are implemented by the selection of a proper communications cable. The following section discusses the how's and why's of cable and connector selection.

III. CABLES AND GENDERS

The RS-232-C signals are transmitted to and from the asynchronous adapter by a *communications cable*. The cable may come in a round shape or a flat ribbon shape. The shape of the cable makes no difference in its ability to support communications, but the types of connectors provided on each end of the cable or the number of wires connected to the pins in the connectors do make a difference.

When purchasing a communications cable for the PC, you should pay special attention to the gender of the cable's connectors, particularly when buying the communications adapter from one vendor and the cable from a different vendor. Almost all modems have a *DB-25 female connector* which requires a cable with a *DB-25 male connector.* Communications adapters, on the other hand, may be made with either a male or female connector. The same vendor may even produce two communication adapters with connectors of different gender. The safest bet is to buy the modem and communications adapter, then buy a cable that matches.

You may want to buy the parts at a local electronics parts supply store and make your own communications cable. You can buy a flat 40 wire ribbon cable, strip off all but 25 wires, then attach compression type connectors on each end. The two advantages to making your own cable are that you can change cable connector gender

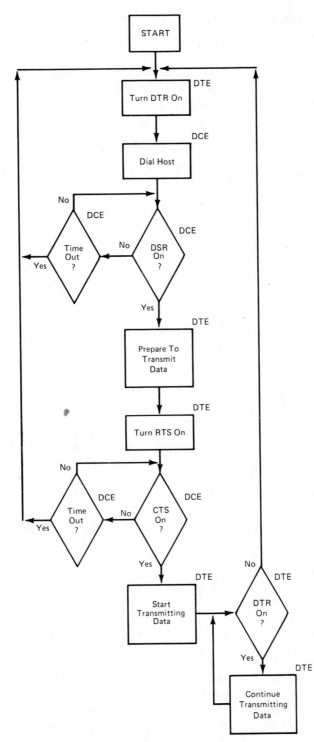

Figure 4–4. Modem signal logic flow chart.

easily if you change communications adapters, and you are assured that all 25 pins in the cable are connected.

As discussed earlier, there is no such thing as standard RS-232-C implementation when it comes to actual hardware production. The number of pins connected in a communications cable fall into this category. The so-called "Basic 8" pins are 1 through 7 and 20 and many communications cables are made with only those pins soldered in place. The IBM communications adapter, however, requires that pin 8 also be connected. Some communications software packages also require that pin 22 be connected for all the software functions to operate properly. So, to eliminate the myriad of pin problems you could encounter in setting up a communications interface, it would be safe to insist on a *full 25 pin cable*.

IV. MODEMS

Modems provide the final link between the Personal Computer and the public telephone system, and their design and costs are changing rapidly. Modem capabilities are increasing and their costs are decreasing with time, making the selection and purchase of just one a complicated matter. The following discussion of the characteristics and capabilities of modems may make that choice easier.

HOW MODEMS WORK

In the simplest terms, a modem converts the *binary electrical signals* it receives from a terminal into *voice-frequency signals* that can be transmitted over the public telephone system. A modem also receives voice-frequency signals transmitted through the telephone system by a remote modem and converts them into binary electrical signals that are forwarded to a terminal. As shown in Figure 4-5, modems *modulate* digital signals (square wave signals) into analog signals (oscillating signals) and *demodulate* analog signals into digital signals. From that *modulate-demodulate* function, the name *modem* is derived.

It is necessary to convert digital signals into analog signals for transmission over telephone lines because of the equipment used in the telephone system. Many pieces of public telephone equipment perform amplifying and filtering functions that will alter *square wave signals* into unrecognizable garbage by the time they reach another computer across town. Modems are used to produce signals compatible with telephone equipment.

Another limitation imposed by the quality of public telephone equipment is the rate at which data can be transferred. Personal Computer hobbyists will find that modems that fall within their budgets operate at 1200 bits per second (bps) or less. Data transfer rates as high as 4800 bps can be achieved using the same telephone equipment, but modems that provide that capability are significantly more complex and expensive than those that operate at 1200 bps.

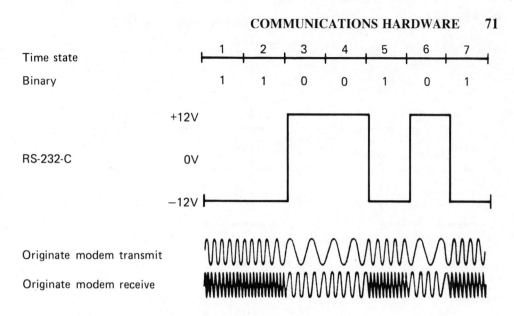

Figure 4–5. Digital signal modulation.

There are several ways of categorizing modems. They can be differentiated by their speed, protocols, features, and intelligence. Figure 4-6 shows the typical methods used to categorize modems.

MODEM SPEEDS AND PROTOCOLS

The speed of a modem is determined by the maximum rate it can transmit or receive data. That rate is measured in bits per second or baud. *Bits per second* is the number of binary digits transferred per second, whereas *baud* is the number of signal events transmitted per second. For most IBM Personal Computer communications applications, these rates will be the same. The rates differ only when digital signals are superimposed onto analog signals, resulting in each signal event carrying two or more binary bits.

The three speed classifications of modems are listed as follows:

Modem Class	Bits Per Second
Low-Speed	600 or less
Medium-Speed	1200–9600
High-Speed	over 9600

The most common modem used in Personal Computer configurations is the *Bell-103 compatible low-speed modem*. Almost every modem manufacturer produces a Bell-103 modem and the cost of these units falls in the range from $80 to $300. The less expensive models do not support *auto-dial* and *auto-answer* and cannot be used to store telephone numbers. Expensive models can be used for auto-dial of telephone numbers stored in disk files or stored in the modem's own memory. The more so-

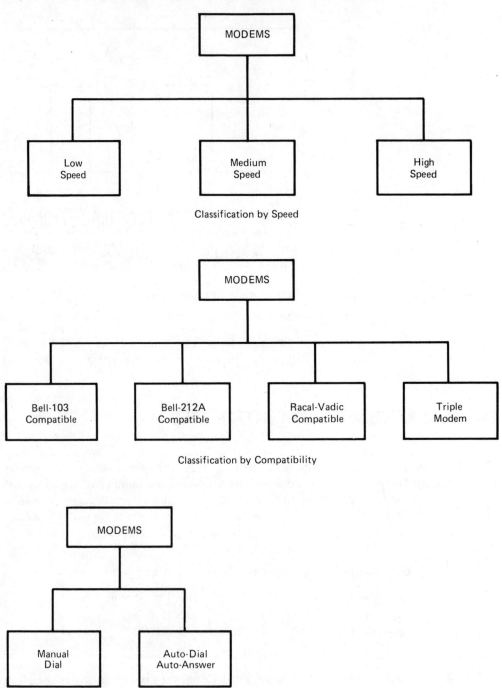

Figure 4–6. Modem classifications.

phisticated Bell-103 modems can also be set up with host software for unattended auto-answer operation.

The distinguishing characteristic of the Bell-103 modem is the way it handles transmitted and received data. As shown in Figures 4-7a and 4-7b these modems use specific *audio frequency ranges* to differentiate between *transmitted* and *received* data. The Bell-103 *originate-mode frequency* information which follows also shows that the binary logic of transmitted and received data is assigned specific frequencies.

Direction	Signal Logic	Frequency (HZ)
Transmit	0	1070
Transmit	1	1270
Receive	0	2025
Receive	1	2225

The originate and answer modes for Bell-103 modems are controlled through *frequency shifting*. The modem that initiates a communications link is set to the originate-mode and the remote modem that responds to the initiation and completes the communications link is set to the answer-mode. As shown in Figures 4-7a and 4-7b, the answer-mode receive frequencies are the same as the originate-mode transmit frequencies. By the same token, the originate-mode receive frequencies are the same as the answer-mode transmit frequencies. Because of the difference in transmit and receive frequencies, one modem always has to be in the answer-mode and the other in the originate-mode for the communications link to be properly established and data transferred.

The important thing to know regarding originate/answer modem designs is that you can get Bell-103 modems that will do one or the other or both. If you never plan to have your modem answer an incoming call from another computer or terminal, then you do not need the answer-mode capability. Originate-only modems are generally cheaper than modems that support both modes.

Low-speed modems are excellent for applications that require a great deal of conversation mode communications or small file transfers. The maximum continuous transfer rate at *300 baud* is *30 characters per second*, which translates into approximately *300 words per minute*. An outstanding typist would have difficulty taxing such a configuration. Another advantage of 300 baud communications is that many people can comfortably read text at that speed. Listing a file on your Personal Computer monitor can be done if you want to read the information but have no need to store it for later use. Time sharing information services generally charge less for low-speed connection time which can also result in cost savings for conversation mode interaction.

For applications that involve frequent large file transfers or the clustering of input from several terminals, low-speed modems are not a good choice. It takes approximately one minute to transfer 2000 bytes of text at 300 baud which translates into 30 minutes of connect time to transfer a 60K file. The transfer of several 60K files results in the computer being dedicated to communications for a significant period of time; operator support is also required during the entire session if the communications software used

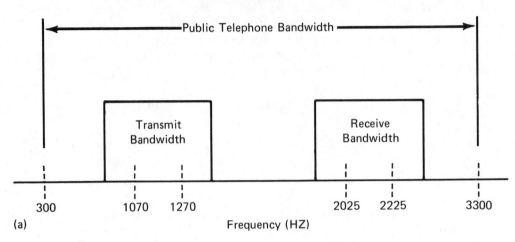

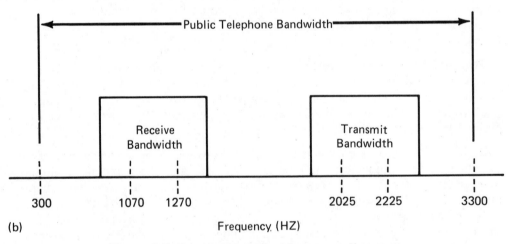

Figure 4–7. Low-speed modem frequency diagrams.

does not provide batch mode or multiple file transfer options. For applications of that type, most businesses and some hobbyists choose *medium-speed modems*.

Most of the medium-speed modems available to the Personal Computer owner operate at *1200 bps*, but their compatibility with other systems varies with the make and model. Some new 1200 bps modems only operate in half-duplex which limits the information systems you can access. For example, THE SOURCE cannot be accessed by anything but a full-duplex system. Other modems offer compatibility with either

Bell-212A or *Racal-Vadic* systems. The more expensive medium-speed modems are compatible with both Bell-212A and Racal-Vadic, and some so-called *triple modems* support Bell-103, Bell-212A, and Racal-Vadic protocols. Generally, you will pay for what you get in modems—the more features it has, the more it will cost.

Medium-speed modems differ in several ways from low-speed modems. Instead of shifting frequencies as is done under the Bell-103 protocol, these modems use a technique called *phase shifting*. Bell-212A and Racal-Vadic protocols use different frequencies, however, and are therefore not compatible. Both protocols use phase shifting to increase *data throughput*, but the signal frequency used as a basis for the phase shifting is different for the two. This simply means that the same modem protocol has to be used at both ends of a 1200 baud communications link, which adds another level of complexity when going from 300 baud to 1200 baud. Fortunately for the Personal Computer user, most information services offer both Bell-212A and Racal-Vadic compatibility so 1200 baud communications can be achieved without purchasing a top-of-the-line medium-speed modem.

Modems that operate at speeds over 1200 bps use more sophisticated electrical signal manipulation to achieve those rates while staying within the frequency limits imposed by public telephone equipment. A technique called *phase amplitude modulation* is used, which is a combination of phase shifting and amplitude modulation. This signal magic is used in the design of 9600 bps modems that are used for synchronous communications.

MODEM FEATURES

Besides classification by speed and protocol, modems are often classified by features or level of intelligence. As the cost of memory and microprocessors decreases, the power and flexibility of modems increase making last years model almost obsolete. This has been the trend over the past several years and is expected to continue into the future.

A "want" list of most of the features available in modems is shown in Table 4-3. Most hobbyists find that a modem offering only a few of these features meet their needs, but some business applications require a *full feature modem* that supports a majority of the listed features. It should be noted, however, that the term "full feature" differs from one modem manufacturer to another. If you need several capabilities in a single modem, you should investigate the actual features provided by available models before purchasing one.

There are also communications applications that do not involve long distance links through the telephone system. Some situations call for the transfer of data between two microcomputers located within the same room. This can be accomplished by placing a short length of telephone line between the modems connected to the two computers, or it can be accomplished by eliminating the modems and connecting the asynchronous adapters of both computers directly together. The first method simply eliminates the necessity of dialing a telephone number before communications begin,

Table 4-3. Modem features.

Direct Connect

Allows direct connection between modem and telephone line and eliminates acoustical coupling equipment.

Auto-Answer

Allows the user to switch the modem into the answer mode by sending it a sequence of characters or signals through the communications link.

Auto-Dial

Allows the user to dial a telephone number either from the Personal Computer keyboard or through software access to a telephone number stored in a disk file. The modem dials the number and establishes the proper carrier signal with a remote host system.

Auto-Redial

Allows the user to redial the last number called by sending the modem a short sequence of characters or signals. Some redial features allow auto-redial if a dialed number was busy or if no carrier was detected.

Telephone Directory

Nonvolatile modem memory allows the user—through software control—to store and automatically dial telephone numbers using a dialing directory.

Auto-Reset

Allows the user to reset the modem to default parameters by sending it a sequence of characters or signals.

Baud-Switch

The modem senses the baud rate of incoming calls and switches to the proper baud rate.

Self-Test

Allows the user to perform software controlled diagnostic testing of the modem's capabilities.

---

but the second method is more complex and requires special equipment, as discussed in the next section.

V. COMPUTER-TO-COMPUTER CONNECTIONS

If you are the proud new owner of an IBM Personal Computer, but you have several hundred programs that you developed on a TRS-80, you are probably interested in transferring some of the software over to your new PC. To do that, you will need to interface the two computers using a device called a *null modem* or *modem eliminator*.

Actually a null modem is not a modem at all—it is a cable that is designed to eliminate the need for a modem. The cable makes each computer operate as if it were communicating with a modem. This is accomplished as shown in Figures 4-8 and 4-9. In Figure 4-8 you can see that the microcomputer and the modem are sending and receiving data over compatible lines, whereas the two microcomputers are both ex-

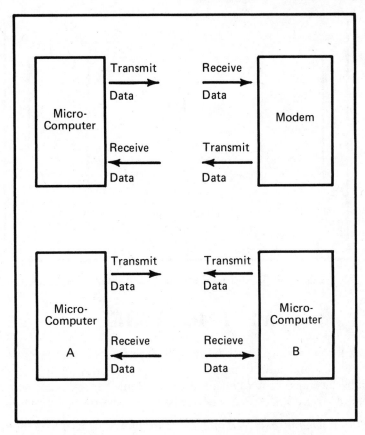

Figure 4–8. Microcomputer-modem interfaces.

pecting to receive and send data on the same lines. Figure 4-9 shows the null modem solution to the incompatibility of micro-to-micro communications. By crossing the Receive Data and Transmit Data lines, microcomputer A is listening on the line microcomputer B is talking on and vice versa.

Null modems can be purchased from a variety of computer electronics stores, but care should be taken in selecting one. There are several ways to connect the cable pins together to get two micros to talk to each other. Figure 4-10 shows a connection diagram that should work between the Personal Computer and most other microcomputers.

By making a direct computer-to-computer connection via a null modem, data can be quickly transferred between two microcomputers. The 1200 baud practical limit of public telephone networks does not exist with the direct connection. Communication software written in the BASIC language can transfer data at rates as high as 2400 baud, whereas some assembly language software can transfer data at a whopping 9600 baud. Direct connections not only allow rapid data transfer, but line noise and other causes of telephone line data transfer errors are eliminated.

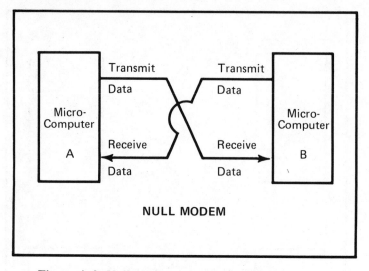

Figure 4–9. Null modem microcomputer interface.

VI. EMULATORS

Emulation is a technique used with the IBM PC to make it behave almost exactly like a specific type of mainframe terminal. The implementation of this technique often requires both hardware and software components. Some hardware and software aspects of emulation are covered here, but an exhaustive discussion is not presented.

Using the PC as a *mainframe terminal emulator* allows the user to do both mainframe access and local processing with the same hardware. Large number crunching programs can be processed on the bigger and faster mainframe, or smaller spreadsheet or word-processor applications can be processed locally.

IBM has three emulation packages available for the PC, and all three packages are designed to emulate IBM terminals. The packages are SNA 3270, SNA 3770 Remote Job Entry (RJE), and IBM 3101. The SNA 3270 and the SNA 3770 RJE require a special synchronous data link control (SDLC) communications adapter, but the IBM 3101 emulator is a software package only that operates with the asynchronous communications adapter.

The SDLC adapter allows the user to participate in networks that use the SDLC protocols. It will also work with a public telephone or leased line network. To operate properly in an SDLC network using this adapter, a PC must be supplied with the IBM SNA 3270 Emulation and RJE Support Program or an equivalent software package from another vendor.

The SDLC adapter is designed to fit into a PC expansion slot and is provided with a 25-pin "D" shell male-type connector—the same configuration used with the IBM asynchronous communications adapter. The SDLC adapter also interfaces with an SDLC modem using an RS-232-C cable. Other SDLC adapter features are listed as follows:

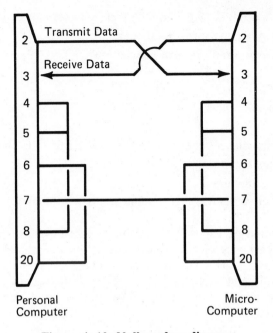

Figure 4–10. Null modem diagram.

- Data transfer rates up to 9600 bps
- Modem control function support
- Program-controlled data transfer support
- Prioritized system interrupt control
- Error detection and reporting
- Field installable and replaceable

With the application of proper software, the SDLC adapter allows a user to participate in an IBM network that is communicating in the EBCDIC character code. The IBM PC can appear to the host system as an IBM 2774 Model 51, Logical Unit Type 2, control unit. The screen formats used with the IBM 3278 Display Station are also emulated.

AST Research Inc. also supplies emulation hardware and software for the PC. Their EM 3780 package comes complete with interface adapter and software that allows the PC to be run as a Remote Job Entry emulator. The EM 3780 uses the binary synchronous (bisync) protocol and allows the PC to communicate with the following host systems:

IBM System 360	IBM 3780 Terminals
IBM System 370	DEC PDP-11 Systems
IBM 2780 Terminals	DEC Vax Systems

The EM 3780 package supports fast file transfers. The maximum baud is 38,400. It also allows PC connections into several network configurations. Some of these configurations are listed as follows:

- Point-to-point (leased) or switched telephone networks via a synchronous modem
- Local networks via a synchronous modem
- Local networks via a null modem connection

The EM 3780 package performs the following:

- Receives data from a host
- Transmits files to a host
- Automatically translates between the ASCII and EBCDIC character codes
- Pads or truncates data to match host systems
- Controls printer functions
- Supports interactive keyboard communications with a host

Several other emulation packages are available for the PC, but will not be discussed here. The previous packages were presented as examples of emulator capabilities. The primary focus of this text is asynchronous communications and local area network participation. The following chapter continues the discussion of asynchronous communications with an explanation of the software required to control the hardware discussed in this chapter.

5

Communications Software

After assembling the pieces of hardware described in Chapter 4, there is one more item that has to be added before the PC can communicate with other computer systems. This last item is the communications software package. Before delving into the subject of communications software, however, it is a good idea to review the relationship between IBM PC software and hardware.

I. SOFTWARE LAYERS

As shown in Figure 5-1, the central processing unit (CPU) is the piece of hardware that directs the flow of communications within the PC, but the commands that control that piece of hardware come from the *operating system*. The operating system is actually several software programs that direct the operation of all internal IBM PC components. Its function is to schedule and coordinate component activities.

The IBM PC has a simple operating system called a *monitor* that is built into the motherboard read-only memory (ROM). This is a bootstrap "hard wired" system that takes over the PC when the unit is turned on; it performs an internal test of the PC including all random access memory (RAM) and reports detected errors. The monitor also starts the A: disk drive operating so that the more powerful *disk operating system (DOS)* loads into memory.

The disk operating system assumes control of the PC after it loads into memory. This system has the necessary commands to control all the peripherals shown on the right side of Figure 5-1. It also controls the transfer of programs and data between disk files and RAM memory (whereby it gets the name Disk Operating System). This system also controls some of the design characteristics of the software that can be loaded and run in the PC; one operating system may support a particular communications function and another may not. Some of the operating systems presently available

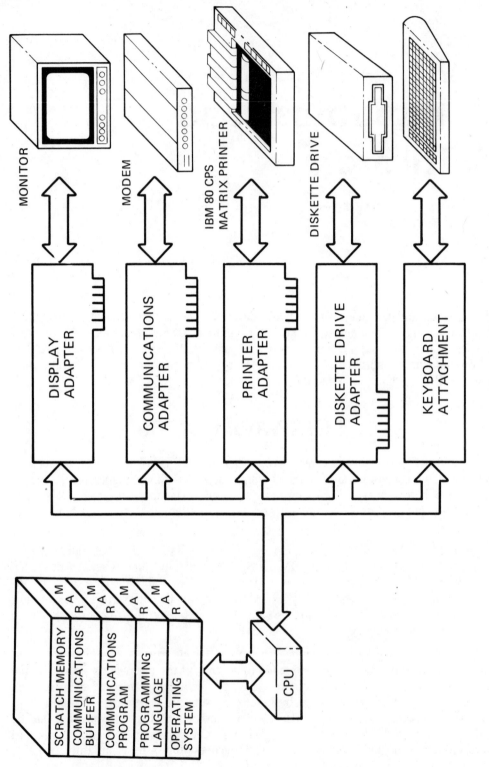

MONITOR

MODEM

IBM 80 CPS
MATRIX PRINTER

DISKETTE DRIVE

DISPLAY
ADAPTER

COMMUNICATIONS
ADAPTER

PRINTER
ADAPTER

DISKETTE DRIVE
ADAPTER

KEYBOARD
ATTACHMENT

SCRATCH MEMORY
RAM

COMMUNICATIONS
BUFFER
RAM

COMMUNICATIONS
PROGRAM
RAM

PROGRAMMING
LANGUAGE
RAM

OPERATING
SYSTEM
RAM

CPU

Figure 5–1. IBM PC communication overview.

for the IBM PC are: IBM's *PC-DOS*; Phase One System's *Oasis-16*; Digital Research's *CP/M-86*; the University of California, San Diego *p-System*, and a variety of Unix type systems.

The next layer of software required for communications is the *programming language*. This layer may be assembly language or a higher level language such as *BASIC*, *FORTRAN*, *Pascal*, or *FORTH*. This layer actually only exists when an *application program* has not been assembled or compiled into machine code. Before a BASIC communications program can be loaded and run, the BASIC language has to be loaded into memory. *High level language* programs that have been compiled and assembly language programs that have been assembled into *machine code* are loaded and executed without loading a programming language. These *directly executable* applications programs (for example, files that have EXE and COM extensions) eliminate the need for the programming language layer shown in Figure 5-1. These machine code programs also operate faster than programs that operate within a programming language because one layer of command translation is eliminated.

In the sequence of software loading from disk to memory, the *communications program* is the last to load. When the communications program is loaded, a certain amount of random access memory is also set aside for the communications buffer described in Chapter 2. Beyond this buffer is a section of memory used for software housecleaning that will not be of concern for most communications users.

The key factor in the software portion of the model shown in Figure 5-1 is compatibility between the operating system that controls the CPU and the next two layers of software. The programming language and the communications program must be designed to operate with the specific operating system the user has chosen for the PC. Commands issued by the communications program must be understood and executed by the operating system to produce the communications results discussed in Chapter 2 and to support the capabilities described later in this chapter.

Besides communicating properly with an operating system, the software must also provide a mechanism for the transfer of data from one device to another. The operating system can control each of the PC's peripherals, but the software must decide which device is to get which data. After the selection of the device to receive certain data, there must be a mechanism for signaling the need to transmit or receive data. There must also be a mechanism for indicating the occurrence of errors and terminating operations when errors occur. The two design techniques used for these data transfer controls and error handling controls are called polling and interrupt driven.

II. POLLING VERSUS INTERRUPT DRIVEN

Although both *polling* and *interrupt driven* communications software accomplish the same objectives of accepting input from the keyboard and transferring data to and from the communications link, they differ significantly in the methods used to accomplish these tasks. They also differ significantly in the speed with which they accomplish the tasks.

The polling technique can result in slow reactions to changes. This method requires that the CPU continually check devices such as the keyboard and the communications adapter to see which devices have data available. If the input buffer for one of these devices contains data when it is polled, the CPU may be required to take all the data from the buffer and process it before going on to check the next device's buffer. If the user wants to interrupt the receipt of a file, the CPU might be emptying the communications receive buffer when the interrupt command is executed. Several characters might continue to display on the monitor before the transfer interrupt appears to occur. A signal received through the communications port might also be acted on slowly because the CPU is polling another device when the signal arrives.

The interrupt driven input/output control technique, on the other hand, causes a program to react quickly to changes under most circumstances. The interrupt technique allows the CPU to continue performing a designated task until data are actually made available which require the performance of a different task. No time is wasted in the polling of devices. When a device has data available, it sends the CPU an *interrupt signal* indicating the desire to be serviced. Whether the CPU stops an activity to service another device depends on the *interrupt priority* given to that device by the communications software. An interrupt such as a minor error indicator that is to be ignored is *masked* by the software. Interrupts that require an immediate response are not masked and are given top priority. For example, the ESC key can be programmed to instantaneously transfer the user from the conversation mode to the command mode regardless of other operations that are being performed at the time. By the same token, the software can be designed to quickly stop the transmission of data on receipt of an XOFF character. Because of the rapid response of interrupt driven software, better speed-matching with host systems can be achieved, resulting in a lower probability of data loss.

The disadvantage of interrupt driven software is the complexity of design required to achieve proper interrupt prioritization. In the polling design, the CPU always knows where data are coming from and interrupts are handled one-at-a-time, based on the *polling sequence*. With interrupt driven design, however, an interrupt can occur at any time during a program execution. The software has to be able to recognize the origin of the interrupt and determine what action to take, based on preselected priorities. The software also has to be designed to preserve the status of the operation in progress when the interrupt occurs, then return to that same point when the interrupt has been properly serviced. The complexity in interrupt driven design translates into longer package development time than that normally required for polling package design, which, in turn, results in higher package cost than the polling design.

Although the design of a communications package is important in the efficiency and speed with which it operates, the internal design of a package will be transparent to most users. Beyond wanting to know whether a particular package is either one type or the other, the user will be more concerned with options that are available with a package. Because of the differences in options offered by the many communications packages now available for the Personal Computer, the selection and purchase of one of these packages can be time consuming.

One element that makes the selection of a package difficult is the jargon used to describe software capabilities. Terms such as *download* and *break signal* are often used without prior definition. Software publishers also use different terms to describe the same process or capability, thus adding to the confusion. To eliminate some of this confusion and to make the selection and use of a communications package easier, a detailed explanation of most of the terms used to describe asynchronous communications software capabilities is provided in the following paragraphs.

III. CHARACTERISTICS AND CAPABILITIES

Communications software is like any other software. No single package is likely to satisfy all wants and needs. The best one can hope to achieve is to obtain a package that provides most essential features and some nonessential but desirable features.

Although business and personal applications of communications software are often different, there are some common communications capabilities that are required. Both applications usually require the capability of sending and receiving disk files and the ability to communicate in the terminal or conversation mode, but because of the volume of large files that are transferred in many business communications applications, business software will often have to support options not required in personal software. The following paragraphs discuss the common capabilities required in these two types of software. The features that are unique to each of these types are discussed later in the chapter. Table 5-1 also provides an overview of the capabilities included in each of these categories.

BUSINESS AND PERSONAL REQUIRED FEATURES

Although the features to be discussed next are common to both business and personal communications software, there are sometimes differences in the way they are implemented. Those differences are discussed briefly.

Communication Parameter Selection

To properly communicate with other mainframe and microcomputers (collectively called *host systems*), a communications user must be able to select the appropriate *communications parameters* required by the host system. These parameters include baud rate, number of data bits, type of parity error-checking, and number of stop bits. The software package may provide *default values* for these parameters, but it must also provide the option of modifying the default values both before and after a connection is made with a host system.

A good communications package also allows the user to modify the standard (sometimes called *global*) default values. A new set of values replace the original default value set. These new default values are normally stored in a disk file for later use. Some software packages also allow the user to store specified sets of parameters for

Table 5-1. Communication package characteristics and capabilities.

BUSINESS AND PERSONAL REQUIRED FEATURES:

Communication Parameter Selection	1200 Bps Modem Support
Duplex Mode Selection	Return to Operating System
Command and Conversation Modes	Disk Directory Listing
Error Handling	Prestored Strings
Data Capture	Password Storage Security
Data Upload	Break Signal
Data Capture To Printer	Operating System Required
XON/XOFF Support	Display Width Selection
Manual and Auto-Dial Modem Support	User Help Files
Dialing Directory	Documentation Manual
Originate/Answer Mode Selection	User Support

BUSINESS PACKAGE FEATURES:

Upload Throttle	Blank Line Expansion
Line Feed Control	Character Filter
Binary Data Transfer	Translation Table
Protocol File Transfer	Case Conversion
Remote Takeover	Tab to Space Conversion
Command Files	Telephone Hangup
Batch Mode	External File Manipulation
Clock Controlled Operation	

PERSONAL PACKAGE FEATURES:

Auto-Redial	XMODEM Protocol
Elapsed Time of Call	Upload/Download Local Echo

each host or service system. A user loads a *parameter command file* or selects a host system from a *displayed directory* to put the specific parameters into effect.

Several communications packages are designed to work with direct connect auto-dial modems, and the communications parameters associated with each telephone number are stored in a file with the number. When the software is instructed to dial a number, the associated communications parameters are automatically put into effect before the number is dialed. These parameters remain in effect until modified by the user.

In each of the aforementioned cases, the default or selected parameters are communicated to the Personal Computer asynchronous communications adapter to set the stage for communications under a specific protocol. The software must *initialize the communications adapter* automatically, or it must be instructed to initialize the adapter before communications with a host is established. If any of the parameters are modified during a communications session, the software must reinitialize the adapter to put the new parameters into effect.

The option of listing selected parameters is another good feature. If difficulty is encountered during a communications session and the selected parameters cannot be listed, trouble-shooting the problem becomes difficult. Establishing proper communications parameters to use with a new system may require some experimentation with different parameters. That trial and error process is difficult to perform without the ability to list the communications parameters.

Duplex Mode Selection

A communications package should allow a user to switch between *half-duplex* and *full-duplex modes* because business and personal communications applications often require connection to both half-duplex and full-duplex host systems. Most information services and bulletin board systems operate in the full-duplex mode, but other microcomputer and mainframe systems may operate in either the full or half-duplex mode.

To properly communicate with a variety of systems, a user must be able to switch between the full and half-duplex modes both before and after a communications link is established. Some bulletin board and host systems may require a user to switch duplex modes after establishing a communications link. If a *host system operator (SYSOP)* answers a page or interrupts your communications session to deliver a message (switches from automatic operation to the conversation mode), the host software may also switch from full-duplex to half-duplex. When this happens, characters are no longer echoed back to the user's terminal. To see the characters typed locally, the user has to make a modem switch to half-duplex or a software switch to *local echo*. A software package that offers a single key stroke toggle switch between full-duplex (remote echo) and half-duplex (local echo) is useful under these circumstances.

Command and Conversation Modes

A user should be able to operate communications software in a *command mode* and a *conversation mode*. The command mode is required for *off-line* communications between the Personal Computer keyboard and the communications software and is used to perform functions that do not involve the remote host system. Certain operations such as changing a telephone number in a dialing directory or viewing selected communications parameters have to be conducted without interaction with the remote host system. When off-line command mode functions have been completed, however, the user must be able to return to the *on-line* conversation mode to carry on with interactive communications with a host system.

Software can be divided into two operation mode categories: *conversation mode predominant* or *command mode predominant*. When the user boots up a communications software package and goes beyond the first screen of introductory messages, the software goes directly into either the conversation mode or the command mode. The user must instruct the software to make a switch to get to the other mode.

Conversation mode predominant software assumes the user will normally be in the conversation or *terminal mode* when communicating. This design is excellent for interactive communications with bulletin boards and information systems. With this type of software, a user only goes into the command or off-line mode when he or she needs to change a communications parameter, select a telephone number, or perform some other non-conversation action. No data are transmitted to the host system while the software is in this mode. When the user completes off-line action, the software immediately returns to the conversation mode.

Command mode predominant software, on the other hand, assumes the user will frequently want to be in the off-line mode when communicating. This type of software is used for business applications that involve a great deal of unattended *batch mode file transfers* or *multiple file transfers*. With command mode software the user remains in either a command or menu mode until he or she requests a switch to the conversation mode. After switching to the conversation mode, the user can return to the command or menu mode at any time during a communications session by striking the required conversation mode escape key. This option allows the user to perform several off-line operations without returning to the conversation mode. The user can list a file, delete a file, or change communications parameters without switching back and forth between off-line and on-line. This type of software also helps to eliminate off-line and on-line *mode confusion*. Conversation predominant software does not always clearly indicate to the user that the mode has changed from on-line to off-line or vice versa.

Error Handling

A software package's ability to handle errors is vitally important. A good package should either warn the user before an error occurs so that preventive action can be taken or provide a clear understandable error message when an error does occur. The package should also allow the user to continue with communications if a minor error occurs. Operations that can result in significant errors should also be designed to give the software user the opportunity to abort a command before the error is made. For example, a user should be told that captured data will be lost when an attempt is made to return to the operating system before the data have been saved. The user should be given the opportunity to go back and save the data before finally returning to the operating system.

Data Capture

Data capture is the process of storing received data in memory or in a disk file. The process is also called *downloading*. Most communications applications will require this capability. Some packages allow data capture directly to a disk file, whereas others only allow data capture to random access memory for later storage in a disk file. Some packages provide both options. Most personal communication applications require *direct-to-disk capture* capability, but many business applications require the *memory capture* option because the captured data must be modified before they are sent to a disk file or because the file transfer rate is too great for capturing data on a floppy disk.

Because of the slow speed of disk I/O, download directly to disk is a slow operation and limits download activities to 300 baud with some software packages. Speed-matching at 1200 baud requires a large *communications receive buffer* to prevent buffer overflow unless file transfers are limited to small files. As discussed in Chapter 2, disk emulation software can be used to set up *electronic disk drives* for download capture to overcome this limitation, but the combination of disk emulators and communications often requires at least 128K of RAM.

Data capture to memory removes the need for disk emulator software to provide communications speed-matching at transfer rates of 1200 baud and higher. The capture buffer is a portion of unused RAM that is set aside to temporarily store received data. Most software designers provide at least 20K of capture buffer for applications in PCs containing 64K of total RAM, but the maximum buffer size may be as high as 128K when the package is used in machines containing at least 192K. To keep the receive buffer from overflowing and to allow operation with small receive buffers, some communications packages may also be set up to automatically dump the capture buffer contents to a disk file when the buffer becomes full. For large file transfer applications a large capture buffer and automatic buffer dump are recommended.

Data capture to a memory buffer has several advantages compared to data capture directly to disk. First, it is at least ten times faster than data captured directly to disk, which allows data transfer rates of 1200 baud and higher. Second, data capture to memory can usually be *toggled* on and off by pressing a single key. The toggle allows a user to capture segments of received data rather than capture and store all incoming data. Third, captured data can be easily and quickly erased if the user decides not to save the data to disk. Hand-in-hand with that advantage, however, is the disadvantage that data captured to memory can be easily lost with the occurrence of power surges or errors that require system reset as part of the recovery process.

Some communications packages also allow the user to select the type of data to be captured. The user can elect to capture only incoming data transmitted from a host system, capture only data entered from the local Personal Computer keyboard, or capture both incoming and outgoing data. This option is good for business applications, but most personal applications do not require it. If only local keyboard input is being captured, a file can be opened and a series of batch mode commands entered into the file. Then the file can be closed and immediately put into operation. Frequent use of this option can improve the efficiency of data communications and reduce communications cost for a business.

Data Upload

The term *upload* is used to describe the process of transferring a local disk file to a remote host system. Both business and personal communications applications make use of this capability to transfer files containing memos, reports, data, or software to remote computer systems.

Some communications software allows data to be transferred directly from memory to the communications port. This option requires the user to first transfer the file to a *memory work area*; then the file can be sent directly out via the communications link.

This capability simply reduces the work load placed on a disk drive when frequent file transfers are performed.

Data Capture To Printer

A communications package should allow the user to send received data to a printer at the same time the data are being displayed on a monitor. Sometimes it is necessary to *log a conversation* with another person or print a download menu contained on a bulletin board, to eliminate repeat listings of the menu during download file selection. A user may also want to log sessions with time sharing systems to refer to later; this is particularly useful when transactions result in fund transfers. Logging conversation mode transactions is also a good way to develop training material for later time sharing or information service system classes.

The simultaneous communications and printing capability offered by most software packages is only usable in the conversation mode. A dot matrix printer can keep pace with conversation mode data transfer rates but may not be able to keep pace with file transfer rates. A good general rule to follow is to only print data that are being continuously transmitted at a rate less than the speed of your printer. An 80-character-per-second printer can keep pace with a 300 bps (30 character per second) modem, but the same printer cannot keep pace with a 1200 bps (120 character per second) modem. A difference in communications speed and printer speed may not be a problem for assembly language software packages because of the way they buffer incoming data, but it will likely be a problem for BASIC language software packages.

Spooler software can be used with the printer option to facilitate simultaneous printing and downloading of data when using a slow speed printer. A user can scan the messages on a bulletin board and mark messages of interest, then go back and list those messages while simultaneously printing them. After listing these messages, the user may go on to other bulletin board functions or download a file while the print spooler continues to send the messages to a printer. A print spooler can also be used to handle print-screens without interrupting data transfer. By pressing the shift and PrtSc keys simultaneously, a user can send screen contents to the printer as communications continue.

A *single key toggle* that allows the user to turn the print function on and off without interrupting the transfer of data is also a desirable feature. This option allows the user to selectively send text to a printer by pressing one or two keyboard keys. Software that requires the user to go into the command mode to turn the print function on is cumbersome and requires either data receipt interruption or a pause in data transfer before printing can be initiated. This frequently results in desired data scrolling off the screen.

Care should be taken when using the simultaneous print option with certain printers. Some non-IBM printers go off-line when they receive XOFF characters, which could cause the Personal Computer keyboard to lock up (not respond to key strokes) until the printer is manually returned to the on-line status. Printers may also respond to format effector characters such as form feeds that are transmitted for monitor control and waste paper.

XON/XOFF Support

Most file transfer applications that involve data transmission rates greater than 300 baud require *XON/XOFF communications speed-matching protocol*. This protocol allows the software designer to use less memory for a communications receive buffer because communications speed-matching will not have to be handled solely by the buffer. Most mainframe computers use the XON/XOFF protocol, so business applications that involve file transfers with mainframe computers can make good use of this capability.

Most assembly language communications software packages provide XON/XOFF support because they can rapidly respond to these characters, but BASIC language software may only support the protocol when they are receiving files. If a BASIC program is advertised as an XON/XOFF protocol package, it should be thoroughly tested before being relied on to perform XON/XOFF speed-matching.

Manual and Auto-Dial Modem Support

Even though a user only has a manual-dial modem, when selecting a software package it is a good idea to get a package that will support both manual and auto-dial modems. Having a communications package that only supports manual dial modems or only supports auto-dial modems limits flexibility in hardware configurations. With the rapid increase in modem capabilities and the rapid drop in modem prices that is taking place, a new auto-dial modem may become a necessity long before expected. An auto-dial modem might also have to be relinquished for repairs for a period of time resulting in the need to use a spare manual-dial modem.

Dialing Directory

When a software package allows the user to store telephone numbers that can be used with auto-dial modems to access remote systems, the package should also allow the user to list the directory of available telephone numbers. Numbers that are buried in command or batch files are inconvenient to locate when the number has to be dialed without use of the command or batch file. It is also good to have a brief summary listing of the major communications parameters that will be automatically invoked when a number is dialed from the directory. Several IBM PC communications packages offer both of these features.

Originate/Answer Mode Switch

It is necessary to switch a modem from the *originate-mode* to the *answer-mode* when receiving a call from a remote terminal or another microcomputer. Manual-dial modems provide a switch that activates the mode change, but intelligent modems may be switched manually or through software control. Communications packages often allow the user to switch from one of these modes to the other by pressing either one or two IBM PC keys. *Menu-controlled* originate/answer mode switches can be more cumbersome to use than single key toggle switches unless the package only contains one command menu.

1200 Bps Modem Support

A communications package should be able to support both 300 baud and 1200 baud communications. The ability to upgrade from a 300 bps modem to a 1200 bps modem without buying a new communications package can save software and business applications training costs. Just about all communications packages use different commands to perform the same function, so going to a new package means communications users have to learn new commands.

Again, because of the faster data handling speed of assembly language software, most communications packages written in assembly language can transfer (send and receive) data at 1200 baud. Some interpreter BASIC packages are advertised as supporting 1200 baud, but their slower operating speed often limits data capture at 1200 baud to files under 10K. Compiled BASIC programs, if properly designed, can capture data to a floppy disk at 1200 baud without the assistance of the XON/XOFF protocol—the PC-TALK package is a good example of this type of software.

Return to Operating System

A communications package's ability to return the user to the operating system is often overlooked when a package is being evaluated. A user should not have to reboot the Personal Computer each time a communications session is completed. A user should be able to terminate communications and return to the operating system to perform other computer operations by entering a simple command. Many packages program a function key or the Alt key combined with another key to provide a shortcut back to the operating system. Other packages require that the user go through a *series of menus* before returning to the operating system. Either option is acceptable, but the single or dual key shortcut is faster to execute and easier to remember.

Some packages allow the user to return to the operating system without breaking the telephone connection with a host system. This allows the testing of a downloaded program to be sure it was properly received before terminating the host system connection. It also allows the user to view a downloaded file, then return to finish the communications session.

Disk Directory Listing

Another useful feature is the ability to list the disk directories of all disk drives. When uploading files, this function allows the user to select files for transfer. When downloading files, this function allows the user to select filenames that are not currently in use. If the package stores communications parameters in disk files, the disk directory listing provides the user with a menu of parameter files. For packages that support batch file operation, this option allows the user to view the menu of available batch files.

Prestored Strings

Frequent communications with systems that require log-on commands can result in repetitive typing. In such cases, *prestored strings* that can be uploaded to a system can be a useful feature for both business and personal applications. Many IBM PC communications software packages allow prestored strings to be uploaded with either a one key stroke or a two key stroke combination, which makes this feature even more convenient. When prestored strings are provided by a package, the user must be able to easily and quickly list the strings while logged on with another system; it is easy to forget which string goes with each key and a quick reminder is sometimes necessary.

Password Storage Security

For software packages that allow the user to store and retrieve character strings, password storage security should be considered. The listing of stored character strings on the monitor should allow the user to omit stored password strings. This keeps onlookers from stealing passwords to time sharing or information services.

Break Signal

Many mainframe and some information services require a *break signal* for program execution interruption. A communications package should be able to send a 200–600 millisecond *sustained high signal* (equivalent to a logical 0) with either a single or a dual key stroke. This signal will interrupt a program execution in progress or get the immediate attention of an information service system. Most software packages fix the duration of the break signal, but some allow the user to specify the signal length.

It should be noted that the break signal is not the same as the IBM Personal Computer *Ctrl-Break* key combination. The Ctrl-Break is actually a Ctrl-C and will terminate the running of a BASIC communications program. The true break is a sustained voltage signal (not a control character) and will not interrupt the operation of the user's software.

Operating System Required

Care should also be taken when selecting a communications package because available packages may operate only under the PC-DOS, CP/M-86, or UCSD-P operating system. Some packages will operate under only one of these systems, but others are available for more than one operating system. A package designed to operate under one system will not operate under another system. Files downloaded using a CP/M-86 communications package cannot be accessed later under PC-DOS because the disk formats are different.

Display Width Selection

Most good communications packages allow the user to operate in either the 40 or 80 column display mode. This is particularly useful when a user is doing a great deal of communicating using a monitor that does not produce easily readable 80 column text.

User Help Files

User *help files* are important for communications packages that are not to be used frequently. They are also helpful for the user who is not accustomed to that particular package. Help files are not a replacement for a good documentation manual, but they provide a *quick reference* for the keys required to perform certain functions. These help files should be readily accessible (single key stroke) and written in clear concise English.

A package should also provide 25th line (bottom of screen) messages and *abbreviated menus* unless the user elects to turn them off. These menus indicate commands that are available under certain modes of operation and help novices learn to use the package more quickly. Expert users may not want to have the menus on the screen and should be allowed to toggle them off.

Documentation Manual

A communications package is incomplete without a good *documentation manual*. A package that contains all the aforementioned features is of little use without a manual that tells how to use the features. A documentation manual does not have to contain the background information on communications provided in this book, but it must fully explain every package feature.

User Support

When all else fails, a user must be able to get support from the software publisher. Good user support means that a technical person is available, when required, to help solve application problems. No communications software package is perfect, particularly new ones coming out on the market, and most of the problems encountered cannot be solved by a software salesman. Before purchasing a software package, check with local IBM PC users groups and other people who own and use the package to be sure it is well supported.

ADDITIONAL BUSINESS-SPECIFIC FEATURES

Business communications applications usually require several software features beyond those described in the previous section. The IBM PC must deal with mainframe communications idiosyncrasies which may include communicating in more than one character code (for example, ASCII and EBCDIC). Business communications may also require frequent large file transfers or multiple file transfers that are beyond the scope of personal communications. Differences in work hours and time zones may also require *unattended-operation* communications capabilities. This section describes these required software features and others that may be needed in business applications.

Upload Throttle

When files are being uploaded to a mainframe system, it may be necessary to match the file transfer rate with the response of the mainframe. Some large host systems will not allow you to send a line of data until you are *prompted* to do so. The prompt may be a letter, a character, a number, or a combination of all three, and it is a signal indicating that the mainframe is prepared to receive more data. Data sent before the prompt is received are usually lost. Uploading a file to such a system without providing a mechanism to wait for prompts results in the *truncation* of each line; a later listing of the file would show the beginning of each line missing. To match the upload speed of the IBM PC with the system response of a mainframe, it is sometimes necessary to throttle the upload.

Communication software packages provide several types of upload throttles. The three major types are time delays, character receipt delays, and character prompt delays. A *time delay throttle* allows the user to select the length of time delay between the upload of each line of data. A *character receipt delay throttle* allows the user to specify the number of characters that must be received from the mainframe before a new line of data is uploaded. A *character prompt delay* allows the user to specify the exact character string that must be received from the mainframe before a new line of data is sent. Of the three types, the time delay throttle is the least effective because it requires the user to specify the longest expected mainframe response; selecting a long time delay to reduce the probability of losing transmitted data could result in long and costly data transfers. The character receipt delay is effective if the mainframe continues to properly receive data. If an error occurs and the mainframe begins to reject data, the IBM PC will continue to transmit data as long as the proper number of characters (error messages in this case) keep coming in over the data line. The character prompt delay is the most effective because it ensures that data will only be transmitted when the proper signal is received from the mainframe.

Line Feed Control

Some communications software packages add line feeds after each carriage return received or transmitted, but others do not. Business communications software should allow the user to decide whether line feeds should be sent following each carriage return or added after each received carriage return. Without this capability, transferred files may have to be edited to remove or add line feeds, and conversation mode communications may be difficult to perform. If a line feed is being added to each transmitted line by a remote system and another one is being added by the PC's communications package, the received data will have a blank line between each line of data. If line feeds are not being added to the end of each transmitted line by the host and the PC's communications package is not adding one, the data received by the PC cannot be listed and edited until line feeds are added. If data are being received in the conversation mode and neither the IBM PC software nor the remote station software is adding line feeds at the ends of data lines, each line will overprint the previous line on the PC monitor, making it difficult for the user to read the data.

Binary Data Transfer

A business communications package must allow the transfer of non-ASCII files. It is often necessary to transfer *machine code* files to protect the source code from being stolen or modified by users. Some BASIC language communications software will not send or receive machine code because some of the binary strings contained in the files appear as *end of file markers* causing the transmit or receive mode to abnormally terminate. Communication software can be designed to overcome this problem and is usually required for business applications.

Protocol File Transfer

The term *protocol file transfer* is used by many software vendors to describe special file transfer techniques. These techniques are different for each package, but they generally do the same thing. The *protocol signals* (sometimes called *handshaking*) used by these packages allow them to transfer text, data, and machine code files, and to perform sophisticated error-checking to be sure files are transferred properly. The handicap in using these protocol file transfer techniques is that the computers on both ends of the communications link must be using the compatible software; there is no standard that controls these protocols and no two are exactly alike. This means that a business must standardize its microcomputer communications software to take advantage of protocol transfers. The *XMODEM protocol* is becoming a default standard in personal communications because of its widespread use on public bulletin boards, but it has not gained widespread acceptance in business communication packages because the protocol is public domain; most business communication package designers use unique protocols to force businesses to use their software on both ends of communication links.

Besides allowing the user to transfer machine code files, the protocol technique offers other advantages. First, multiple files can be transferred by invoking "wild card" commands in much the same way as multiple files can be transferred from one disk to another on the IBM PC. All files with a particular extension or with a specific string as part of their filename can be transferred by entering one file transfer command. Second, data are transferred in blocks and the size of these blocks can be selected by the user. Each block is checked for transmission errors and blocks containing errors are retransmitted. For transmission over noisy telephone lines, the file transfer block size can be set small to force frequent checks for errors. For transmission over low-noise telephone lines, the file transfer block size can be set large to speed up file transfers. Third, the error-checks performed under protocol file transfer are usually of the cyclic redundancy check (CRC) type described in Chapter 2. The CRC is a mathematically computed checksum, and its value is uniquely calculated for each block of data. This type of error checking is superior to asynchronous parity error checking. The presence of CRC error checking also allows the user to set parity to None, thereby increasing the throughput of data with the elimination of the parity bit.

Remote Takeover

Some IBM PC communications packages allow remote users to call in and take over the operation of a computer. To perform this function, both systems usually have to employ the same software. Businesses can use this capability to transfer files without having to provide computer operators at both ends of the communications link. A branch office can send a file to a branch office in another time zone either before or after the normal working hours of the receiving office.

Command Files

Command files allow a user to store several parameters in a disk file for repeated use. These files can contain many or all the software package commands that can be entered from the keyboard. Communication parameters such as parity and number of data bits may be modified, and a telephone number can be automatically dialed by a command file.

Command files offer several advantages for business applications. First, they save users from repetitive typing of commands, Second, different user disks can be set up, containing passwords and system log-on information specific to certain individuals. Third, command files can contain telephone numbers and passwords, eliminating the necessity for separate lists that have to be kept to call and log-on with remote systems.

Batch Mode

Batch mode operation is similar to command file loading and execution, but it supports several commands that are not supported by command files. A *command file* can modify communications parameters and dial a telephone number when used with an auto-dial modem, but a communications operator must take over to continue the session after the communications link is established. A *batch file* can modify communications parameters and dial a telephone number, but it can also continue the communications session after the connection is established with a remote system. Log-on messages can be sent and files transferred between the IBM PC and any other system without operator assistance. A batch file can also be written to delay execution until a specified period of time has elapsed; unattended file transfers can be performed late at night when telephone rates are at their lowest. This capability could be a valuable asset for a business with branch offices in different time zones.

Clock Controlled Operation

Clock controlled operation can combine the capabilities of either the command file loading or the batch mode operation with operation that is controlled by an internal IBM PC clock so that file transfers can be accomplished at specific preset times. The user can set up the software to dial a remote system at 3:00 AM, perform all log-on functions, upload a text, data, or program file, log-off the remote system, then return the IBM PC to the operating system—all without the attendance of a local or remote system operator. Clock controlled operation can be used to take advantage of low late-night public telephone rates and to transfer files outside normal working hours, freeing-up the machine for other tasks during business hours.

It should be noted that clock controlled operation is sensitive to proper communications when it is used for unattended operation. The software has to be able to perform rudimentary *artificial intelligence*. After a command string is transmitted to a host, the software must be able to check to see that the host response indicates proper receipt of the command and repeat the command if the response is not correct. This eliminates the problems encountered with noise-generated command transmission errors.

Blank Line Expansion

Some host computer software packages change modes of operation in response to blank lines; this requires the use of communication software that eliminates undesired mode changes. The message receive functions of many electronic mail systems change from the message input mode to the message edit mode when a blank line is received. The file creation mode of some mainframe editors also change from the input mode to the edit mode when a blank line is received. A line containing only a carriage return means "end of text" to these systems. To avoid mode changes when the user wishes to upload text containing blank lines to such a system, a communications package must convert lines containing only a carriage return into a space followed by a carriage return.

Character Filter

Some mainframe and microcomputer communications software transmit control characters. These characters do not print on most computer terminals, but the characters are printed on an IBM PC terminal. To eliminate these annoying and sometimes confusing characters, it is necessary for software to *filter* them out of the incoming stream of data. Some PC software packages allow the user to turn the filter on or off by executing a command string. Business applications that require remote demonstrations of software running on a computer that transmits control characters would benefit from the filter option.

Translation Table

Translation tables allow the user to redefine incoming or outgoing character codes. Any of 256 different codes can be redefined so that a different character is passed back to the IBM PC than the one represented by received data or a different character is sent out the communications port than the one entered at the keyboard. EBCDIC code can be converted into ASCII code. Certain characters can be redefined as nulls or spaces or can be left out of the translation table entirely to filter them out of incoming or outgoing data.

Case Conversion

Many older computer systems—and some new computer systems—do not recognize lowercase letters. Some of these systems will automatically convert lowercase to uppercase, but many systems will not perform that function. To overcome this problem, an IBM PC software package must perform the conversion from lowercase letters to uppercase letters before the characters are transmitted.

Tab to Space Conversion

The IBM Personal Computer sometimes uses tab (Control-I) characters to represent spaces in stored files. These tab characters save valuable disk space by representing up to eight spaces each. Other systems, however, do not always follow the same convention. To keep files that contain tab characters intact, it may be necessary to *convert tab characters into spaces*. Several IBM PC communications packages allow the user to turn this automatic conversion on and off by executing a command from the keyboard.

Telephone Hangup

Some business communications involve systems that do not automatically break the telephone connection when a user logs off. To break a connection with one of these systems, the user should be able to execute a software command that ''drops the line'' when an auto-dial/auto-answer modem is being used. Without this option, the modem might have to be turned off to break the connection, and frequent off/on cycling of a modem could shorten its life.

External File Manipulation

It is often necessary to delete old files as new ones are being created during a communications session. It may also be necessary to rename files that have been created by a communications software package (for example, a command file) or files that have been improperly named during file downloading. It may also be necessary to run a BASIC program or execute a DOS command (for example, a FORMAT or CHKDSK command) during a communications session. These operations can be done more quickly and easily if the user can perform them without exiting the software package. The IBM PC communications packages that provide these options can save a company time and money when file transfers are frequently performed.

ADDITIONAL PERSONAL FEATURES

Personal communications are often limited to bulletin board, private host, and time-sharing information system interactions. These communications links may result in file transfers, but those transfers are generally limited to small programs, program patches, or text files. This limitation mainly results from the slow operating speed of the systems contacted. Most of these systems operate at 300 baud, which results in long connect times for large file transfers. Because of the types of services used and the types of files transferred by the hobbyist, this category of communications user has special needs. The following paragraphs address these needs.

Auto-Redial

Some local information services used by the hobbyist run on microcomputers and allow only one user at a time, whereas others have a limited number of incoming connections. The telephone numbers of these services are frequently busy. Instead of manually redialing a number from the keyboard, an auto-dial modem can be software-controlled to redial a telephone number until a connection is made. Software packages that offer this capability also provide an alarm signal that gets the user's attention when the carrier of a remote system is finally detected. It is often necessary to use an *auto-redial* to get through to a bulletin board system on weekends or holidays.

Elapsed Time of Call

It is convenient to have an *elapsed time of call indicator* when communicating with a time-sharing information service. Information services generally charge a rate based on *connect time*, so the elapsed time indicator can help a user save connect-time costs. This feature can also serve as a reminder of costs when calling a long distance number to get in contact with a host computer system.

XMODEM Protocol

Many public bulletin board systems use the *Ward Christensen XMODEM protocol* as a file transfer option. This protocol is similar to the protocol file transfer technique described earlier in this chapter in that it requires a *protocol-matched system*. Software that supports this protocol during file receipt allows the user to take advantage of 99.6% error-free file downloading from bulletin boards that support XMODEM file transfer. The XMODEM protocol performs checksum error detection for transferred blocks of data, and blocks containing errors are automatically retransmitted. The decreasing quality of voice grade telephone lines expected with the increase in telephone system competition will make this error-checking protocol more attractive. Its inclusion in the PCMODEM and PC-TALK communication packages used in many personal applications may cause this protocol to become a default standard for the IBM PC.

Upload/Download Local Echo

Home-based communications often involve novice communications users and file transfers that are not locally displayed (listed on the local monitor as the transmission takes place) can be confusing to these users. The wrong file can be selected and uploaded to a host or bulletin board system, but the user will not realize the mistake unless the transferred file can be listed after the transfer is completed. With local echo of the file during transmission, operator errors can be noted and file transmission aborted saving the user time. The same is true for downloading. While viewing a file being downloaded, a user can elect to abort the download process if the file turns out to be the wrong one or contains unexpected data.

IV. EVALUATING COMMUNICATIONS SOFTWARE

The evaluation and selection of a communications package may not be an easy task. Changing needs and capabilities in a business environment and changing budgets in a personal situation contribute to the complexity. But, as is the case with other software packages, decisions have to be made—based on the best information available at the time.

The initial approach to selecting a software package is to first assess communications needs. A list of all essential features should be developed. This should be followed by the development of a list of nonessential but desirable features. Only then should available communications software packages be considered.

To place communications packages in proper perspective, it is a good practice to produce an *evaluation matrix* similar to the one shown in Figure 5-2. Information can be recorded on such a matrix by reviewing the manuals provided with software packages. Newsletters and magazines also publish software reviews containing data that can be used in completing the matrix. Local IBM Personal Computer user groups often have a special interest group (SIG) dedicated to communications. Information can be obtained through conversations with the members of such a group. Software vendors can also be solicited for information; many of them have toll free telephone numbers.

As part of the evaluation of communications software, experience using a package is valuable. Public domain and inexpensive BASIC programs are excellent learning tools. A user can experiment with these simple programs and learn a great deal about communications through trial and error. There are many bulletin board and private host systems operating in major metropolitan areas that can be used as guinea pigs during this learning process. To provide the communications novice with a place to start, a simple BASIC communications program called PC-SPEAK.BAS is provided in Appendix E. A flow chart for that program is contained in Appendix F.

```
Communication Software Feature             Pkg #1   Pkg #2   Pkg #3   Pkg #4
-----------------------------------------  ------   ------   ------   ------
Data capture direct to disk file
Data capture to memory buffer
On-line display of capture buffer
On-line editing of capture buffer
Filtering of received control characters
Blank line expansion
Optional add/delete of linefeeds
Upload wait for host prompts
Upload text throttle (delay between lines)
Menu of prestored uploadable strings
Transmission of prestored strings
Transmission of a true break signal
Tab to space conversion
XMODEM protocol file transfer
Protocol error-checking file transfer
XON/XOFF support during file send/receive

Non-ASCII (binary) file transfer
Operation with non-autodial modem
Autodialing telephone directory
Autodialing modem support
Auto-redial of last telephone call
Auto-redial of last call until connect
Modem/telephone hangup
Return to operating system without hangup
Elapsed time of call display
On-line switch between originate/answer
On-line selection of duplex with toggle
On-line selection of comm parameters
On-line listing of selected parameters
On-line printer on/off toggle
On-line viewing of disk directories
On-line viewing of disk files
Deletion and renaming of disk files
1200 baud receive/download operation
Save/reload of customized parameters
Batch operation from operating system
Command file power/flexibility
Remote takeover and operation
Efficient use of available memory
Display of help files
Line 25 abbreviated help menu
Opional 40 or 80 column operation
Ease of command key use
Quality of user manual
---------------------------------------------------------------------------
Features: E = Excellent, G = Good, F = Fair, and - = Not Supported
```

Figure 5–2. IBM PC communication software comparison.

6
Local Area Networking

Thus far this book has dealt with general purpose communications on the IBM Personal Computer—the technology of exchanging information and data between IBM PCs or between PCs and larger computer systems. The scope of communications has ranged from neighborhood networks to those extending from coast-to-coast. The primary communications media discussed has been the ordinary public telephone system. This telephone system consists of local exchanges connecting low-grade voice lines to subscriber phone outlets; the local exchanges are in turn connected to each other via microwave links, long lines, or special high-grade digital trunk lines that carry much of the nation's computer communications traffic. As Chapter 2 pointed out, this system forms a network of varying quality voice and data lines that are commonly used for personal computer modem-based data communications.

The appearance of low-cost, 16-bit microcomputers in increasing numbers in a wide diversity of businesses has led to significant growth in the application of data communications to everyday business problems. Many of these applications utilize the telephone networks as just described to exchange information and data over relatively long distances. Businesses are discovering, however, that 75–80% of their communications requirements occur across relatively short distances, such as within the confines of a group of offices or a building. The newer generation of microcomputers has provided a low-cost and convenient means to automate "internal" communications— the result has been the rapid rise in popularity of a branch of data communications commonly known as *local area networking*, or *LAN* for short. To differentiate between distant and local data communications in subsequent discussions, the former will be referred to as *modem networking*. This is not a standard term but conveys the fact that virtually all long-distance communications rely on modems, whereas local area networks commonly used with PCs do not. The purpose of this chapter is to explore the significance of local area networking—distinguishing characteristics, criteria on which to base a selection, basic hardware and software design, and most importantly, applications. The relationship between modem networking and local networking and how

103

they work together to increase the range of applications available to a business will be discussed.

I. INTRODUCTION

As just discussed, local area networking is a form of computer communications generally used for the internal transfer of data and information within an organization. *Internal* in this context refers to the confines of an office, a group of offices, a building, or a closely spaced group of buildings. In its most elementary physical form, a local area network is two or more PCs connected together by some type of wire or cable to form a data path between the computers. Once physically established, a local area network allows the exchange of program and data files between users connected to the network. It also allows a user to send a file to a printer or hard disk attached either to another PC or directly to the network. Figures 6-1a and 6-1b illustrate basic physical and file transfer concepts underlying LAN operation. The printer and hard disk are "shared" resources since any of the three users have access to those devices. The example shows a hard disk attached to the network as a separate device through an interface box; in some networks, the hard disk is attached directly to a specially designated IBM PC, just as the printer in Figures 6-1a and 6-1b.

To illustrate basic LAN principles, Figures 6-1a and 6-1b show two types of logical processes that occur on these networks. Figure 6-1a depicts a user at PC #1 sending a word processor file to the user at PC #3. This transfer could have been initiated by either user. The user at PC #3 would have the option to interact with this file as if it had been originated at his or her own PC—for example, writing the file to a local floppy disk drive or using it as input to a word processor, etc. Figure 6-1b shows the logical process of a user on PC #3 printing a file on the printer attached to PC #1. Similarly, it shows the user on PC #2 storing a locally created file on the remotely connected hard disk. An interesting consideration relating to PC #1 in Figure 6-1b is the degree to which network software will allow PC #1 to support a local user while at the same time controlling access to its attached printer. We will return to this question later in the chapter.

The more fundamental question is, What benefits do local area networks offer for business applications? First, local area networks allow the sharing of expensive resources such as letter quality printers and high-capacity hard disk drives among a number of users. For the cost-conscious manager, this is a direct economic benefit. Second, local area networks allow the high speed exchange of essential information between key people in a business. If properly utilized, this sharing will promote greater efficiency and productivity and will lead to more sophisticated applications such as electronic mail. Finally, local area networks provide the catalyst to increase the range of potential applications for the IBM PC.

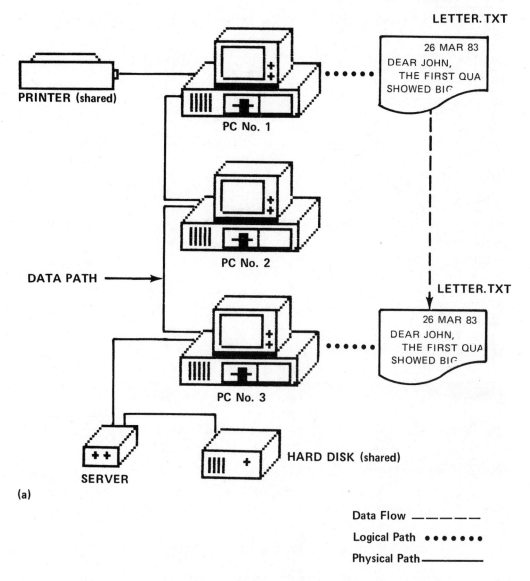

LETTER.TXT

26 MAR 83
DEAR JOHN,
    THE FIRST QUA
SHOWED BIG

LETTER.TXT

26 MAR 83
DEAR JOHN,
    THE FIRST QUA
SHOWED BIG

PRINTER (shared)

PC No. 1

PC No. 2

DATA PATH

PC No. 3

SERVER

HARD DISK (shared)

(a)

Data Flow — — — — —
Logical Path • • • • • •
Physical Path _____

Figure 6–1a. Basic local area network.

II. VARIATION ON A THEME

There are two ways to look at a local area network—as a communications technology and as a multi-user computer installation. Before proceeding further in the discussion of LAN fundamentals, it would be useful to characterize LANs in comparison to other communications systems and to other types of multi-user data processing systems.

Local area networks are in fact communications systems, and as such are a logical extension of the principles and systems covered earlier in the book. However, there

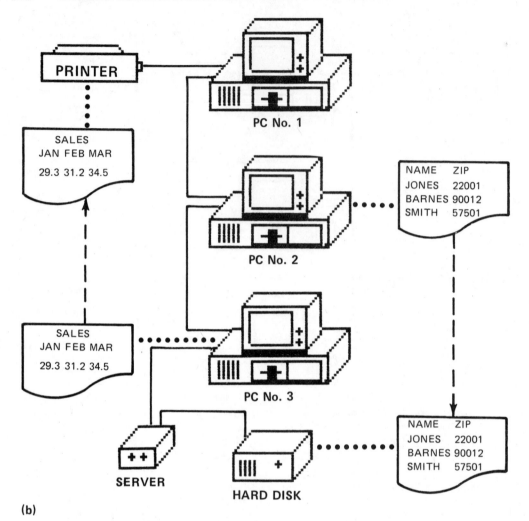

(b)

Figure 6–1b. Basic local area network

are two primary characteristics of LANs that distinguish them from modem networks such as TELENET, TYMNET, ARPANET, and the public telephone system. First, LANs are designed to work in a restricted geographic area, generally limited to thousands of feet or closely spaced building complexes. Second, LANs operate at relatively high speeds when compared to the typical modem networks currently in use. LAN data transfer speeds may be as high as 50 million bits per second (50 megabits/sec), or slightly more than 6 million characters per second. Compare this to the maximum data transfer speed of 56 kilobits/sec (7000 characters per second) for high-grade telephone company digital trunk lines, or the 300/1200 baud (30/120 characters per second) transmission speed used by most personal computer communication systems. At these megabit speeds, LAN operation exceeds the rate at which many current microprocessors conduct data transfers to and from random access memory (RAM).

In a general sense, LANs are in fact multi-user data processing installations. As such they are a logical alternative to the "classic" multi-user system consisting of a central processing unit (CPU), several terminals connected to the CPU, and a multi-user operating system such as MP/M-86, OASIS-16, or XENIX. Terminals in a multi-user system are generally not capable of stand-alone data processing. Instead they rely on the central computer to assign a portion of main memory (RAM) to, and execute applications programs for that terminal's user. Conversely, each work station in a LAN is an independent, stand-alone computer capable of executing its own applications programs. Both types of systems can share resources such as printers and hard disks to reduce peripheral costs.

There are obvious physical differences between a multi-user system and a LAN—these are illustrated in Figure 6-2. Multi-user terminals are physically connected to serial input/output ports on the central computer and their users are usually assigned segments of main memory for program execution and data storage. Additionally, each user in a multi-user system is typically assigned a private area for mass storage on a shared hard disk. This last statement is also true for each user in a LAN. The combination of a multi-user terminal, its assigned area of main memory, and a share of the CPU execution time is functionally equivalent to a single work station on a local area network.

III. FUNDAMENTALS

OVERVIEW

For purposes of illustrating basic concepts, the simplified LAN depicted in Figure 6-1 will be briefly described. Hardware components consist of three IBM PCs, a printer attached to PC #1, and a hard disk unit. In each PC, an adapter card is required in one of the five expansion slots—this card is commonly referred to by an assortment of names, depending on the particular network vendor. Some of the more common names are *transporter card*, *network adapter card*, *bus interface unit*, or *communications interface unit*. It functions much the same for this network as the RS-232-C asynchronous communications card functions for a modem/telephone network. The network data path is commonly formed by a coaxial cable, similiar to that used on a 75 ohm TV antenna. Some systems use a cheaper means of data transport, the twisted-pair wire, similar to that used in telephone installations. The data path for this example is terminated at both ends. In some network systems, the data path forms a closed loop. The usual method of making connections from each PC to the data path is by standard T-connectors on the back of each adapter card, as shown in Figure 6-3. There are no modems or connections to modem networks shown in this example in order to simplify this preliminary discussion of LANs. The purpose of this network is very straightforward—it allows all the PC users to access shared resources, in this case the printer attached to PC #1 and the hard disk drive. In addition, any PC user is able to transfer files or data to any other PC user on the network. These operations occur at high speeds as previously mentioned.

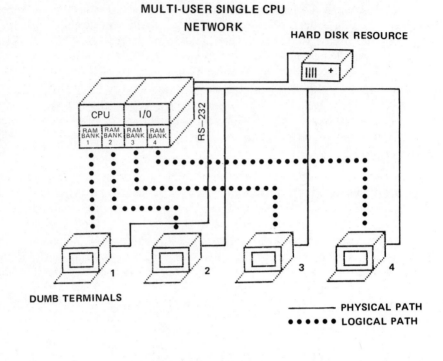

MULTI-USER SINGLE CPU NETWORK

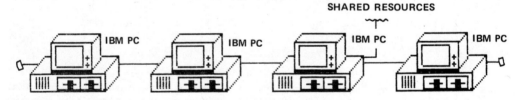

LOCAL AREA NETWORK

Figure 6–2. Shared resource architectures.

TERMINOLOGY

At this point let us introduce some of the terminology associated with the design and implementation of LANs. Again refer to Figure 6-1. The PCs and the hard disk server are known as network *devices*, or network *nodes*. In general, a device or node is connected directly to the network cable, or data path. The terms *transmission media* and *bus* are commonly used synonyms for data path. To illustrate another use of the word *bus*, the IBM PC *system bus* is the data path by which the 8088 processor communicates with RAM and with I/O devices attached to the PC. The term *server* refers to any device that interfaces a non- or semi-intelligent peripheral to the network, as shown in Figure 6-1. The most common are *disk servers* (also known as *file servers*), *print servers* and *modem servers* (also known as *communications servers*). The IBM

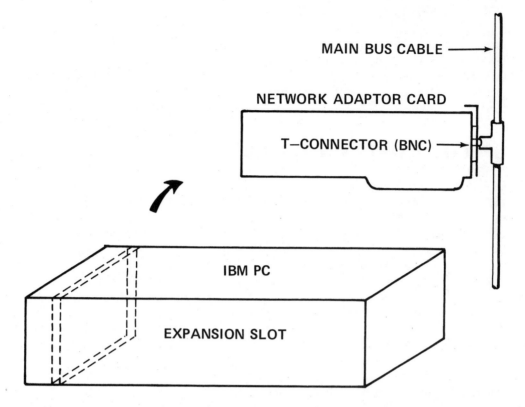

MAIN BUS CABLE ——→

NETWORK ADAPTOR CARD

T—CONNECTOR (BNC) ——→

IBM PC

EXPANSION SLOT

Figure 6–3. Local area network hardware (typical).

PCs included in a LAN are commonly called *work stations*, particularly in an office automation context. The body of rules that allows an orderly, reliable transfer of data among all the network devices is collectively known as a *protocol*. These concepts will be explored in more detail in the following paragraphs.

The terms *transparent* and *virtual* are often used in discussions on local area networks (and other data processing subjects as well). A process is transparent if it exists but does not appear to; a process is virtual if it does not exist but appears to. For example, a *virtual memory* process writes text to a floppy drive when the RAM text buffer overflows—a word processor operator never knows that internal memory has been used up. Another use of the term is illustrated in the multi-user installation of Figure 6-2. The combination of terminal, RAM segment, and CPU time slice for a single user forms a *virtual work station*. LAN data movement is a good example of trans-parency—it is obviously occurring, but how it occurs is not apparent to a LAN user. The term *throughput* is a measure that describes the quantity of useful data that can be handled by a local area network in a given time interval. Contrast this with the term *data rate*, which is merely how fast data move on a network. The term *multi-user* has already been introduced as referring to the use of a single computer (CPU, memory, and I/O devices) by multiple users. *Multi-tasking* is the sharing of a single CPU by more than one process; the term *concurrent* is sometimes used in the same context as multi-tasking.

The final term to be defined is *direct memory access (DMA)*. This is an important concept because it is commonly used in local area networks. Simply stated, direct memory access allows input/output devices to conduct data transfers directly with RAM without CPU intervention. In the local area network context, the I/O device is the PCs network adapter card which contains the necessary logic chips to conduct DMA data transfers. DMA is a prerequisite for the high speed operations typical of local area networks.

SPEED OF DATA ON THE NETWORK (DATA RATE)

One of the major factors that characterizes a LAN is the speed at which data move on the network. Table 6-1 contrasts the speed of a 1 megabit/sec LAN with speeds of other forms of data movement to and from, or within an IBM PC. The important conclusion to be drawn from this table is that network data movement is about as fast as computer data movement, considering that parallel transfers use eight data lines simultaneously. However, the higher throughput of data in the computer requires *buffering*, or temporary data storage, to prevent the loss of data as it goes into the network. It is the job of the network adapter card to sort out data rate and throughput mismatches. The table also shows the advantage of the higher speed *Ethernet* with its 10 megabit/sec network data rate. The bottom line is that a well-designed network works best with a hard disk in order to use its inherent speed to best advantage.

Table 6-1. Data transfer rate comparison.

Transfer Type	Operation	Maximum Speed (megabits/sec)
Serial	Network data flow	1.0/10.0*
Parallel	RAM read/write	9.5
Parallel	DMA transfer	9.5
Parallel	Processor-initiated I/O	7.6
Parallel	Hard disk I/O	6.5–8.0
Parallel	Floppy disk I/O	0.25
Serial	Multi-user terminal (RS-232-C)	0.0192
Serial	MODEM at 1200 Baud (RS-232-C)	0.0012

*Ethernet

HOW DATA MOVE ON THE NETWORK (DATA STRUCTURE)

Since the network in Figure 6-1 must distribute processing and data storage tasks among a number of users who may require near-simultaneous access to the network, it is necessary to structure data flow in a controlled manner. Control implies an orderly means of allowing each device to access the network; it also implies some degree of service that allows data to arrive at its destination virtually error-free and in the same sequence it was transmitted. A prerequisite to logical network control is the placement of data streams into formatted *packets* which are then transmitted in accordance with network protocol. The format of the data as it travels from one network adapter card to another is similar to the SDLC data packets discussed in Chapter 2.

The demands on a local area network system follow the irregular patterns of individual user processing requirements. The irregularity or randomness of data transmission associated with these demands constitutes a form of data transfer called *bursty* communications. Network speeds are designed so that system demands such as requests for file access are fulfilled with no apparent delay attributable to the network itself. This type of system design, incorporating random bursts of data packets traveling at high speeds, stands in stark contrast to modem network communication systems. Communications over a modem network are limited by the low speed capability of that network; thus modem network sessions tend to be continuous in nature and typically last for at least several minutes, tying up a communication channel for the duration of the connection.

LANs AND DISTRIBUTED PROCESSING

Once a local area network is physically assembled and the communications rules established, some interesting challenges present themselves. These concern the concepts and rules by which the shared resources operate. One obvious problem concerns access to the hard disk drive—Which user has priority, and how are multiple requests to access data from the same open file(s) arbitrated? The answer lies more in how the accompanying software (operating system or applications program) is designed than in the mechanics of how the data move from point to point on the network. One popular solution to this dilemma is to partition the hard disk drive into segments and assign each segment to a specific user. Each segment could contain several files which would then be accessed just as a user accesses floppy diskette files. Such segments will be referred to in the future as *volumes* and are logically equivalent to a floppy diskette.

In local network usage, it is important to distinguish between drives, volumes, files and records since most network applications involve data storage and retrieval. Figure 6-4 illustrates the logical relationships between these storage entities. In summary, the degree to which data storage is protected from unauthorized network user access must be specified through appropriate software design.

Another design challenge in local area networks is how network support software will handle requests for floppy disk or printer access from the network while the PC work station to which those devices are attached is being used by its operator. In Figure 6-1, this would apply to the peripherals (floppy and printer) attached to PC #1. This problem is best handled by interfacing the network to multi-tasking or multi-user operating systems on the host IBM PC; examples of these operating systems are Concurrent CP/M-86, MP/M-86, or UCSD p-System. Existing solutions range from not allowing local use of a PC when it provides a shared device to the network to not using an IBM PC for attaching shared resources. It is important for a prospective user

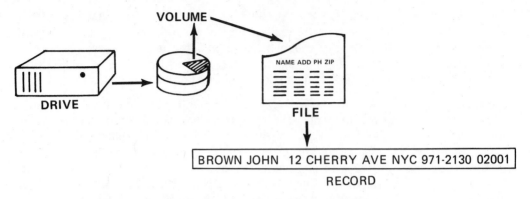

Figure 6–4. Data storage terminology.

to carefully investigate the operating systems that a particular network will support and any restrictions in the use of a network PC as a shared resource.

LAN SPECIFICATION

There are many more network configurations than those illustrated in Figure 6-1; this example is simplistic, but useful for a conceptual overview of local area networks. There are other factors that must be considered besides the physical connection of networks. Some of the key decisions that must be made when designing or specifying a LAN are the operating system(s) to use on the host PCs, the design of applications programs to exploit the power of local networking, the mass storage size to include on the network, and the need for modems and modem network resources. For the cost-conscious business user, another even more fundamental decision must be made—whether to use a multi-terminal, multi-user system or to use a LAN design to provide the required distributed processing. The relevant variables that should be considered in selecting a local area network are summarized in Figure 6-5. Capacity, physical connection, and access rules are described in the next section.

IV. NETWORK TYPES

The type of network selected has a major bearing on its cost and capabilities; thus the prospective user should carefully weigh the inherent strengths and weaknesses of a particular network configuration. Three methods of classifying networks are by data path capacity, physical network structure, and the set of rules by which the network controls access by its devices. The commonly used terms for these concepts are *bandwidth*, *topology*, and *protocol*, respectively.

BANDWIDTH

Bandwidth is the measure of a network's ability to move data. The concept of bandwidth is graphically illustrated in Figure 6-6. In the *baseband* system shown in Figure 6-6a,

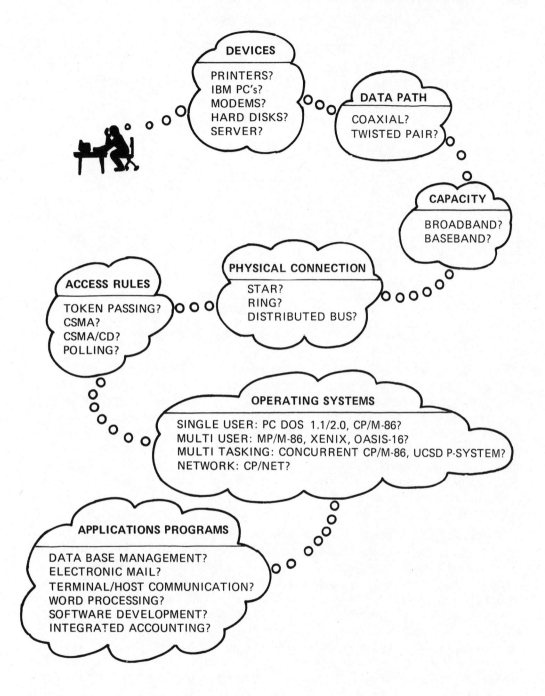

Figure 6–5. Factors in local area network selection.

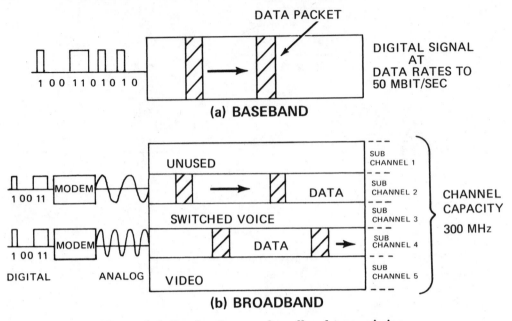

Figure 6–6. Baseband versus broadband transmission.

a single digital signal is input to the network—a serial stream of bits packed into formatted data packets as previously discussed. The serial data packets are sent and received at a specific design data rate—typically 1–50 megabits/sec. Two of the networks discussed in greater detail later in this chapter use a nominal data rate of 1 megabit/sec. This is equivalent to about 125K characters/sec. The third uses a data rate of 10 megabit/sec, or about 1.25 million characters/sec. In contrast to this high speed, the ordinary telephone system (not including segments upgraded for digital data transmission) can support a data rate of about 120–240 characters/sec with reasonable error tolerance. In a baseband system, the transmission is all digital and operates at half duplex (a node can either send or receive, but not both simultaneously).

In contrast, a *broadband* system such as the one illustrated in Figure 6-6b, makes efficient use of high capacity Cable TV (CATV) distribution media. This type of cable has a bandwidth of 300 megahertz (Mhz). The high bandwidths on CATV cables were designed to accommodate 50 channels of 6 Mhz TV video for community distribution. This high capacity can be fully utilized in broadband local area networks. The *channel capacity* (another term for bandwidth) is normally partitioned into sub-channels, each of which is assigned a specific service or function—for example, high speed data, low speed data, video, or switched voice. This technique is known as *frequency division multiplexing,* or *FDM*. FDM allows the using organization to select sub-channel bandwidths according to the desired service in each sub-channel. In a broadband LAN, data packets are transmitted as analog signals just as they are on the long distance modem networks; therefore, modems are required for digital-to-analog conversion. A high speed data channel also requires a commensurately high speed (and expensive!) modem. An example of how the sub-channels on a broadband network could be allocated is shown in Figure 6-7.

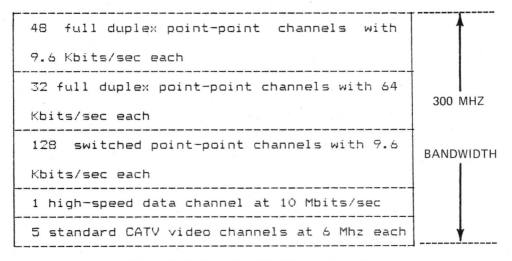

Figure 6–7. Broadband LAN sub-channels.

The added capacity and service diversity provided by broadband LANs comes at a price. The tradeoff for this highly capable type of local area network is a substantial increase in cost and complexity. The requirement for relatively expensive variable frequency and high speed modems is a major cost driver, as is the increased complexity of the communications interface units (network adapter cards). Installation of broadband LANs is difficult because of the criticality of component placement and the careful tuning that is required for each network on a sub-channel. For these reasons, it is not likely that broadband technology will soon find its way into low-cost personal computer LANs. The local area networks discussed in detail in this chapter are baseband networks because of their ease of installation and relatively low cost. Examples of baseband systems are the XEROX/INTEL/DEC Ethernet, the Corvus Omninet, and the Orchid Technology PCnet. Examples of broadband systems are Wang Laboratory's Wangnet and Sytek's Localnet 20.

TOPOLOGY

Topology is a fancy word for a simple concept—the way networks are physically connected together. There are three common LAN topologies illustrated in Figure 6-8: star, ring, and distributed bus. There are, as always, variations and combinations of these configurations; however, the following discussion will be limited to the basic types shown.

A desirable feature in any local area network is the absence of a *critical node*. A critical node is one whose failure will cause the entire network to fail. The worst topology from this aspect is the star network, illustrated in Figure 6-8a. The central computer is an obvious critical node. In the ring topology of Figure 6-8b, critical nodes may or may not exist, depending on the particular network in question. IBM's local area network for the PC has not been announced as of Spring 1983 but will in all likelihood be a ring topology. The distributed bus topology shown in Figure 6-8c and featured in the example LAN of Figure 6-1 does not have a critical node. The inherent

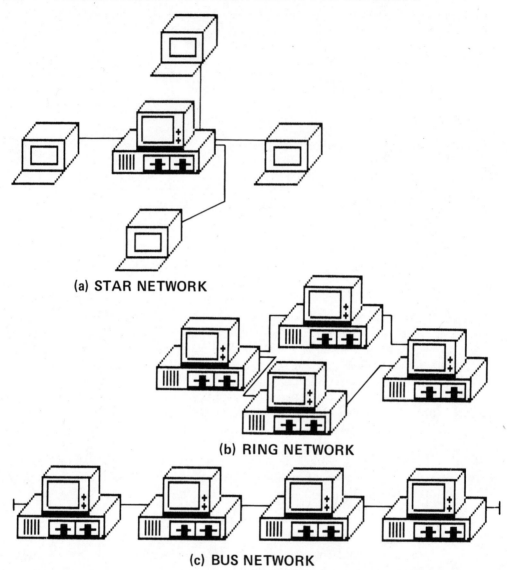

(a) STAR NETWORK

(b) RING NETWORK

(c) BUS NETWORK

Figure 6–8. Local area network topologies.

reliability of distributed bus networks and their flexibility in adding new devices make them a logical choice for low-cost networking applications. All the IBM PC networks to be covered later in the chapter are of the distributed bus topology. The key features that a manager should be aware of in selecting a network topology are reliability and ease of expansion.

PROTOCOL

In Chapter 2, a protocol was defined as the set of rules by which data communications are conducted. This definition also applies to local area network communications. Also in Chapter 2, the concept of the International Standards Organization (ISO) 7-layer data communications architecture was discussed. This network layering concept is receiving greater attention and plays a major role in the LAN field. The significance of a layered communications model is ultimately economic—without an attempt to standardize protocol within layers or interfaces between layers, no two communications systems would be compatible. The desired goal is to establish a local area network specification with recognized interface and protocol standards that will allow networks and devices from different vendors to communicate with each other. This of course may be an unattainable goal in practice, but at least the proliferation of hardware and software can be held to reasonable levels. The best effort to date is the work being done to develop the IEEE 802 local net specification—IEEE 802 is evolving into a dual specification for distributed bus (i.e., Ethernet) and ring (IBM) systems since no agreement could be reached on a single specification.

As an example of the importance of standard protocols, consider the case of a businessman who has purchased a low-cost local area network from vendor A. This LAN is advertised as "Ethernet compatible," which means that the protocol for layers 1 and 2 follow the Ethernet specification. If in the future the same businessman desired to expand his operation into a full-blown Ethernet supplied by Vendor B, his existing system would still be usable in the larger LAN. The operating system software might very well change but the physical components and the protocol implemented on the network adapter card would not. Another example of this compatiblity will be seen later in the discussion of 3Com Corporation's *EtherLink* network.

At the current time, the protocol of greatest concern to a manager seeking to choose the best LAN for the needs of his or her business is the one governing access to the network. This protocol is found both in the physical and data link layers. The most common of these are *polling*, *token passing*, and *carrier sense multiple access (CSMA)*. These protocols are most commonly found respectively in star, ring, and distributed bus networks. CSMA protocol can also include *collision detect* features—the complete protocol would then be referred to as *CSMA/CD*. The emphasis in this chapter is on the CSMA technique because currently available IBM PC networks are of the distributed bus type. The presence of higher layer protocol (layers 3–7) in a local network design varies depending on the particular network; Omninet (to be described in detail below) implements layers 1 through 4, while the Ethernet specification defines layers 1 and 2. The interfacing of applications programs to local networks will be an area of great interest as the user base of LANs grows—thus it is likely that layers 6 and 7 (presentation and application layers) will receive increasing attention in future local network design. Layer 6, in particular, is important to the communication of graphics images and will be discussed in Chapter 7.

SUMMARY OF LAN NETWORKS—CHOICE FACTORS

Earlier in this discussion on local area network types, cost versus capability was mentioned as a motivating factor for becoming more conversant with certain characteristics of local area network technology. Table 6-2 is a summary of the foregoing discussion and is presented as a general overview of cost, flexibility, growth, and capacity of network types. When analyzing the needs of a small business or an office automation project, these are only the starting points for consideration—other major factors are the maximum number of work stations allowed, the cost of the expansion slot adapter card required, cable characteristics and installation, maximum cable length allowed, and interfaces with existing applications software. As more and more systems become available for the IBM PC, choosing the "right" system for a specific application will require increasing sophistication.

Table 6-2. Summary of LAN features—an overview.

Category	Variable	Least Cost	Most Flexibility	Most Growth	Most Capacity
Bandwidth	Baseband	X	X		
	Broadband			X	X
Topology	Star	X			
	Ring				
	Bus		X	X	X
Protocol	Polling	X			
	Token Pass			X	X
	CSMA		X	X	

V. THE NETWORK SOFTWARE CONNECTION

As with most computer applications, the ultimate success of local area networks relies upon good software design. The relationship of the software required to operate a LAN to its host operating system and to the applications programs that it supports may be the most crucial characteristic of a local network. The definition of what constitutes "network software" would be appropriate at this point. Network support software generally consists of four parts:

- Communications (networking) support
- Input/output and file handling support
- User management support
- Applications program support

Figure 6-9 illustrates a typical way in which network software integrates into an existing installation. Communications support is provided by the network adapter card and is usually in the form of *firmware* (software that is permanently written on a ROM chip) and/or direct hardware circuitry. The trend in the future will be to place the standard network protocols into a single chip on the adapter card. This is one of the benefits of network protocol standardization and will lead to radically lower costs to implement LANs.

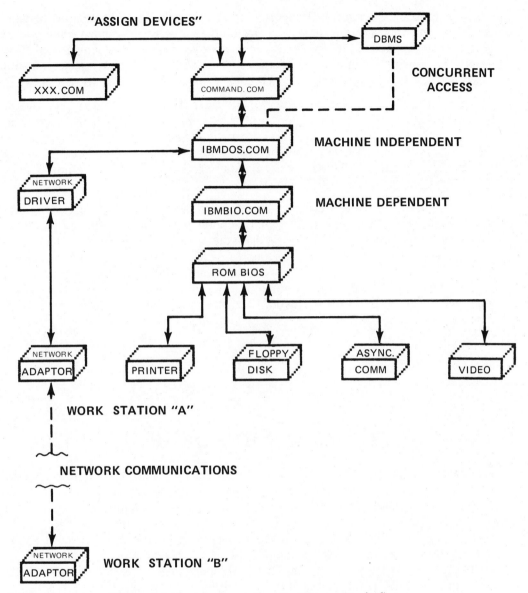

Figure 6–9. Local area network software (typical).

The next level of support is for the file handling and input/output routines. In Figure 6-9, this is accomplished through a patch to the *machine independent* portion of PC DOS—the hidden file, *IBMDOS.COM*. This patch to IBMDOS.COM makes the network appear as just another I/O device, as if it were a device supported by the *machine dependent* part of PC DOS—IBMBIO.COM. As far as the Command Interpreter is concerned, any legal I/O command in PC DOS will apply equally to remote devices served by the local network.

The third level of support is to the users to carry out the task of managing network configuration. This would include such functions as attaching and unattaching shared devices, partitioning hard disk volumes, controlling user access, and similar jobs. This support is shown in Figure 6-9 as a unique COM file and/or a patch to the existing COMMAND.COM interpreter that works in conjunction with the patch to IBMDOS.COM.

The final level of support by network software is to the applications programs to be run on the network. These might be data base management systems, accounting packages, electronic mail, or long-distance communications. The main task of this type of network support is to enable the applications package to effectively make use of the inherent features of a local area network. The biggest challenge at this level is to manage concurrent access to shared files.

From the user's point of view, the desired situation is to have little or no visibility into normal network operation. The configuration management required should be user-friendly and occur infrequently. Furthermore, an application program should have easy access to that level of network support for the creation of customized systems. Once the hooks are made into the network, applications program operation should be virtually unchanged for the user. Communications protocol handling should be totally transparent to all users on the network. Transparency is achieved if an application process uses the normal operating system commands; for example

A>DIR C:

instead of

A>DIR C: ON SERVER1

VI. IBM PC LOCAL NETWORKING SYSTEMS

Having introduced the reader to the fundamental principles and considerations involved in local networking, let us now turn to the practical side and review three of the first LANs to be implemented on the IBM PC. The objective of doing this is twofold: to explore the latest in personal computer communications technology and to create an awareness of potential applications using a network of intelligent work stations. The three systems chosen for a more detailed look are all available on the market and are relatively low cost implementations. There will undoubtedly be a sharp increase in the total number of LAN installations throughout 1983 and beyond, particularly as applications software packages are designed to exploit distributed processing systems. As more local area networks are developed for the IBM PC, the focus will shift away from hardware considerations to the need for increased integration of communications into business applications. This will be discussed further in Chapter 7.

PCNET

PCnet System Overview

PCnet was designed specifically for the IBM PC and its native operating system, PC DOS. It is classified as a *distributed bus, baseband* local network with *CSMA/CD* access protocol. The network is capable of addressing up to 64,000 devices and can therefore easily accommodate practical network sizes from a physical point of view. PCnet also supports many IBM PC plug compatible computers such as COMPAQ, Colby, Columbia MPC, Eagle 1600 and their MS DOS operating system. It is compatible with PC DOS version 1.1 and will be compatible with version 2.0 by mid-1983. PCnet software interfaces directly with PC DOS and makes the network look like another input/output device to the operating system. There are no servers required on this network—instead shared printers, modems, and hard disk devices are connected directly to designated PCs. PCnet will support any plug compatible hardware that is supported by PC DOS.

PCnet Hardware

The PCnet hardware consists of a single network adapter card that plugs into one of the available expansion slots on each IBM PC in the network. On the back of this board is a BNC-type connector which plugs directly into the network cable via an inexpensive T-connector, as shown in Figure 6-3. The network cable is a standard 75-ohm CATV type coaxial cable. It runs end-to-end throughout the area where the networked PCs are installed. Depending on cable rating, wire runs of up to 7000 feet are possible, allowing an entire work area to be pre-wired and PCs to be added to the network or easily moved. Hooking up the cable is almost as easy as plugging in the power. The PCnet adapter card contains proprietary CSMA/CD logic to control access to the network by attached PCs. A nominal serial data rate of 1 megabit/sec provides high speed operation and optimizes direct memory access operations with the PCs in the network.

PCnet Software

Each PCnet adapter card comes with software that integrates the network into PC DOS. This DOS interface is designed so that standard single-user PC applications can use the network without change. More advanced multi-user systems can be developed from single-user applications software with only minor program modifications. The three main features of the DOS interface are *disk sharing, file locking*, and *remote execution*.

Disk Sharing. Disk sharing allows PCs to share hard disks or floppy drives installed in other PCs. The shared disks appear to be locally attached. For example, if a PC has one diskette drive and shares a hard disk via the network, the user can access the *local floppy* as Drive ''A:'', and the *shared disk* as Drive ''B:'', ''C:'', or ''D:'' as shown in Figure 6-10. Drives B:, C:, and D: then become volumes on the shared hard

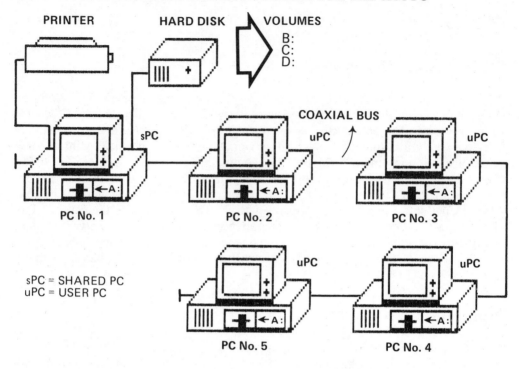

Figure 6–10. PCnet installation and components.

disk for this particular example. Any future reference to B:filespec, C:filespec, or D:filespec while loading or saving programs or accessing data files will activate the *hard disk* as if it had been attached to the requesting PC. The assignment of *drive designations* (A: or B: for example) to local and shared drives is completely flexible, so that a user's Drive ''A:'' does not have to correspond to their local floppy drive. Figure 6-10 shows a typical PCnet installation and *logical drive relationships*.

This sharing is immediately useful to a multiple-PC installation in many ways. First, it provides each user with the capacity and speed of a hard disk at the lowest possible cost. Second, it simplifies the *backup* problem—only one hard drive requires backing up, and the one backup can cover the data from all users. Third, each PC requires only one diskette drive to perform the initial system boot. Finally, it allows users to examine other users' data files and transfer files between shared and local (floppy) storage. The disk sharing interface has the inherent advantage of being able to work with any hard disk that is compatible with the IBM PC, whether internally or externally mounted.

File Locking. In order to implement a multi-user, multiple-PC application sharing *common data files*, there must be a mechanism to ensure that these files are only accessed by one user at a time. The denial of access to a file that has been opened is known as *file locking. Access denial* can be specified at the file or the record level. The term *unlock* refers to the removal of the access denial when the file is closed.

Since PC DOS does not support file locking (remember that it is a single-user system), the DOS interface includes function calls to lock and unlock files by name, or by name and record number. These assembly language *function calls* can be used from within an application program to provide the required file access protection. If two or more PCs try to modify a common file at the same time, one will simply wait until the other is finished with its access before proceeding. This is essentially the same principle used in installations running multi-user operating systems. Another means of file locking is through the use of three supplied utility programs that can be executed from a batch file. This provides a degree of protection at the operating system level without requiring modification of an applications program.

Remote Execution. In order to create a truly distributed processing system with PCnet and PC DOS, there must be a way to share expensive resources such as printers, modems, and plotters and to perform what amounts to multi-tasking operations. The DOS interface does this with a feature called *remote execution*. Remote execution allows a user on one work station to run a command on another PC as if the command had been entered on that PC's keyboard. After the command executes, the remote caller is informed by a short "beep" on their PC. This feature has a rough analogy in modem network systems. This analogy is commonly known as a *host communications* program in which the host computer can be controlled by remote commands coming into its modem. The analogy is not complete since the PCnet remote execution feature does not provide the requesting user a view of the process while it is executing. In PCnet an IBM PC with specialized peripherals can act as an "execution server" for other PCs and can print files, assemble programs, or plot graphs while the requesting user is performing other work. As long as the host user is not trying to do an I/O operation to the same peripheral, the network access is transparent. *Software compatibility* is guaranteed, and any hardware that is *plug compatible* with the PC can be remotely accessed.

There are distinct limitations to this scheme. Any remote command issued must terminate with a return to DOS in order to work properly. For example, a command to run VisiCalc will not work with the remote execution feature since there is no way to return to DOS without user intervention from within VisiCalc. In addition to the preceding, any program that requires interaction with the user will not work with remote execution. However, *batch processing* jobs will run properly if the .BAT file is carefully constructed to return to the DOS prompt upon completion. Any program that takes a file, processes it, and rewrites the results to an output device should also work. This would typically include such applications as sorts, compiles, assemblies, and similar.

PCnet System Specifications and Operation

Hardware Specifications. The hardware adapter card communicates with the PC's *system board* through the use of *interrupt lines, DMA channels*, and *I/O ports*. The adapter card uses those lines, channels, and ports not used by any other peripherals in order to avoid *contention* with such devices as floppy drives and hard disks. One result of this allocation is that DMA access can only be made to the lowest 64K of RAM. The impact of this restriction is not significant from a practical standpoint.

Maximum cable length is determined by signal loss; for *RG-59B/U* coax the maximum length is 3000 feet. The heavier *RG-11/U* coax will support a cable length of up to 7000 feet, but is more difficult to install. Cable taps and terminators are standard BNC hardware, available at any electronics supply store. There are no restrictions on where expansion PCs can be tapped into the *main bus cable*. Again referring to Figure 6-3, the T-connector tap on the main bus cable is designed to attach directly to the BNC connector on the adapter card at the PC back panel.

Software Operation. The operating system for the network is supplied as a patch to the existing PC DOS code. Network software uses 16 *interrupt service addresses* not otherwise used by DOS. An interrupt service address is a location in RAM that contains another address called a *pointer*. This pointer is the location of a routine that carries out a particular network function. PCs in a network must be initialized as either *shared PCs* or *user PCs* (contracted to *sPC* and *uPC*, respectively). Each sPC and disk drive volume is assigned a maximum 14-character name to simplify command and software references.

There are some restrictions in the sharing features of the PCnet software. In general, user PCs can access shared PCs, but neither user PCs nor shared PCs can access users. This is a reasonable restriction, given the design of this network, in that user PCs should not be arbitrarily interfered with. Also, an sPC may not directly access another sPC; however, this is a temporary restriction and will be removed in later versions. If there are multiple sPCs, a uPC with access privileges to appropriate sPCs can copy files between any two of them, in effect acting as a "go-between."

Upon initialization, each sPC user assigns a name to their work station and to each volume on the attached hard disk (if present). Floppy drives on an sPC can also be assigned a volume name for shared access. A list of uPCs that can access that sPC is also entered. Finally, for each shared volume, the allowable users and their read/write access are designated. Each user with a uPC enters the names of the sPCs they desire to access. The uPC operator must also map his local drives and all shared drives to volume designations (PC DOS allows drives A: through J: to be assigned). In order to use a shared printer or modem, a uPC user enters the command,

ASSIGN device_name TO sPC_name device_name

All subsequent file I/O commands to the local device (LPT1: or COM1:, for example) are then executed on the shared printer or modem attached to an sPC (PC #1 in Figure 6-10). PC DOS version 2.0 has increased flexibility for I/O device assignment—this makes shared peripheral use even easier on PCnet.

The file locking mechanism, which the reader will recall was used to allow *concurrent access* to shared files, is accessible at the operating system level or by applications programs, and is based on a symbolically named lock, known as a *semaphore*. The semaphore is a 16-byte identifier large enough to contain a full 11-byte filespec and a 5-byte record number. A typical semaphore would look like the following:

filenameext00055

Since the locks apply to files on shared mass storage devices, they are maintained in RAM on all sPCs having those resources. The locks can be set, reset (cleared), or tested by the function calls discussed earlier. Table 6-3 lists the allowed function calls

Table 6-3. PCnet function calls.

Type 0.   LoopLock (sPC_name, lock_name)
- Lock the given name at the given sPC—if locked already, wait and try again—keep trying until free
- Return codes: "OK", "sPC down", "bad arguments"

Type 1.   Lock (sPC_name, lock_name)
- Attempt to lock the given name at the given sPC
- Return codes: "OK", "lock in use", "sPC in use", "bad arguments"

Type 2.   Unlock (sPC_name, lock_name)
- Attempt to unlock the given name at the given sPC
- Return codes: "OK", "lock not found", "sPC down", "bad arguments"

---

with the activity performed and the possible results of the call. Certain restrictions are applicable to the use of this concurrent access technique: if any user program creates a new file or changes the length of an existing file, the entire volume containing that file must be closed to multiple access. The use of the full 16-byte semaphore to lock a record will work on *indexed files* if the 5-digit "record number" is considered to be the first five characters of a designated *key field*. A planned enhancement is the increase in semaphore size to 32 bytes to accommodate larger or multiple *index keys*.

File access control at the PC DOS level is through the utility programs LLOCK.COM, LOCK.COM, and UNLOCK.COM. These programs have the same effect as (and use) the internal function calls of the same name. They are designed to be used within batch files, as shown in the following example that uses dBASE II and a data file named RECORDS.DBF:

```
A>COPY CON: ACCESS.BAT
LLOCK RECORDS.DBF Rem Test file and lock when free
DBASE Rem Enter dBASE II and "Use" RECORDS
UNLOCK RECORDS.DBF Rem Release lock on RECORDS.DBF
```

The choice between LLOCK and LOCK is dependent on whether the user desires a one-time request to lock a file (LOCK) or a continuous loop request until a file becomes free (LLOCK).

The remote execution mode of PCnet allows a uPC user to execute a DOS command on an sPC provided that user is placed on the sPC's access list. The remote command line looks like the following:

```
re [sPC_name] <command string>
```

The sPC name is optional and, if specified, sends the command string to the designated sPC for execution. Otherwise, the destination sPC is determined by the network software using the list of sPCs with their volume assignments. If one volume is designated a *network default volume* during system startup, it would execute all commands where no sPC name was indicated. For example, consider the following DOS COPY command typed on a uPC:

```
re copy b:filename1 c:filename2
```

In this case, assume that drives B: and C: are assigned to the shared hard disk. If the network default volume were initialized as C:, the command would execute on the sPC containing volume C: since no sPC name was included in the command. File locking against multiple access is preserved on remotely executed commands so that a user cannot use the system to bypass volume or *file protection*.

PCnet Application Examples

Shared IBM PC Word Processing System. This example describes a four-user word processing system that shares a hard disk and both letter and draft quality printers. In this example it is assumed that a hard disk that allows partition of its available space into multiple volumes is used. The system uses five PCs; one acts as a shared printer/mass storage work station, whereas the other four are used by operators to input and modify stored text. The shared PC contains a diskette drive, a *fixed media* hard disk unit (12 megabyte capacity), and a tape cartridge unit (5 megabyte) for backup purposes. The hard drive is formatted into 1 *public volume* with 2 megabytes of capacity and 4 user-owned *private volumes* with 2.5 megabytes apiece (approximately 1600 pages of text per user). It also contains printer ports to which the two printers are attached. The volume-to-disk assignments (or *mapping*, as the process is sometimes called) on the shared PC (sPC) is shown in Table 6-4.

Table 6-4. Shared PC hard disk volumes—word processing example.

Volume	Drive	Contents
A:	Fixed 2 Mbyte	Common programs including the word processor, mail merge, spelling checker, etc. Read only by all uPCs
B:	Fixed 2.5 Mbyte	Read/write file storage for user #1
C:	Fixed 2.5 Mbyte	Read/write file storage for user #2
D:	Fixed 2.5 Mbyte	Read/write file storage for user #3
E:	Fixed 2.5 Mbyte	Read/write file storage for user #4
F:	Cartridge 5 Mbyte	Used exclusively for backup. Can backup two users at a time
G:	Floppy	Used to boot and copy programs to shared volume A:

Each word processing operator's uPC is configured with only one floppy diskette drive (used primarily to boot the system). These uPCs have a volume-to-disk drive mapping as shown in Table 6-5.

These sPC and uPC assignments are illustrated in Figure 6-11. Since volume A: on the shared hard disk drive contains the common applications programs, all users will need access to that volume. Volume A: is also designated the network default volume. Typical applications programs located on Volume A: are the word processing package (WordStar, for this example), mail-merge, spelling checker (Word Plus, for this example), grammar checker, indexing program, and footnoter. Volume A: might also contain universal boiler plate files for insertion into documents, although each user

Table 6-5. User PC disk volume mapping—word processing example.

Local Volume	Mapped Drive	Contents
A:	PCnet shared volume A:	Volume containing read-only programs
B:	PCnet shared volume X: (X = B:, C:, D:, E:)	Volume assigned as read/write storage for this user
C:	Local floppy drive	Volume for local storage

will likely have his or her own such files as well. Each word processing operator will have a dedicated volume for the storage of required document files. For purposes of clarifying this application, the following sequence of events is presented for the user on PC #3 as a document preparation task is carried out:

PC #3 operator directs printer output to the shared draft quality printer on PC #5 and requests the word processing program from the hard disk:

```
A>assign lpt1 to PC #5 lpt1
A>ws
```

In response to the WordStar prompt for an edit file, the operator then requests a document file from his or her private volume:

```
d:chapter6.doc
```

When editing is complete, the revised document is saved back to volume D:. The operator then desires to run the document through a spelling check sequence while editing on a second document is begun:

```
A>re spell d:chapter6.doc
```

This places a file on drive D: called *errwords.txt* and signals the user on PC #3 when complete. After reviewing *errwords.txt* and inserting corrections for misspelled words, that user now has the option to issue another remote command to mark his or her file with words to be corrected:

```
A>re markfix d:chapter6.doc
```

Finally, when the operator is ready to print the draft manuscript, a WordStar print file command is issued and the desired file will print automatically on the draft quality printer attached to PC #5. During this time, the operator is free to continue further editing work.

Mainframe Program Development. Many large mainframe-oriented time sharing systems are not optimized for maximum productivity in the creation and development of software. Many systems lack good, interactive full-screen editors and often provide poor response when heavily loaded. An alternative is to use IBM PCs to write programs and review results. However, mainframe communications lines are expensive and are poorly utilized if one line is provided for each PC.

A solution could be structured using PCnet to make the process more productive for a programming staff. This solution would consist of connecting a shared PC (sPC)

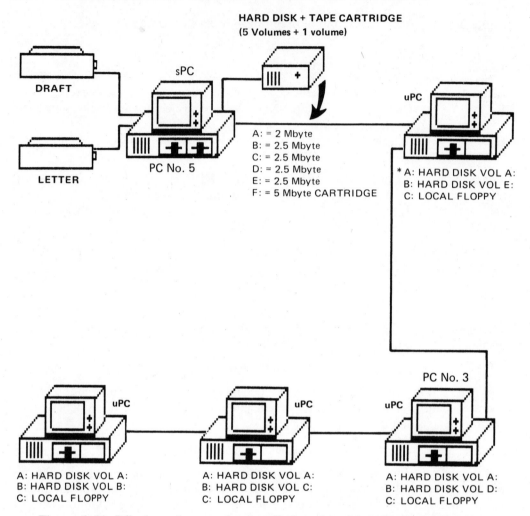

HARD DISK + TAPE CARTRIDGE
(5 Volumes + 1 volume)

sPC

DRAFT

uPC

A: = 2 Mbyte
B: = 2.5 Mbyte
C: = 2.5 Mbyte
D: = 2.5 Mbyte
E: = 2.5 Mbyte
F: = 5 Mbyte CARTRIDGE

PC No. 5

LETTER

* A: HARD DISK VOL A:
B: HARD DISK VOL E:
C: LOCAL FLOPPY

PC No. 3

uPC

uPC

uPC

A: HARD DISK VOL A:
B: HARD DISK VOL B:
C: LOCAL FLOPPY

A: HARD DISK VOL A:
B: HARD DISK VOL C:
C: LOCAL FLOPPY

A: HARD DISK VOL A:
B: HARD DISK VOL D:
C: LOCAL FLOPPY

Figure 6–11. PCnet word processing installation. Asterisk indicates local drive designators mapped to hard disk volumes by uPC initialization.

with hard disk and modem to the mainframe and linking user PCs to the sPC via the network. The communications link from the sPC to the mainframe would be via any means compatible with the attached modem. Modem network connections to a local network will be discussed in more detail later in the chapter. If a *file transfer program* exists to *upload* and *download* files from the mainframe system, it should be kept on volume A: of the hard disk. Upon completion of source code editing, a user would run the file transfer program on his or her work station, using the modem attached to the sPC to upload the file to the mainframe. After the program is processed on the mainframe, the user requests downloading to the hard disk where it is accessible via the network for further development. In most cases, this technique is limited to source code editing on the PCs; program compilation or assembly would in all likelihood be done on the mainframe itself.

The volume assignments for this example are virtually identical to those in the word processing situation. Volume A: is the network default volume and contains the required text editors, syntax pre-processors, file transfer programs, and other software development aids. Each programmer has a private volume for source code and related development files. The aforementioned volumes should all be located on the shared hard disk drive.

PCnet Economics

The final topic of discussion in this review of PCnet will be the cost factors involved in the installation of the network. A starter system is available—this consists of two network adapter cards, two BNC-type "T" connectors, one finished 20 foot coaxial cable with two 75 ohm terminators, one distribution diskette each to initialize and manage shared PCs and user PCs, and one user's manual. This is the complete kit required to network two IBM PCs and would be considered entry level cost for PCnet. Prices for individual network components are as follows:

- PCnet Adapter Card (w/ BNC connector and user PC software) $695
- PCnet Finished 20 foot Coaxial Cable $ 20
- PCnet Finished 50 foot Coaxial Cable $ 29
- PCnet Custom RG59/U Coaxial Cable $ 44 + .30/ft
- PCnet Custom RG11/U Coaxial Cable $ 44 + .60/ft
- Tri-Hex Tool (used for BNC insertion) $200

The installation in Figure 6-12 requires the following hardware and software:

- 1 Starter Kit $1490
- 6 PCnet Adapter Cards + BNC Hardware $4170
- 760 feet of Custom RG59/U Coaxial Cable (measured length of bus cable plus 50% for corners, routing, taps, etc.) $ 272

                                        Total $5932

Communications cost is $742 per user for this example. Additional costs for this installation would be any peripherals attributable to networking requirements, typically a hard disk unit. Since PCnet uses any IBM PC plug-compatible peripherals, these costs will vary widely. The release of electronic mail and print spooling software will increase network costs by $750 and $600 respectively. Assuming the base case of a 760 foot pre-wired installation with a two-work station starter kit (cost = $1762), cumulative costs for adding additional work station capability are as follows:

Work stations:	3	4	5	6	7
Cumulative $:	2457	3152	3847	4542	5237
Cost per User:	819	788	769	757	748

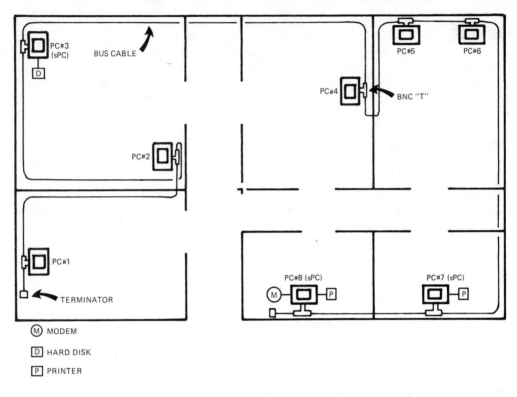

Figure 6–12. PCnet local area network installation.

OMNINET

Omninet System Overview

Omninet is the more mature of the networks reviewed here in detail. It was initially released for the Apple II, Onyx, and DEC LSI-11 in mid-1981 with over 1000 systems installed as of late 1982. It is capable of addressing up to 64 devices, which can be any combination of IBM PCs, Corvus Concepts, Apple IIs, and others to be supported by Omninet software. *CONSTELLATION II* is the name of the software supplied with Omninet. It supports resource sharing and file transfer and differs from the earlier *CONSTELLATION I* software by the extension of support to computers other than Apple II. Omninet operates at a 1 megabit/sec data rate and interfaces to PC DOS on the IBM PC. It will also support IBM PCs using the UCSD p and CP/M-86 operating systems. It can be classified as a baseband, distributed bus network with CSMA access protocol. Omninet does not support a collision detect feature—instead it uses a *Transport Layer protocol* (Layer 4 of the ISO 7-layer model) to seek an acknowledgment of successful receipt of message packets at the destination device. The network currently makes use of *disk servers*; a disk server is an interface device that allows many computers to access a common hard disk drive. This use of servers will eventually be extended to include *print servers*, *communications servers*, *Mirror servers*, and *gateways*. Figure 6-13 illustrates the general layout of an Omninet system.

Inasmuch as Omninet makes use of servers in its networking philosophy, a brief explanation of Omninet servers is in order before proceeding further. Recall that a server is a device that interfaces any non- or *semi-intelligent* peripheral to a network. Disk servers and print servers are the more familiar devices. They are used to allow file transfers or printing to and from expensive network resources such as hard disks and letter quality printers. In Corvus systems, a Mirror server is an interface to a *video tape data backup* capability; this mass storage technique is a low-cost method of *archiving* (storing) large amounts of data by using ordinary video tape recorders. A communications server provides shared access to a number of modems attached to the network—more about this capability will be discussed in the section on interfacing LANs with modem networks. A gateway is a special case of a communications server—it is a device that interfaces dissimiliar networks by the use of *protocol translation* software and/or firmware. The networks involved may be any combination of LANs and modem networks. Depending on the complexity of the networks being interfaced, gateways can become relatively expensive devices. Again, more on these will be said in the discussion to follow on interconnecting LANs and modem networks.

Omninet Hardware

General. Omninet is implemented on an IBM PC adapter card called a *transporter*. The transporter functions in much the same manner as the PCnet network adapter card. PCs are interconnected using a twisted pair wire (you will recall that PCnet uses a coaxial cable). The *electrical signaling* standard of RS-422 is used on the twisted pair just as it is on the PCnet coax. This wire can be supplied using low-cost telephone wire; the maximum segment length of Omninet is 1000 feet. Wire from the transporter card to the main network bus is connected to the bus through a simple terminal box. The disk server is the interface between the hard disks and Omninet. It also manages multiple-user access to its connected hard disk drives. Up to four Corvus hard disk drives may be connected to one disk server, each with up to 20 megabytes of storage. Any number of disk servers may be connected to Omninet (within the total device limitation).

Transporter Card. The transporter card implements the *collision avoidance* protocol for Omninet. The card is capable of determining when the network is available for starting a transmission. The card also computes a randomized transmit start time for data packets in order to minimize collision possibilities. As mentioned earlier, the transporter also implements a Transport Layer protocol that provides an economical form of *virtual circuit* between the two communicating devices (an IBM PC and disk server, for example). This virtual circuit guarantees that either a data packet on the network will get to its destination or that a non-delivery notification will be made to the sending device. The protocol also discards duplicate messages and ensures that data packets are received in the same order transmitted. If an acknowledgment is not received, the transporter will attempt a user-specified number of retransmissions. *Retransmission* will not be attempted if the CSMA circuitry detects that data are already on the network.

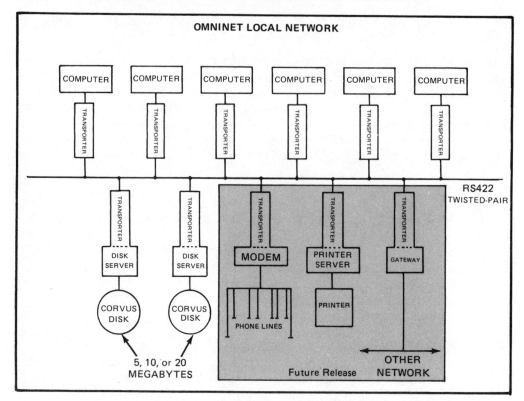

Figure 6–13. Omninet system installation.

All of the aforementioned functions are performed without CPU intervention, thus unburdening the computer's valuable memory and processing time. The transporter card is also responsible for the control of data flow into and out of its host PCs RAM. The technique used is direct memory access, which was explained earlier in the chapter.

Disk Server. The disk server consists of a transporter for network interfacing and a Corvus disk system interface for hard disk access control. The transporter allows the disk server to function in a manner similiar to any other device on the network. The disk interface ensures the proper routing of hard disk file accesses to the requesting PC work station. It also maintains a file on the hard disk drive called the *network active* table. This file relates Omninet user or server names to host numbers—it is used by software to locate active Omninet users and servers. A *host number* is the permanent identifier for each device on the network.

Other Servers. A print server will be added to the list of Omninet devices and combined with a communications server in one enclosure. The print server function will be to *buffer* print files from multiple network users and to maintain a prioritized *print queue* for *batch printing*. The communications server will allow the connection of modems to the network; the modems will be addressable from user PCs using the PC DOS I/O device COM2:. This combined server will be configurable using a Z-80 on-board processor—adapter cards will determine the number and types of modems and printers supported by the server. Another device, similar to a server, is the Omninet gateway computer for interconnecting Omninets or linking them to systems such as *Ethernet, SNA*, and other modem networks.

Hard Disk Drives. The hard disk drives are Corvus drives; other makes of hard disk drives are not supported by the disk server. Drive sizes can be 6, 11, or 20 megabytes. Firmware in the disk drive supports multi-computer file transfers (pipes), concurrent file access (semaphores), backup (Mirror), and network initialization.

Omninet Software . . . CONSTELLATION II

The main, high-level networking software provided by Corvus for use with Omninet is collectively known as CONSTELLATION II. CONSTELLATION II is just one of many protocols that can be supported by Omninet. Its significance lies in an ability to allow single-user operating systems to share resources in a local area network environment without extensive software modification. The functions of CONSTEL-LATION II are threefold: to allow access to shared resources such as hard disks, to transfer files between network users independent of the type of computer or operating system, and to support concurrent file access. CONSTELLATION II will also support *print sharing*; until print servers are available, the printers must be attached to an IBM PC or other work station supported by Omninet. Two significant differences exist between PCnet and CONSTELLATION II software: the support of multiple operating systems by Omninet, and Omninet's use of detached hard disk drives with their accompanying servers. These differences tend to make the Omninet software somewhat more complex to understand than that of PCnet, although this complexity only manifests itself to the individual designated as the *System Manager*.

CONSTELLATION II software has four levels of support to the Omninet system. These levels are:

- Hard disk firmware
- Disk server firmware
- Operating system ''drivers''
- Support software

The functions of the hard disk firmware are to perform disk sector read and write housekeeping, establish and maintain a common buffer area on the hard disk for dissimiliar DOS file transfers (this buffer area is referred to as the *pipes*), manage file-locking procedures for concurrent access, and maintain *boot* areas on the hard disk for the use of individual operating systems. These boot areas contain assembly language programs that allow each supported DOS to initialize itself with the appropriate Corvus disk interfaces.

The disk server firmware has two relatively simple tasks—to ensure that the originator of any data access request is identified so that the return data flow goes to the correct work station, and to communicate with other servers and users in order to maintain a table of active network users.

Drivers allow each operating system to access the Corvus hard disk as if it were a mass storage peripheral attached to the host work station. A driver is nothing more than an assembly language program that is attached to the IBMDOS.COM file of PC DOS to provide communications with the Corvus hard disk. The normal method of implementation is to make a volume on the hard disk look like a floppy drive to the host operating system. This function of the driver has the same result as the shared disk allocation scheme used in PCnet. The Corvus drive is partitioned into several volumes that are assigned to the users on the network. Each work station's driver maintains information on the location of its associated volumes, their individual sizes, and the read/write access allowed.

Several support programs are provided with CONSTELLATION II. These programs, along with their grouping according to specially designated users who would execute them, are listed in Table 6-6. Figure 6-14 illustrates the location of the component parts of CONSTELLATION II and their interrelationship.

Table 6-6. CONSTELLATION II support software.

System Manager
- Drive Manager .... creates volumes
- User Manager .... creates users
- Access Manager .... specifies user/volume matching
- Boot Manager .... sets up hardware boot data

Maintenance Manager
- Installation program
- Disk diagnostic
- Omninet diagnostic
- Recovery programs
- Mirror programs

Individual Network Users
- Mount Manager .... sets up user's volumes
- Library procedures

Omninet Operation

In order to gain an appreciation for the capabilities and limitations of Omninet in a working environment, a more detailed look at disk sharing, operating system interfaces, network operation, and the transporter is presented in the following pages.

Disk Sharing. Disk sharing is the bread-and-butter element of any network application that requires multiple-user access to data bases or files of any type. The following discussions use terminology that is defined in Table 6-7. The housekeeping chores required for shared disk access are somewhat higher in Omninet than in PCnet. Nine separate tables are required to organize users and their assigned volumes on the network, to assign specific access levels, and to permit the coexistence of up to 63 operating systems and computer types. Figure 6-15 shows the location of these tables

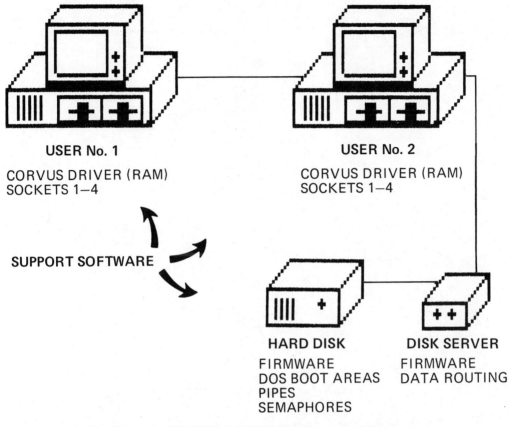

USER No. 1

CORVUS DRIVER (RAM)
SOCKETS 1–4

USER No. 2

CORVUS DRIVER (RAM)
SOCKETS 1–4

SUPPORT SOFTWARE

HARD DISK

FIRMWARE
DOS BOOT AREAS
PIPES
SEMAPHORES

DISK SERVER

FIRMWARE
DATA ROUTING

Figure 6–14. CONSTELLATION II software and firmware.

on a daisy-chained drive system. The design of this scheme for controlled disk access has evolved from the original *Corvus Multiplexer* system, which allowed a number of computers to access a hard disk drive through an electrical multiplexer. The Multiplexer was a form of local area network with a star topology. CONSTELLATION II software will work with Omninet or the older Multiplexer systems. In fact, the organization of the tables required by CONSTELLATION II is independent of the Omninet communications protocol.

Table 6-7. Omninet definitions.

Network	an Omninet network, with 1 or more disk servers
System	daisy-chained drives on 1 disk server
Drive	one in a set of daisy-chained drives
Volume	a contiguous area on a drive
Mount	associate a disk disk volume belonging to a user with that user's hard disk driver
Unmount	clear any association with a driver

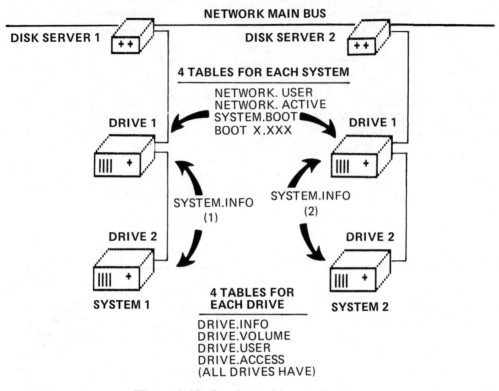

Figure 6–15. Omninet table organization.

Disk sharing is more than just the maintenance of volume-user-access relationships. Another aspect, which has been discussed previously in the review of PCnet, is concurrent access. All of the operating systems supported by CONSTELLATION II are single-user systems. This means that the operating system provides no protection against concurrent access to an application program's file structure. CONSTELLATION II provides a set of routines that can be accessed from some applications programs to lock and unlock files on the hard disk(s). The usage of these routines would be similiar in principle to the equivalent routines in PCnet.

Operating System Interface. A Corvus hard disk driver integrates into PC DOS in such a way that interference with normal operating system functions is minimized. Version 1.1 of PC DOS has no provisions for user-installed drivers as does CP/M-86; with no specific procedures to be concerned with, the DOS/driver interface is done at the lowest level possible. In other words, the user should never be aware of the presence of the driver. This situation may change with Version 2.0 of PC DOS since it does have provisions for user-supplied I/O device drivers. The driver software must do three things:

- Preserve the transparency of its existence to the user
- Send Corvus drive and transporter commands in a machine-independent manner
- Read and change the mount table

The mount table lists, for each volume accessible by that user, the disk server number, a drive number, the physical limits of that volume on the disk, and a read/write protect status. You will recall from Table 6-6 that each user maintains his or her own mount table. PC DOS uses volume designations A: through J:; other operating systems use different conventions. Part of the job of the *drive access* table is to strip away DOS-dependent volume naming conventions.

Network Operation (under CONSTELLATION II). Having said little to this point about the movement of data around the network, it is appropriate that the more communications-oriented functions of CONSTELLATION II software running on Omninet be explained. When a device powers up on the network, it sends a "Hello" message to all other active devices to announce its activation. The host number, device type, and the name of the device are transmitted. In addition, any device on the network can query any other device with "Who are you?" and "Where are you?" message packets; the response is a "My ID is" message, which is virtually identical to the "Hello" message. If the query is by device type, only those devices respond; otherwise, all devices will respond. These messages are used by network management software to determine the configuration and status of the network.

Device addressing within the Omninet local network allows a message to be sent to any device attached to the network or to all devices on the network. In addition to device addressing, Omninet supports the concept of a *socket*. A socket provides additional addressing capability by allowing a message to be sent to a particular buffer in the host computer. Up to four sockets can be defined for each computer on the network. With appropriate host computer software, the socket concept can be very powerful, particularly in a multi-tasking environment.

Transporter. The transporter accepts two major types of commands from the host computer to control the overall flow of messages within the local network. These commands are *SEND message* and *RECEIVE message*. An Omninet message contains two fields which are accessible by the host computer: *user data* and *user header*. Refer to Figure 6-16. The user data field may be up to 2047 bytes long; the user header up to 255 bytes long. A SEND message command specifies a result and header address, a destination host number, destination socket number, data address and length, and the header length.

The transporter utilizes DMA to transfer the message and optional message header without further involvement of the host software. When the message reaches its destination, one of the following four results is sent back to the sender:

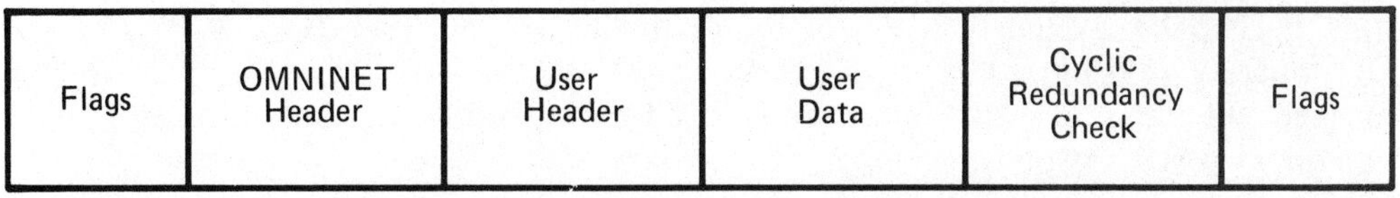

Flags	OMNINET Header	User Header	User Data	Cyclic Redundancy Check	Flags

Figure 6–16. Omninet data packet.

- Message delivered successfully
- Message failed after N retries
- Receiving socket not set up
- Message too long for receiving socket

RECEIVE message commands prepare host sockets to receive incoming messages. The RECEIVE message command specifies a result address, a socket number, a data buffer address, and maximum message length. The optional user header length is also specified. When this optional header is used, the header and the actual message can be placed into separate locations in the destination host's memory. This would allow, for example, the CONSTELLATION II software to keep track of the optional user header while the data proper is placed directly into a socket for use by an applications program.

Omninet and CONSTELLATION II Configuration Example

The elements of Omninet and CONSTELLATION II have been covered in enough detail to give the reader the background necessary to understand the manner in which this IBM PC networking system operates. Because Omninet is conceptually more difficult to comprehend than PCnet, a specific example of network setup, logical and physical device assignments, and representative data transfer events will be described. In this particular example, all the work stations are IBM PCs, but the operating systems are different. This may not be the most practical setup in actual use but it serves to illustrate the general functioning of a network configured for different DOSs. Figure 6-17 illustrates the following discussion and shows the sequence used to initialize the example network. As a starting point, the Corvus disks and the disk server have been powered up, but no PCs are on line. In this example, user LARRY on PC #1 has volumes on both drives 1 and 2, but his PC DOS boot program is located on drive 1 only. Remember that all data being transferred follow the message conventions just described.

Assuming that users BRUCE and DON on PC #2 and PC #3 boot up in the same manner as PC #1, the network should be ready to operate with all users logged on and the assignment of volumes to users made. The given volume assignments to drives and users would have been made at an earlier session using the *Installation Program*. From this point on, one user should be designated the System Manager, responsible for drive, user, access, and boot management. Table 6-8 lists the functions of each of the four areas of System Manager responsibility. The System Manager support software runs in UCSD p-System Pascal—therefore, if the System Manager is using the PC DOS operating system, a change of operating systems is required. Typically, the system manager functions are performed during initialization and infrequently thereafter. The individual user is responsible for mount management and the usual processes of file management. Table 6-9 lists the functions of the mount manager software available to each user on the network.

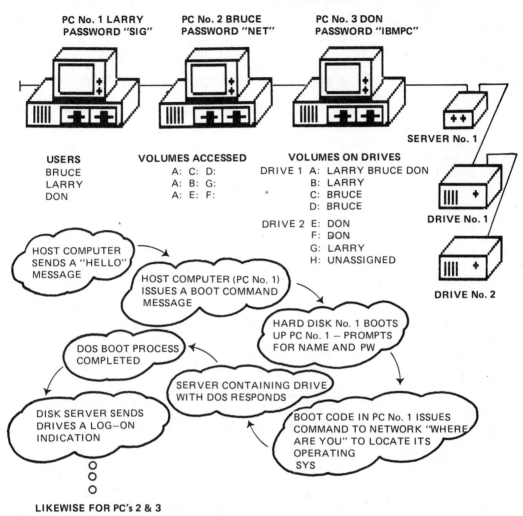

Figure 6–17. Network initialization process.

Multiple Operating System Support

Omninet provides for dissimilar operating system file transfer through the Corvus hard disk "pipes" scheme. This means that a user on one IBM PC running under PC DOS can communicate with another user on an IBM using CP/M-86 or with someone on another personal computer supported by CONSTELLATION II. The example in Figure 6-17 does not indicate which operating system LARRY, BRUCE, and DON might be using—for discussion purposes let us assume that LARRY is using CP/M-86 and BRUCE and DON are using PC DOS. These dissimiliar operating systems therefore coexist on the same net. The decision on whether or not to use dissimilar operating systems in a specific application should be part of the overall system design. It is conceivable that a PC DOS user might in fact desire to access a CP/M-86 file since

Table 6-8. Support programs—system manager.

Drive Manager. . . . .requires system password

- List drives on line. List the drive number and capacity of all drives on line. Indicate if they are not initialized.
- List volumes. List the name, address, length, and operating system type of all volumes on the specified drive. List all unused space on the drive
- Add a volume to a drive
- Remove a volume from a drive
- List free space on all drives
- Protect. Specify system-wide access: none/read-only/read-write

User Manager. . . . .requires system password

- List user name, password, boot DOS type, and home system
- Remove user from user directory
- Add user to user directory
- Change user information

Access Manager. . . . .requires system password

- Specify user access to several volumes
- Specify volume access for several users

Boot Manager. . . . .requires system password

List file names and CPU types for all boot files
- Add boot file to volume
- Remove boot file from volume

---

many of the evolving 16-bit applications programs are being written for both CP/M-86 and PC DOS. A good example of this is the well-known data base management system, dBASE II. Any request to transfer a dBASE II file, for example, from user LARRY to user BRUCE, would not be a direct PC-to-PC file transfer; instead it would go via the "pipes" area of the appropriate Corvus hard disk as discussed earlier.

Omninet Applications

Applications supported by Omninet are very similiar to those described earlier in the discussion of PCnet. For the mainframe program development example, the link to a mainframe computer from Omninet would require each work station to have its own modem connection. If modems are attached to one or more PCs on the network, mainframe links would be set up just as if the network were not present. There is no communications server currently available for this system, although such a device will be a future addition to Omninet. Unlike the scheme used in PCnet, the Omninet modem server will attach directly to the main bus and will be configurable to the desired

Table 6-9. Support software—individual users.

Mount Manager. . . . .no password required

- List drives on line. Same as drive manager function
- List volumes accessible to this user
- Mount a volume (identify to the driver)
- Unmount a volume
- Save mount table—located in the driver
- Change user's password
- Protect: specify individual access privileges: read-only/read-write
- Specify secure or release of a volume

number of modem channels. This configuration is illustrated in Figure 6-13. A number of applications programs specifically designed to take advantage of Omninet and CON-STELLATION II network features should become available during 1983. At least one electronic mail system is already planned.

Omninet Economics

Our final discussion on Omninet concerns cost factors to install a practical network such as that illustrated in Figure 6-12. Unit prices for Omninet components used in this installation are as follows:

- Omninet Transporter Card $ 495
- Disk Server $ 990
- 1000 feet Twisted Pair Cable $ 250
- 6 MByte Corvus Hard Disk $2295
- 11 Mbyte Corvus Hard Disk $3295
- 20 Mbyte Corvus Hard Disk $4295
- Mirror Backup Option $ 790

The system shown in Figure 6-12 requires the following material:

- 8 Transporter Cards $3960
- 1 Disk Server $ 990
- 1000 feet Twisted Pair $ 250

         Total $5200

The communications cost for this installation, with material equivalent to the PCnet system, is $650 per work station. In this case the additional requirement for mass storage is fixed within a known range since Omninet only supports Corvus hard disks. As in the PCnet base case, we start with minimum configuration of two work stations, a disk server, and a pre-wired bus cable, resulting in a starting cost of $2230. Cumulative costs of adding additional work station capability are as follows:

Work stations:	3	4	5	6	7
Cumulative $	2725	3220	3715	4210	4705
Cost per User	908	805	743	702	672

ETHERLINK

Overview

EtherLink is a hardware and software package that connects IBM PCs and allows the sharing of floppy drive and printer resources. EtherLink is the first IBM PC local area network designed to Ethernet specifications. EtherLink uses PC DOS and is transparent to the user, except for the additional operating system level commands necessary to establish links between user PCs and server PCs. As few as two or as many as 100 PCs may be connected to a single *segment* of network cable. Because EtherLink is an Ethernet-compatible LAN, it supports multiple segments—these segments are connected by devices known as *repeaters*, which make several physical segments appear to be one *logical network*.

With the addition of the *EtherShare* network server, up to 72 megabytes of shared hard disk storage are supported. Two software packages, *EtherPrint* and *EtherMail* are available to run on the EtherShare server. If no EtherShare server is present, a printer can be attached to one or more PCs designated as *servers*; the *server PC* also provides shared floppy disk resources. EtherLink software supports the sharing of floppy disk drives and printers, but not hard disks. Each PC in the EtherLink LAN requires a network adapter card containing standard Ethernet logic circuits and firmware. *EtherLink* is the official name for the basic network and its supporting software—this does not necessarily include EtherShare, EtherPrint, or EtherMail. We will extend the term EtherLink to describe all the components provided by 3Com Corporation to set up a LAN; this includes not only the basic system, but also the extra server(s) and their software packages.

EtherLink Hardware

The hardware associated with EtherLink is composed of network bus components, the EtherShare network server and adapter cards. Each of these will be discussed next in more detail.

Network Bus Components. The EtherLink data path is formed by coaxial cable—either RG-58A/U *thin coaxial* with BNC-type hardware or the commercial grade Ethernet *thick coaxial* with N- type hardware. Thin cable can be connected directly to the adapter card with a BNC T-connector, similar to the hardware connections in PCnet; thick cable requires an external *transceiver* and a cable tap. Thick and thin cable may be intermingled on the same network as long as basic network configuration rules are followed. These rules, which conform to Ethernet specifications, are summarized in Table 6-10 and illustrated in Figure 6-18. Although thick cable allows longer segments,

Table 6-10. The Twelve Commandments of Ethernet.

I.   100 nodes maximum on any single segment
II.   Nodes must be at least 2.5 meters apart
III.   Node is defined as an addressable entity connected via:
● Cable Tap   {T-connector for thin cable}
● Transceiver   {on adapter card for thin system}
● Controller   {on adapter card for thin system}

IV.   Any number of devices may be connected to a node
V.   Repeaters may be placed at any or every node position
VI.   Maximum length of cable between any 2 nodes = 1500 m
VII.   Maximum segment length:

● 300 m   Thin Ethernet
● 500 m   Thick Ethernet with non-3Com transceivers
● 1000 m   Thick Ethernet with 3Com transceivers

VIII.   Maximum length of transceiver cable = 50 m {Adapter card to thick cable transceiver}
IX.   Maximum of 2 repeaters in a path between any 2 nodes
X.   Maximum of 1000 m for a point-to-point link
XI.   Maximum end-to-end network length = 2800 m
XII.   Maximum of 1024 nodes on a complete network

it is considerably more difficult to install. Thick cable is also more costly, both because of increased cost per linear foot and the requirement for extra hardware at each device connection point. Examples of network installations for both the thick and thin bus cases are shown in Figures 6-19 and 6-20.

EtherShare Network Server. This hardware component is a general-purpose microcomputer, although it does not function as a network work station. The server uses an Intel 8086 processor operating at 10 MHZ and has 512 Kbytes of parity-

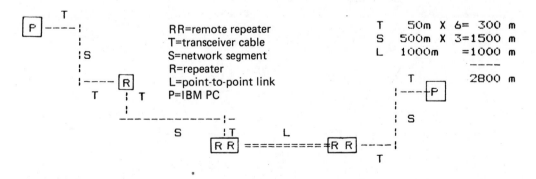

Figure 6–18. Ethernet multi-segment network.

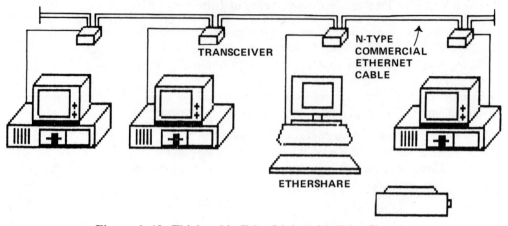

Figure 6–19. Thick cable EtherLink (with EtherShare).

checked, random access memory. Each network server station can be equipped with either 10 or 36 megabytes of hard disk storage, with external expansion to 1 additional drive of equal capacity. The choices of hard disk storage are thus 10, 20, 36, or 72 megabytes. The server has a 1 megabyte 5-¼ inch floppy disk drive for backup purposes. A 17-megabyte cartridge tape drive is another optional peripheral. Either one or two printers may be attached to each server. There is no limit on the number of servers that can be placed on EtherLink, although the cost of this device would be a limiting consideration. The server is supplied with a keyboard, video display, and EtherLink adapter card.

Adapter Card. Each device, or node on the network, must have an EtherLink network adapter card installed. The adapter card contains the circuitry and firmware required to implement Layers 1 and 2 (Physical and Data Link) of the previously

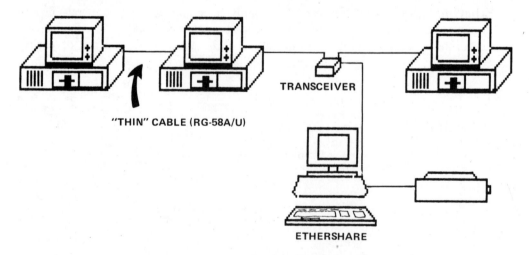

Figure 6–20. Thin cable EtherLink (with EtherShare).

discussed 7-layer ISO model. The card includes a transceiver, which is capable of driving the thin Ethernet cable. As previously mentioned, the thick Ethernet installation requires an external transceiver, which can be supplied by either 3Com or XEROX Corporation. The adapter card is responsible for a number of functions that are required for proper network operation: DMA data transfers with the host computer's RAM, data formatting into Ethernet packets for transmission, passing received data packets to the host PC's operating system, data error checking, data encoding and decoding, and access control according to the Ethernet CSMA/CD protocol. Because of the popularity of the Ethernet CSMA/CD access protocol, it will be described in greater detail.

The adapter card implements the full CSMA/CD protocol in the Ethernet specification. With packet sizes ranging from 64 to 1518 bytes, this protocol will support a network configuration of up to 2.8 km between any two work stations. A multi-segment Ethernet (or EtherLink) LAN is shown in Figure 6-18; the Ethernet packet format is shown in Figure 6-21. The maximum packet size is based on efficiency and the desire to minimize collisions (two or more data packets on the network simultaneously). Minimum packet size is chosen to guarantee collision detection (CD) at maximum network sizes. Figure 6-22 illustrates how minimum packet size and maximum network size interact to provide collision detection under the worst case condition.

The time required to transmit 64 bytes is 51.2 microseconds at a 10 megabit data rate. This is approximately equal to the time required for a bit of data to make the round trip between two PCs at the network extremities in Figures 6-18 and 6-22. If PC "A" commences a packet transmission on the network, "B" will not sense the carrier until "A's" packet begins to arrive. If PC "B" were to start a transmission just prior to the arrival of "A's" packet (which would be allowable with the CSMA/CD protocol), a collision would be generated at "B" when "A's" packet arrives. "B" would then transmit a collision signal, which would begin to arrive at "A" while "A" was still transmitting the original 64-byte packet. Thus the adapter card in "A" would also detect a collision and begin its collision recovery routine. This consists of continuing transmission for a short interval in order to generate the collision signal just mentioned (this is known as a *jam transmission*) followed by a random silence period before reattempting to send the packet. Since this was the worst case example, any longer packet size or any two nodes closer together on the network will also have guaranteed collision detection.

This logic is the most difficult part of the CSMA/CD protocol to comprehend. The remaining aspects of this access control method are relatively straightforward. If the

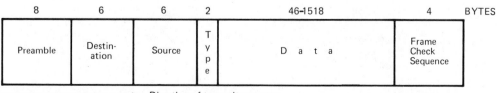

Figure 6–21. Ethernet packet format.

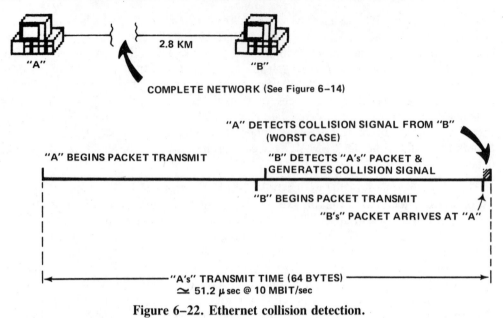

Figure 6–22. Ethernet collision detection.

physical layer of a station does not sense a carrier, it signals the data link layer to begin transmission of one or more data packets. On a baseband network such as EtherLink, a "carrier" is actually the presence of digital signal transitions from bit-to-bit. Once the packets are transmitted, the collision detect logic works as just described. With Ethernet packet sizes, the percentage of collisions is quite low (less than 1%), even on relatively large and busy networks (in excess of 100 work stations). The end result is that a business user of EtherLink or similar LANs need not be overly concerned about degraded performance due to collisions.

EtherLink Software

Basic System. EtherLink software is supplied in the basic system (without EtherShare) to allow designated PCs to be set up as *server* PCs. A server PC cannot be used to run other applications programs while it is so designated. There are no limits on the number of PCs that may be set up as servers. Any printer or floppy I/O device that can be attached to a PC can become a shared resource. For example, the following sequence will establish an IBM PC as a server named SERVER1, with drive B: (write protected) and line printer LPT2: available as shared resources:

```
A>PCSERVER    {executes PCSERVER.COM program}
Server name? SERVER1
Server drive ID? B:
Write protect? Y
Server printer ID? LPT2:
```

This could have also been entered as:

```
A>PCSERVER SERVER1 B: /WP LPT2:
```

From this point on, any PC in the EtherLink network can access SERVER1, but only one at a time. The using PC LINKs a local drive designator (in this case, C:) to the shared floppy disk with the following command:

A>EL LINK C: SERVER1

The effect of this command is to make drive B: on SERVER1 available as logical drive C: on the using PC work station. Local drive designators A: through D: can be linked to the named server's shared drive. Only one drive and one printer on a server PC may be designated as shared resources. Although *linked access* to a server PC is exclusive (only one user PC linked to a resource at a time), the user PC may link to the floppy and printer simultaneously. Figure 6-23 illustrates the general capabilities and limitations of EtherLink's basic software.

It should be obvious from this simplified example that the capability for multiple users to access the basic EtherLink network is limited when only one server is designated. In fact, with more than one server designated—three, for example—only three virtual circuits can be in use at any given moment, regardless how many PCs are connected to the network. This is wasteful of EtherLink's capacity on networks with a relatively large number of user PCs. This problem would not exist on an EtherLink network that contained an EtherShare server.

Compatibility of existing IBM PC software must be carefully assessed before planning applications on an EtherLink network. In general, the following criteria must be met for a software package to be compatible:

- Runs on IBM PC DOS
- Uses standard floppy disk and printer drivers
- Is relocatable in user RAM
- Sufficient room in RAM exists for program code and data
- Does not require physical insertion of a diskette during program operation

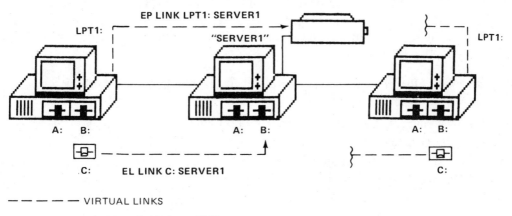
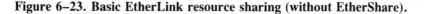

Figure 6–23. Basic EtherLink resource sharing (without EtherShare).

Representative programs and the degree to which they meet the aforementioned criteria are listed in Table 6-11. Keep in mind that newer versions of these programs may change the applicability of the listing—the programs are shown here to give the reader a feel for compatibility requirements.

Table 6-11. EtherLink software compatibility.

Compatible Software	Incompatible Software
Visicalc*	EasyWriter 1.0
Supercalc	Visitrend/Plot 1.0
WordStar	Visidex 1.0
EasyWriter 1.1*	VisiSchedule
Pfs:File*	Time Manager
Pfs:Report*	
Pfs:Graph*	
Visi Desktop/Plan*	
Visifile	

*Note: These programs are self-booting and are loaded with the command *EL BOOT*—this allows the network linkages to remain intact between the user and server PCs. A normal warm boot would break any existing links.

EtherShare Software. The addition of EtherShare to the EtherLink network adds a new dimension to its utility in the business environment. Hard disk drive resources require the addition of this separate microcomputer and the EtherShare software package. The hard disk drives are provided by 3Com Corporation with the EtherShare server—other types of drives are not supported by network server software. EtherShare is made up of three distinct parts:

- The EtherShare server, which manages all EtherShare resources such as hard disk volumes and printers
- The EtherShare administrative program, which performs housekeeping jobs on the server
- EtherShare commands, which execute from a command file on each user PC's local drive (usually A:)

There are 14 EtherShare commands accessible by each user on the EtherLink network. These commands allow the user to

- Log-in and Log-out from the server by user name
- Create or delete EtherShare volumes
- Link local floppy drive designators to EtherShare volumes
- Modify user access and volume parameters
- Display directories of network users and volumes

Volumes can be established on the hard disk as either 160 Kbyte or 320 Kbyte areas. In this context, a volume simulates the presence of an additional single or double-sided floppy drive. A 10 megabyte drive can accommodate about 30 double-sided floppy equivalents, or a proportionately higher number if some volumes are single-sided equivalents. Any user on the network can link one to three local drive designators to the EtherShare server. The allowable drive designators are A:, B:, C:, or D:, just as in the basic EtherLink software. The normal assignment would be to allocate drive A: to the local floppy and then to LINK B:, C:, or D: to appropriate hard disk volumes. A single user would then have access to a maximum of 1.28 megabytes of combined floppy and hard disk mass storage.

A single user may only establish one set of links (drive designators to volume names) to a given server at a time. Over the entire network, however, any number of links may be set up from multiple users, up to the limit of the server capacity. The job of the EtherShare housekeeping software is to sort out the flow of data to and from the server with multiple users accessing the hard disk.

File protection is accomplished by passwords and a simple scheme of access control. Protection is provided only to the volume level of storage. Individual files and records are not protected. A volume can be *public* or *private*. If public, everyone on the network has access, unless a password is assigned; if private, only the creator of the volume has access. Passwords can be assigned to any volume. Table 6-12 summarizes the protection scheme managed by EtherShare software.

Table 6-12. EtherShare volume protection.

Volume Access	Password Assigned	No Password
PUBLIC—many users; shared access	Password required	Anyone can use
PRIVATE—only 1 user can access; exclusive access	Password required	Only the creator may use

EtherPrint. EtherPrint is supplied as a software utility package that runs on the EtherShare server and on user PCs. It performs in similar fashion to the print sharing software on the basic EtherLink network. The commands to link and unlink printer resources are identical. The major difference is that EtherPrint allows the use of two printers on the server. Print files are queued in the EtherShare server on a first-in, first-out basis until the selected printer is available. Once a printer link is established between a PC and one of the two print devices, normal PC DOS or BASIC print commands can be executed on the selected printer.

The following sequence will illustrate the use of EtherPrint to print a final report on a letter-quality printer attached to the server, which will be named SERVER1. The report has been prepared with WordStar. The first step is to establish the printer link:

```
A>EP LINK ?
Your printer ID? LPT1:              {what printer device to link}
To whom?  SERVER1                   {designate the proper server}
SERVER1 linked to LPT1:             {confirmation of link}
```

In the event that a review of EtherShare printer assignment is desired, the following sequence will list printers attached to the server:

```
A>EP DIR ?                          {list printers on the server}
Server?  SERVER1                    {designate the proper server}
A>EP LINK LPT1: /?                  {what printers are attached?}
Printer(s) supported by the server:

   1—DIABLO
   2—EPSON

Selection?  2                       {use the Epson printer}
SERVER1 linked to LPT1:             {confirmation}
```

The next step would be to load WordStar from a shared volume on the hard disk. Let us assume that WordStar is located on PUBLIC volume WORDPROC which is linked to drive B:. The file to be printed, REPORT.DOC, is on PRIVATE volume MYFILES which is linked to drive C:.

```
A>B:WS                              {Load WordStar from the hard disk}
P                                   {Print file from "Edit No File" menu
                                    of WordStar}

Name of file to print?   C:REPORT.DOC

                                    {Now answer the print file questions
                                    as desired}

Ready printer, press Return
```

The report file on hard disk volume MYFILES will now begin printing on the Epson printer attached to the server as printer #2.

EtherMail. EtherMail is an application package designed to run on the EtherShare server and on network PCs. The server acts as a post office and mail administrator for the network; each PC runs an EtherMail program that provides its user with network mail capabilities to be described next. EtherMail is an internal message processing system—there is no tie-in to modem networks through gateways or modem servers. EtherMail allows the network user to

- Get new mail from the "post office"
- Open and read a message
- Compose a new message
- Reply to a message
- Forward a copy of the message
- Send a message
- File a message (send it to yourself)
- Print a message
- Save a message in progress (to be finished later)
- Delete a message

Up to 26 DOS files may be attached to an EtherMail message for sending—common uses of this feature might be to send a WordStar document file for comment or perhaps a Visicalc budget model to update a cost center's entries. Distribution lists may be created and used to automatically send mail to predefined groups of recipients by entering only a file name. A text editor is included in the software and is automatically invoked when messages are created, replied to, or forwarded. The editor may also be used off-line. Any other editor or word processor may be used and the resulting file sent as an attachment to a normal message.

The EtherShare server has two primary functions in the EtherMail process: it accepts and distributes a user's messages, checking every server on the network to find the proper addressees. Each active user on the EtherLink network must be logged on to a specific server, if there is more than one present. Message routing is accomplished transparently to the user. The server also accepts messages addressed to all its logged-in users, and holds them in the "post office" until the recipient(s) desire to retrieve their mail. In addition to the "post office," the EtherShare server also maintains personal "mail folders" for the users who normally log-on to that server. The mail folders are managed by the users, not by the EtherShare "post office."

EtherLink Economics

In keeping with our effort to give a network installation cost comparison using equivalent requirements, again refer to Figure 6-12. Available EtherLink hardware and software that could be used on this system are as follows:

- EtherShare Disk Server (10 Mbyte) $11500
- EtherLink Network Interface $ 950
- Thin Ethernet Cable $ 20 + $1/meter
- Thin Ethernet Terminator Kit $ 25
- Thin Ethernet Loopback Plug $ 25
- EtherMail Software $ 1500
- EtherPrint Software $ 750

The required hardware and software for the eight work station setup in Figure 6-12 would be: (again, exclusive of hard disk)

- 8 EtherLink network interface cards (includes T-connectors and software) $7600
- Thin Ethernet Terminator Kit $ 25
- Thin Ethernet Loopback Plug $ 25
- 760 feet Thin Ethernet Cable $ 252
                                      Total $7902

The resulting communications cost per user for EtherLink is therefore $988. The starting minimum for EtherLink (two work stations and 760 feet of pre-wired bus cable) is $2202. Incremental costs as additional work stations are added are:

Work stations	3	4	5	6	7
Cumulative $	3152	4102	5052	6002	6952
Cost per User	1051	1026	1010	1000	993

As in the Omninet case, hard disk requirements are dependent on the vendor's supplied options. Third party drives are not supported.

SUMMARY

In this section of the chapter, currently available local area networks for the IBM PC have been thoroughly reviewed. It is our hope that the reader, having been exposed to the fundamentals of the technology early in the chapter, will now have a better appreciation for the power and versatility of LAN communications. Furthermore, the reader should be able to better evaluate the merits of new networks that become available for the IBM PC—certainly there are many more to come. New networks may differ in detail from the three reviewed here; however, the ability of a network to adequately support file transfer, disk and printer sharing, and concurrent access should be closely examined before significant resources are committed to the system. In addition, the availability of applications software utilizing network features (concurrent access data base, for example) should be determined. The economic factors of network installation given at the conclusion of each system's description should be interpreted as representative costs only since prices are very sensitive to the volatility of the microcomputer marketplace.

During the course of examining each network, certain similiarities and differences have emerged. Table 6-13 summarizes the salient features of the three networks. The intent is not to show one network as being "best" in all situations, but to illustrate that each of the systems may best match a given requirement. The strengths of the PCnet system are ease of use and simplicity of configuration. Omninet excels in its flexibility to connect dissimiliar computers and operating systems and in the cheaper cost of adding new work stations to an existing net. EtherLink has the advantage of its compatibility with standard Ethernet components and networks. The comparative pricing with Figure 6-12 as a reference should only be used as a jumping off point for a much more detailed study of the alternatives available. The comparison only encompassed pure local communications costs—shared peripheral requirements are equally important and are likely to be the pacing items when considering the total distributed processing cost.

VII. INTER-NETWORK COMMUNICATIONS

Up to this point, the reader has been introduced to personal computer communications using the telephone system over long distances and local area networks over short distances. The next logical topic in this progression is communications between networks. Three catagories of inter-networking suggest themselves: two or more similar local area networks, dissimilar local area networks, and local area with modem networks. The latter is of the most interest from a practical point of view and the one most likely to be encountered in business applications. The first two will be briefly described in order to provide a complete overview of the subject. Three key terms are introduced in this section: *repeater*, *gateway*, and *modem server*—or *communications server*—as it is frequently called.

Table 6-13. Summary of network features.

Feature	PCnet	Omninet	EtherLink
Transmission media	Coaxial	Twisted pair	Coaxial
Adapter cost	$695	$495	$950
Cable cost	$44 + 0.30/ft	$250/1000 ft	$20 + $1/meter
Access protocol	CSMA/CD	CSMA	CSMA/CD
Higher protocol	No	Layers 3/4	No
Max length (ft)	3000/7000	1000	300m-2.8km
Servers	No	Yes	Yes
Multiple DOS	No	Yes	No
Multiple computers	Yes	Yes	No
Data rate	1 Mbit/sec	1 Mbit/sec	10 Mbit/sec
Mass storage*	IBMPC/? Mbyte	$900/80 Mbyte	$11500/72 MB
No. of devices	64,000	64	1024
Gateways	Future	Future	Repeater
Printer sharing	Yes	Yes	Yes
Bandwidth	Baseband	Baseband	Baseband
Topology	Dist'd Bus	Dist'd Bus	Dist'd Bus
Concurrent access	Record level	File level	By Volume
Multi-user DOS	No	No	No

*This is the connection cost for mass storage and max capacity per server. A shared IBM PC is required for PCnet. PCnet mass storage depends on shared PC hard disk controller board drive capacity and number of sPCs. There may be multiple servers on Omninet at $900 each.

SIMILAR LOCAL AREA NETWORK CONNECTION

The device that accomplishes the linkage between two LANs of the same type is known as a *repeater*. The main purpose of a repeater is to increase the coverage and scope of a local area network. Repeaters are common in the design of Ethernet-based LAN systems. On the 3Com EtherLink, repeaters are merely transceivers—these devices provide the Layer 1 (physical layer) connection between multiple segments of an EtherLink network. The ultimate use of repeaters is to provide additional flexibility in the physical layout of a local area network and to allow the inclusion of additional work stations. There are restrictions: in the EtherLink version, no more than 100 devices, including repeaters, may be attached to any network segment. A network segment is any portion of the network terminated on both ends. No more than two repeaters may be in the path between any two work stations. Figure 6-24 illustrates the use of repeaters to extend a single type of LAN.

DISSIMILAR LOCAL AREA NETWORKS

A *gateway* is a device designed to interface two dissimilar networks. The two dissimilar networks may both be LANs, or one may be a LAN and the other a modem network.

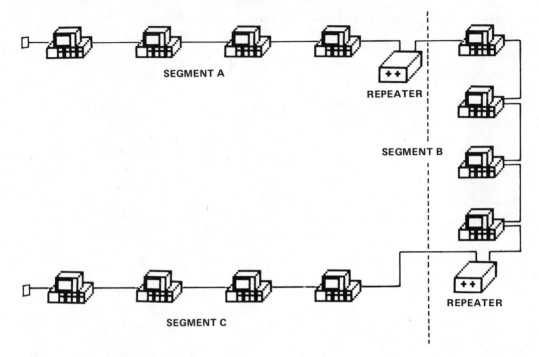

Figure 6–24. The use of repeaters for multi-segment local area networks.

The LAN/modem network interface will be described more fully in the next section. A gateway is literally a device on both the networks it seeks to connect. One side of the gateway communicates via the protocol of its connected network; the other side communicates according to its connected network's protocol. A diagrammatic example of a gateway is shown in Figure 6-25. Although not strictly necessary, gateways are

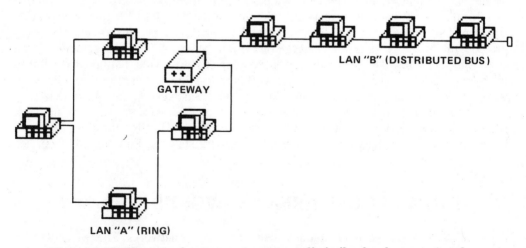

Figure 6–25. The use of gateways to connect dissimilar local area networks.

normally co-located within a single enclosure. An example of a gateway application is the interconnection of an Omninet network to an EtherLink network. Omninet's planned gateway device will undoubtedly include Ethernet as one of its connection options.

Some gateways also have another protocol translator, known as an inter-net protocol. This is shown in Figure 6-26. The function of such a protocol is to provide an orderly means of accommodating the simultaneous operation of two networks. Within the framework of the ISO model, inter-netting is most likely to occur in the network (3), transport (4), and session (5) Layers. The reason for this is straightforward: Inter-netting is very closely linked to communications routing methodology, and these three layers are primarily involved in moving data to the correct recipient via the most economical path. An inter-net protocol is one that will allow the establishment of *virtual circuits* across two dissimilar networks. Thus, a user on an EtherLink network could establish a virtual circuit with an OMNINET user through a gateway device.

LOCAL AND MODEM NETWORK RELATIONSHIPS

As previously mentioned, gateways are capable of tying together dissimilar networks. This includes local and modem networks since in virtually every case the protocol and bandwidth are quite different on these types of networks. There is, however, a simpler way to connect LANs with modem networks—through the use of a *modem server*, or *communications server*. This technique is illustrated in Figure 6-27. Modem servers will in general be more prevalent in business applications due to their relatively low cost compared to gateways. A modem server may be thought of as a special case of a gateway, but a modem server exists primarily to provide (a) modem channel(s) to

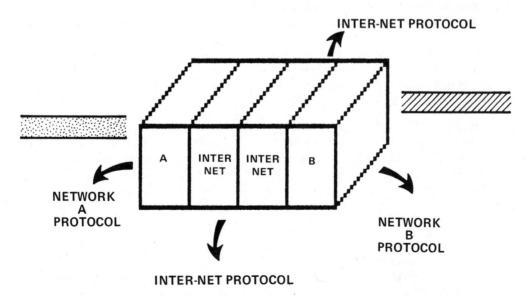

Figure 6–26. Gateway with inter-net protocol translation.

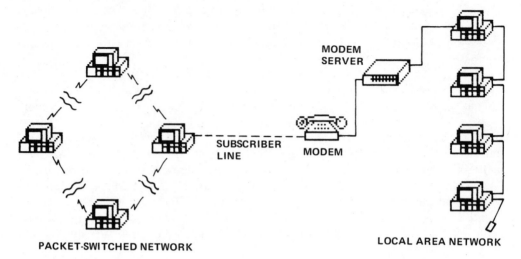

PACKET-SWITCHED NETWORK

LOCAL AREA NETWORK

Figure 6–27. Modem server connecting packet-switched network with LAN.

multiple users on the local area network. This device is most appropriate when the local area network is connected to a subscriber telephone line for low-to-medium speed communications.

At this point we will introduce a new term—the *packet-switched network*. Up to this point, telephone-based data communications have been referred to as modem networks since modems are the most visible aspect of those networks to the average user. When the data get to one of the many digital trunk lines that carry high volumes of long-distance computer communications, the technology used to route traffic is known as packet-switching. This term reflects the fact that the data packet itself carries the required routing information to get to its intended destination rather than relying on a fixed-route physical circuit (circuit-switching). A node on the packet-switched network would be connected to many potential users in a service area via either dedicated leased lines or, more commonly, via local subscriber telephone lines. As indicated in Figure 6-27, the local modem may be quite some distance from the nearest packet-switched node, although it will itself be a node or device on the local network.

You may have perceived yet another characteristic of modem servers and gateways: the mixing of widely different data rates, or bandwidths. In Figure 6-27, the dissimilar data rates might range from 56 kilobits/sec on the packet-switched network to 1 megabit/sec on the local area network. The mismatch for a modem server, as shown in the Figure 6-27 installation, is even greater, with 0.3 Kbit/sec on the modem and 1 Mbit/sec on the LAN.

From the perspective of the user, the operation of a modem server does not differ from normal IBM PC asynchronous communications usage as long as data are originated from their work station within the local area network. The modem becomes a shared resource just as printers and hard disk devices. Any user on the LAN can address the modem with the appropriate I/O file designation (COM2: in PC DOS or BASIC, for example). Once the modem establishes a circuit on the telephone line or directly on a packet switched network, it becomes unavailable for other requesting users (unless the owners can afford multi-channel modems!). If the modem is so-equipped, all the appropriate auto-answer and auto-dial features are usable in the normal fashion. Once a modem network session is begun, as in the case of a SOURCE or CompuServe access, the virtual circuit remains busy until the call is terminated. Network planners should select a communications server that accommodates sufficient modem cards to handle the estimated requirements for long-distance data communications.

The interesting challenge for modem servers begins when a party on one local area network desires to establish a circuit with a colleague on another local network, located several hundred miles from the first. The applications that could be supported by such communications include electronic mail, file transfer, access to specialized data bases, document transmission, and software distribution to name but a few. In order for these applications to be practical, there must be a scheme whereby each user can uniquely address the desired recipient—at least to the point where the recipient's work station is identified. Figure 6-28 shows an example of how an inter-net protocol, known as a *PUP inter-net datagram*, is constructed. The information required for routing after receipt into a network is contained in this *datagram* format. This particular format is used in the U.S. government's packet-switched network, ARPANET—a large, world-wide network commonly used by universities and research establishments. This par-

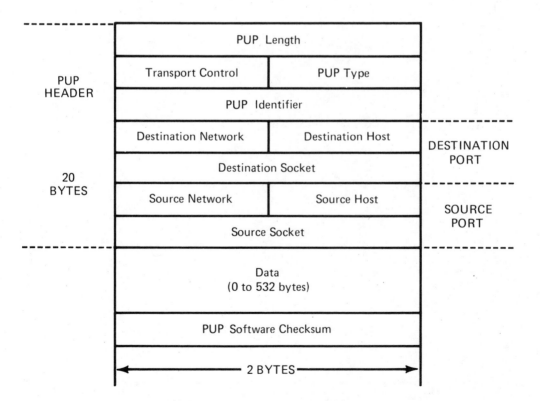

Figure 6–28. PUP inter-net datagram.

ticular format can also be used within the Ethernet data packet and thus provides a means to interconnect an Ethernet with a packet-switched network such as ARPANET.

A properly designed local area network should be able to support advanced applications such as unattended file transfer and electronic mail. In this case, an accurate time-keeping device is also required in order to initiate the process. Even better for such an application would be a network running under a multi-tasking or multi-user operating system. The advantage of this arrangement is that a network user could be doing independent processing while a virtual terminal or "process" was handling the background communications tasks. Background communications could be either on the local area network or on a modem network. This would include the automatic sending and receiving of data files and mail. Another candidate for a background communications process would be maintaining an active bulletin board for incoming calls. The reader should be aware of the importance of such devices as gateways and modem servers and how they fit into the overall process of designing a functional local area network. As always, the role of software, designed to exploit existing communications technology, is crucial to the ultimate success of any business communications system.

7

Current and Future
Applications of IBM
PC Communications

Throughout the course of this book, communications technology as applied to personal computing—specifically to the IBM PC—has been explored and it appears to have limitless potential as software support expands. The increasing availability of terminal emulators, protocol adapter cards, local area networks, and applications software spanning the universe of communications usage presents a challenge for the creative use of this information machine. The goal of this chapter is to provide the reader with the key features and potential usage of popular applications that rely on some form of data communications. No attempt is made to cover all conceivable applications; instead, a few representative uses of communications, some still in their infancy, are described.

To receive maximum benefit from the following pages, the reader should subscribe to a basic principle of personal computing: Only through the interaction of personal computer users, either in "local" or geographically widespread environments (or both) will the true potential of mass accessibility to computing power be realized. Electronic mail, graphics "videotex" technology, electronic publishing, teleshopping, and bulletin board services are some of the activities that have yet to reach their full potential. These are covered in the pages to follow. The more mature applications such as Bulletin Boards and Electronic Mail are covered first, followed by those that are less developed in the context of everyday use. Finally, a case study of a medium size business is presented in order to put the information in this book into a real-world context.

I. BULLETIN BOARD AND HOST
COMMUNICATION SYSTEMS

Bulletin Board and Host Communications systems are related in the sense that a remote operator has some specified degree of control over the host computer system. The Bulletin Board System (BBS) is the more specialized application of the two, in that the remote caller is given access to a menu of allowable activities; these activities are in turn determined by the features that the System Operator (SYSOP) desires to provide the intended users of the BBS. A host communications system on the other hand, allows remote operators more freedom in their access to the facilities of the host computer—typically, a host program allows remote operation at the operating system level, the use of any available language compilers or interpreters, or the direct execution of an applications program resident in the host. A BBS is itself an applications program, whereas a true host utility works at the operating system level.

A host communications utility operates under a very simplistic concept—the output from the remote keyboard is trapped and sent to the RS-232-C port; upon receipt at the host computer, it is treated as a keyboard character input stream and is sent to the COMMAND.COM processor in DOS. The resultant video output on the host is paralleled to the RS-232-C port and eventually displayed on the remote video monitor. The benefits of this mode of communications are clear—with the possible exception of graphics displays, PC users have access to any software that will run on their home computer and can be placed on a readible storage media. The ideal media to use with this application is a hard disk, inasmuch as a remote user would like to have as many programs available without requiring a media change as possible.

There are both operating system and applications program considerations when using a host communications system. The calling computer need not be using the same operating system as the host computer—in fact, the remote work station might be a *dumb terminal*, capable of only display and communications functions. The most effective remote work station would be another IBM PC—this allows the remote caller access to most of the IBM PCs unique keyboard and display capabilities, if the host communications software is written properly. One operating system restriction concerning remote access is the necessity for the host communications program and any desired applications programs or language compilers to run under the same operating system. For example, one could not run a CP/M-86 program if the host communications software were running under PC DOS.

The IBM PC has many applications programs that write their output directly to screen memory rather than using DOS function calls for video I/O. These programs include such favorites as VisiCalc, MultiPlan, and 1-2-3, all of which make extensive use of the IBM PC's display capabilities. In general, these programs will not operate properly when remote access is attempted. The next level down in sophistication is the use of full screen operations, such as would be found in dBASE II and WordStar. If the host communications software is designed to recognize full screen cursor codes from a remote terminal and to transmit those codes back to the calling station, then full screen operations are possible with a host system. In addition, a method of simulating IBM PC function keys, "alt" keys, and other unique keyboard functions adds considerably to the usefulness of a host communications software package. An example of a host program that accommodates both full screen operations and IBM PC-unique keyboard functions is *Remote Access* from Custom Software in Bedford, Texas.

The most basic level of host communications interaction on the IBM PC is remotely running software that uses only standard TTY, line-oriented output. PC DOS commands and most interpreters, compilers, and assemblers would fall into this catagory, for example. PC DOS Version 2.0 has a function called *CTTY* that accomplishes this task by allowing a remote data stream (from a modem) to be considered as the local console (keyboard). Another example of a communications program with this capability is *Lync*, from Midnight Software in Goleta, California. One very important consideration for any host communications software is that it should provide password-controlled access to the host computer. The reason for this is obvious: Uncontrolled access to the host operating system could allow extensive damage to be done to valuable files and applications programs.

Since BBSs are feature-oriented and tend not to allow unlimited control over the host computer, it is worthwhile to analyze this application in the same manner that terminal communications were reviewed earlier. Many well known BBSs have been available for other computers, such as the FORUM-80 for the TRS-80 family, ABBS for Apple IIs and IIIs, and CBBS for CP/M-oriented microcomputers. The oldest of these systems have five years of experience under their belts. As expected, BBS software for the IBM PC is in its infancy and the range of products available may not match some of the more established systems. The characteristics described next are generic, however, and provide a yardstick for future comparisons. Table 7-1 summarizes features that currently exist or will undoubtedly appear in future IBM PC BBS releases. No one software package is likely to have all of these features. Highlights of the more unique BBS features are described next.

Table 7-1. Bulletin board system features.

User Functions

Sign-on bulletins	Leave message
Auto-Log-on	Expert mode
Marked scanning	Graphics mode
Downloading	Uploading
Bidirectional retrieval	Selected retrieval*
Help mode	SIG support
XON/XOFF support	SYSOP paging
Text editing	Multilevel access

Message password protection
Remote program execution
Multiple download directories
Multiple command interpretation
Mail notification at sign-on
Communications parameter selection

SYSOP Functions

System customization
Directory maintenance
Message data base maintenance
Chat mode control
Single and multiple addressee messages
Special feature program creation
File conversion utilities

---

*Note: By number, subject, or marked

Marked Scanning/Selective Retrieval by Mark

This feature allows the BBS caller to scan through the existing message file and mark those that he or she desires to read in detail. This translates into significant time (hence dollars) savings for a busy user.

System Security and Access Control

These functions are accomplished in several ways, some of which are interrelated. Access to and deletion of messages may be controlled by passwords. Passwords may also control access to different levels of capability on the BBS and may be linked to unique download/upload directories. Passwords can be both user-controlled (in the case of messages) or SYSOP controlled (in the case of function and directory access).

Bidirectional Scan/Read by Designated Entry Point

This feature allows the message reader to enter the data base at a selected message number and either read or scan messages forward or backward by numerical sequence (equivalent to chronological order in most systems).

Remote Program Execution

Some BBSs allow the caller to directly execute selected programs on the SYSOPs computer. One of two methods might be used: Running the program outside the BBS environment, such as in the host communications system described earlier, or staying within the direct control of the BBS such as is done with the HOSTCOMM BBS (see Chapter 1). A good example of such a program is the LOGOUT program under HOSTCOMM which allows a caller to review the activity of the 15 most recent people logged on to the BBS.

Mail Features

Typically these will not be nearly as extensive as in a full-fledged *computer-based mail system (CBMS)*. Common features are the ability of the SYSOP to address mail to system users either privately or by a designated group. Each such user logging on is then informed that he or she has mail waiting in addition to the general bulletins that are normally present. The better systems will indicate the fact that the mail or message has been read by the intended recipient. A major difference from the way most CBMS systems work is the lack of direct station-to-station mail delivery—the SYSOP's computer in effect becomes a store and forward facility, and the SYSOP must do the forwarding.

SYSOP BBS Management

Most, if not all BBS systems will give the SYSOP a fair degree of flexibility in configuring and managing the BBS. Maintenance of the download directories and message data base are essential features for a well-managed system, particularly when mass storage capabilities are limited. Customization of the communications parameters is a must—particularly important is the ability to change from 7-bit to 8-bit operation to support the exchange of data such as WordStar files or graphics. A well-designed BBS system will allow the SYSOP to change such parameters as baud rate and word length while the program is running. The ability of the SYSOP to initiate a "Chat" mode in response to a caller page lends an air of friendliness to the bulletin board.

After reading the next section, the reader will note a similarity to Electronic Mail functions—this is not by accident as Electronic Mail and BBS applications are close cousins. As will be pointed out in the next section, Electronic Mail has more structure and is targeted to designated individuals and groups within an organization; additionally, management of an Electronic Mail system is usually more decentralized (many SYSOPs to contend with!) than a BBS. There are no doubt many applications in which the distinction between BBS and CBMS operations becomes rather academic.

II. ELECTRONIC MAIL

Electronic Mail, or *Computer-Based Mail System (CBMS)*, is riding a crest of new-found popularity as microcomputers become more and more prevalent in small business and corporate activity. Not a particularly new or innovative application—it has been available on the packet-switched network ARPANET, for example, for many years—it nevertheless has taken on a new significance with the advent of more powerful microcomputers and their increasing acceptance in business. Electronic mail can be defined simply as the ability of persons to exchange communications addressed to a particular individual or group through the use of computer communications facilities. Strictly speaking, electronic mail should be differentiated from *Bulletin Board Systems (BBS)*, wherein messages are often left for a general or unspecified audience. The structure of a CBMS is generally more formal than that of a BBS. This is reflected by the existence of a draft specification (National Bureau of Standards) for CBMS message structure.

The vehicle for "carrying" CBMS traffic can be local area networks, modem networks, or a combination of the two. CBMS systems can be completely self-contained or they may use commercial *store-and-forward* facilities such as THE SOURCE or *CompuServe*. Figure 7-1 illustrates a simplified CBMS transaction using a combination of LAN and modem network services. The store-and-forward facility depicted allows a number of widely dispersed users to deposit mail in a value-added network service—SOURCEMAIL on THE SOURCE and EMAIL on CompuServe—for delayed retrieval by the intended recipient(s). The advantage of this system is that users do not have to purchase sophisticated CBMS software; they merely dial in to the store-and-forward service and send or retrieve their mail as required. The tradeoff is network service

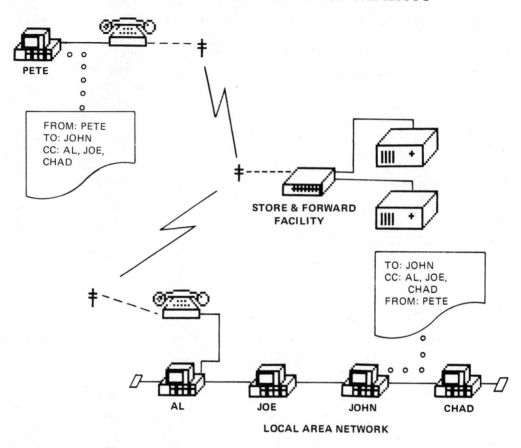

Figure 7–1. Electronic mail service (local and remote).

subscription and connection costs for a commercially operated store-and-forward facility versus long distance telephone rates and dedicated software required to operate a private CBMS.

In the example shown, the assumption is made that the local area network depicted had electronic mail software capability available when the overall CBMS system was designed. There is at least one electronic mail package designed to work with a local area network: the EtherMail application for 3Com's EtherLink LAN. EtherMail is not designed to work with a network external to EtherLink, although it would be relatively easy to link it with a modem system if a modem server were available. There are at least two companies that have designed CBMS software for the Corvus Omninet on the Apple II/III, and it is reasonable to assume that such software will soon follow for the IBM PC on that network.

If the CBMS application is in a relatively confined area, it can be implemented on a local area network or on an "in-house" mainframe network. This geographically limited context of CBMS activity might better be termed an *electronic intra-office memo*. Limited in scope of geographic coverage, however, does not mean lack of usefulness. Electronic Mail can be a real boon to productivity when properly used. The best examples of increased productivity in this environment are virtual elimination of "telephone tag" and a reduction in scheduled meetings

Electronic mail can be attended or unattended. If the former, at least either the originator or recipient must be present to send, receive, or otherwise process the message. The store-and-forward facility is considered an attended system because this service provides the equivalent of a full time "attendant." With the proper software, a service such as THE SOURCE can be accessed from an unattended terminal or work station, thus blurring the distinction between the two types of mail service. A completely unattended CBMS allows the automatic exchange of messages at a predetermined time and requires access to an internal real-time clock in the PC (typically provided by an expansion card) or use of an external chronograph. A newer generation of modems is now starting to appear—these typically contain full provisions for operating an unattended mail or file transfer system.

In Chapter 5, the generic features of terminal communications programs are defined so that the interested reader can make informed evaluations of existing software packages. Since IBM PC users will make similar evaluations when selecting CBMS software, the general features of this communications application will be described in the following paragraphs. Table 7-2 lists the features found in a complete implementation of a CBMS service. Not all of these features are required for a successful electronic mail application; the desirability of each should be weighed carefully against the cost of the package. There are no standardized terms used to describe CBMS features so the following discussions cross-reference equivalent terms in parentheses.

Table 7-2. CBMS features.

SEND Options	FILE Options
Carbon Copy	Selective Read
Blind Copy	Selective Scan
Reply Requested	Editing
Express	Merging
Registered	
Delayed Delivery	
RECEIVE Options	ADDRESSING Options
Forwarding	Group Addressing
Immediate Reply	Standard Distro
Delete	Hidden Distro
Save To File	Named Accounts
Scan Pending Mail	

MISCELLANEOUS Options

Password Security	Multi-Level Security
Encryption	TELEX gateway
Templates	On-Line Help
Prompting	Customization
Calendar	Withdrawal
DBMS Integration	

Send Options

A well-designed electronic mail service allows more than mere sending of a letter or document. The SEND process controls the originator's intended distribution and disposition of the mail. Some typical SEND capabilities are:

Carbon Copy	Send a copy of the correspondence to any designated account(s), including own
Blind Copy	Send a copy of the correspondence to an addressee without indicating such to other recipients
Reply Requested	The correspondence should be responded to
Express (Special Delivery)	Mail will receive some type of special handling on receipt, such as alerting the destination work station, etc.
Registered	Indicate delivery to intended recipient
Delayed Delivery	Deliver mail at a future specified time/date

Receive Options

Receive options allow readers of the message a degree of flexibility in dealing with received mail. The FORWARD and REPLY features make the CBMS a fully interactive application. The FILE capability is required for archiving or post-processing activities. The SCAN feature is particularly useful when the electronic mail application has a high traffic load.

Forward	Send the letter (with comments as appropriate) to another account not on the original addressee list
Reply	Allows an immediate reply to the correspondence, whether or not requested
Save (File)	Retains the message in an existing or new file for later editing, merging, review, etc.
Delete (Discard)	Dispose of the message after reading
Scan	Browse through pending mail, looking at only originators, subject lines, lead-in sentence, etc.

File Options

Since mail is just a form of information, a CBMS must have an archival facility to be truly useful. It should have all the usual filing features such as selected retrieval, file transfers, editing, and merging. A well-designed file system also allows the off-line preparation of correspondence, essential to the economic use of CBMS services. Retrieval can be by date intervals, by subject, by originator, by keyword, or any combination of these categories. Merging allows insertion of boiler plate text or non-text material, such as VisiCalc spreadsheets, into the outgoing mail. On-line editing is done during an attended session and should allow modification of the message header (see the following) while composing the text. Scanning allows a rapid survey of pending or stored mail.

Retrieval (Search)	Allows you to scan or read a message by date interval: all before, all after, or between designated dates. Search by keyword, by subject line, by originator
Scan	Allows you to browse through filed messages, looking at only originators, subject lines, or perhaps lead-in sentence of correspondence
Editing	Provides edit capability—either line- or character-oriented. Off-line or on-line; the latter allowing alteration of message header
Merging	Allows the insertion of pre- formatted information into a message during preparation, usually off-line

Addressing

Addressing schemes use a *message header* to route mail. Generally a message header consists of a "TO:" line, a "SUBJECT:" line, the number of lines of text in the message, posting information (date and time sent), and acknowledgment indication. A good CBMS system provides complete flexibility in its addressing. In addition to the carbon copy and blind copy provisions mentioned earlier, there should be group addressing and hidden distribution features.

Group Addressing	Allows the use of multiple account numbers on the TO: line
Standard Distribution	In conjunction with the filing capability, allows pre-stored distribution lists. Lists referred to by file name
Hidden Distribution	A variation of blind copy. No addressee sees the distribution
Account Number/ Name Association	Address by name rather than by account number

Miscellaneous Features

Beyond the basic features of sending, receiving, filing and addressing, CBMS systems begin to increasingly depart from commonality. There are a number of features that are more properly catagorized as nice-to-have, although some of these may be important for a specific application.

For corporate or other large CBMS installations, correspondence security and access control are a must. Generally, a one-level password scheme is sufficient; this requires that all participants in a given group have a unique password. Security of any such password scheme can pose a problem over time. Multi-level access is another means of achieving security. It allows more flexibility and control in message retrieval and can be combined with a message classification scheme. Another approach is to use message encryption; such protection is more costly since each work station in the CBMS network must have a data encryption device. With the recent emphasis on the prevention of computer misuse and fraud, encryption is becoming a very popular security measure. Some additional CBMS features are:

On-Line Help	Provides description of CBMS functions and usage
Prompting	Leads the user through the procedure of sending, receiving, or filing mail
TELEX Gateway	Sends messages to an unattended TELEX machine
Templates	Provides pre-stored formats for certain specialized correspondence
Customization	Allows the tailoring of certain CBMS features to meet specific group or organization needs
Calendar	Automatically notifies the originator of an intended recipient's schedule or absence
Withdrawal	Removes messages from a recipient's mailbox before acknowledgment, reading, or scanning
Data Base Update	Places selected portions of a message into a data base

As electronic mail becomes more widespread and sophisticated, an increasing number of cleverly designed features will become available. Integration of CBMS into other applications will be an area of continued growth.

A well-designed CBMS should make the addressing function transparent to users. In other words, the sender should only be concerned with the account number or name of the recipient. The message should find its way to the proper work station no matter what combination of modem or local area networks are in use. The address information required may be an account number, a name, a job title or combination of those. Provisions must be made for the common occurrence of an individual or a job moving from one physical work station to another in the same building or even to another city. The software and communications protocols required to make this happen are not trivial and would be a major factor in the cost of a CBMS software package.

As an example of the way an electronic mail system works in practice, a short session on SOURCEMAIL, the electronic mail service of THE SOURCE Telecomputing Corporation, will be described in Figures 7-2 and 7-3. The example is designed to show an overview of SOURCEMAIL capabilities and illustrates typical operation of an electronic mail system.

```
>MAIL SEND

 TO:  TCB647, TCA123, CC TCC213, BC TCD301

 SUBJECT:  PROPOSED MEETING
 TEXT:
 Gentlemen,

 I propose we have a conference on the applications of
 telecommunications to the retail distribution industry.
 We might want to look at such things as salesmen entering
 orders into an inventory system from their customer
 sites, an electronic mail application for our dispersed
 warehouses, methods whereby we can connect to the
 mainframes of our suppliers, etc. Please give me your
 thoughts on such a conference by Friday. I think if we
 do this, it should be within the next three months.
 Thanks.
                              Bob Jones, TCE421

 .S

 TCB647   TCA123   TCC213   TCD301 - SENT
```

Figure 7–2. SourceMail example—send.

```
>MAIL READ

 TO: TCB647
 FROM: TCE421   POSTED MON 16-DEC-82   09:26
 SUBJECT: PROPOSED MEETING

 Gentlemen,

 I propose we have a conference on the applications of
 telecommunications to the retail distribution industry.
 We might want to look........ by Friday. I think if we
 do this, it should be within the next three months.
 Thanks.
                              Bob Jones, TCE421

 DISPOSITION: REPLY
 TEXT:
 Sounds great Bob. I would welcome the chance to assist
 in such a project.           Bruce

 .S
 TCE421 - SENT
```

Figure 7–3. SourceMail example—receive.

III. VIDEOTEX AND TELETEXT

The inauguration of THE SOURCE in mid-1979 brought a new dimension to the world of personal computing—for the first time, people had access to large data banks such as UPI and the New York TIMES from the privacy of their homes. Since that time, several competing information services have opened to the personal computing market. At the same time THE SOURCE began its pioneering operation, related events were occurring in Europe. In Britain, public telephone and broadcasting authorities began operation of the PRESTEL *videotex* and CEEFAX and ORACLE *teletext* services. The British services were, and remain, graphics- and television-oriented, providing a wide variety of consumer-oriented information in the form of sequential graphics and text frames. THE SOURCE and similarly structured information services in the United States are currently text and personal computer-oriented. The purpose of this section is to discuss the role of the personal computer, specifically the IBM PC, in the future development and applications of electronic information exchange. There appears to be substantial merit in combining technologies from these ''information brokers'' and applying them to the new generation personal computers.

Any discussion of *VIDEOTEX* and *TELETEXT* should begin by making the reader fully aware of the essential difference between these systems. TELETEXT uses the broadcast TV media to transmit alphanumeric and graphic information to data base subscribers, whereas VIDEOTEX uses the equally familiar telephone system to interactively communicate information. VIDEOTEX allows a fully interactive exchange of information while TELETEXT limits the subscriber to viewing a choice of video frames (normally called ''pages'') on a TV set. The use of Cable TV for TELETEXT can be interactive if a subscriber feedback channel is provided. This is done, for example, with the Warner QUBE system in the United States, which provides a 1200 baud feedback capability. In some cases the feedback capability might be provided by an associated telephone circuit, in which case the Cable TV system is both VIDEOTEX and TELETEXT.

Both systems use large data bases at the source; both systems require specially modified TV receivers, although in the case of VIDEOTEX, stand-alone personal computers can be adapted to receive alphanumeric or graphics information. VIDEOTEX response may be simple, such as selecting information categories from a menu, or more complex, such as making interactive queries to a data base. Services such as THE SOURCE, CompuServe, and *Dow Jones News Service* are special cases of VIDEOTEX technology—these and similar systems do not currently use graphics, but instead rely on alphanumeric data and display formats. The more ''classic'' VIDEO-TEX services are represented by the British PRESTEL and the Canadian TELIDON systems. Examples of TELETEXT services are the previously mentioned British CEE-FAX and ORACLE systems and the French TELETEL system. TELIDON and PRES-TEL are also standards, in addition to being services.

VIDEOTEX in its most general sense is a technology which promises to play a large role in the growth of communications applications for the IBM PC. Today's applications (in the United States at least) are alphanumeric—tomorrow's will become increasingly graphics-oriented. As the use of graphics increases, both the providers and the users of information will have a stake in how the technology is implemented. Key factors to watch will be the choice of transmission media, the protocol adopted for graphic representation, and the technique used in the terminal to display graphics. Of particular concern in this section will be the Presentation Level Protocol (ISO Layer 6) and terminal (IBM PC) intelligence requirements. Because of the greater flexibility and growth potential of VIDEOTEX, and conversely the limited two-way communications capability in TELETEXT, the latter will not be discussed further in this section.

A VIDEOTEX system can be characterized in two ways—by breaking it into constituent parts and by placing it within the context of the ISO 7-layer architecture described in Chapter 2. The first of these provides a point of departure for discussion of the policy and economic aspects of VIDEOTEX, whereas the ISO model is useful as a frame of reference to discuss standards and protocols. Table 7-3 illustrates the component parts of a VIDEOTEX system and some current examples of each. Table 7-4 shows the seven layers of the ISO model with a VIDEOTEX service interpretation.

Table 7-3. VIDEOTEX systems—who's involved.

Information Sources	*Distributors*
UPI	THE SOURCE
AP	CompuServe
NY Times	NewsNet
Dow Jones	DJNS
Media	*Users*
Cable TV	Home
TELENET	Business
TYMNET	Government
AT&T	Corporate

In Table 7-3, the information source is the corporate entity that provides the publicly accessible data bases. In some instances the data base operator and the distributor are one and the same—Dow Jones, for example. Other data base owners market their information to companies that provide an independent subscription service for the general public or for business and government users. Information distributors provide this value-added service. The communications media is independently provided by

Table 7-4. VIDEOTEX systems—ISO 7-layer architecture.

Layer 7 (Applications)	VIDEOTEX service protocols
Layer 6 (Presentation)	Character/graphics representation
Layer 5 (Session)	Log-on/security/billing
Layer 4 (Transport)	Communications media routing
Layer 3 (Network)	Packet-forming protocols
Layer 2 (Data Link)	SDLC, HDLC, CSMA, etc.
Layer 1 (Physical)	RS-232-C/RS-449, etc.

regulated and private packet-switching network operators. These media operators provide both information source-to-distributor and distributor-to-subscriber connections. End users are the owners and operators of the many terminals and intelligent work stations that can be used to display and process information. The end user normally deals only with the distributor of the information; the information provider and communications operator deal with the distributor in a manner that is transparent to the user. The end user, however, should be alert to regulatory policy issues and economic factors concerning the owners of data base and communications resources. Ultimately, these entities have a significant impact on the economics of VIDEOTEX usage since the distributor bears the costs of both data base access and the transport of that data.

The IBM PC's role in VIDEOTEX technology has been well-established in the context of alphanumeric data base access. Any terminal communications program will allow the PC access to the services described briefly in Chapter 1. As the VIDEOTEX concept expands into graphics, however, the PC's role is not as well-established. At this point, the ISO Presentation Layer (Layer 6) becomes relevant. The presentation layer protocols will determine the manner in which graphic data are formatted, communicated, and displayed in a VIDEOTEX service—for such protocols to be effective, they must be machine independent. There are three general classes of graphics transmission technology in which most, if not all, such protocols fall: *alphamosaic*, *alphageometric*, and *alphaphotographic*.

Alphamosaic representation has the least resolution of the three. Its image construction is illustrated in Figure 7-4. This figure represents the British PRESTEL VIDEOTEX system and standard. This example of alphamosaic graphics indicates a maximum

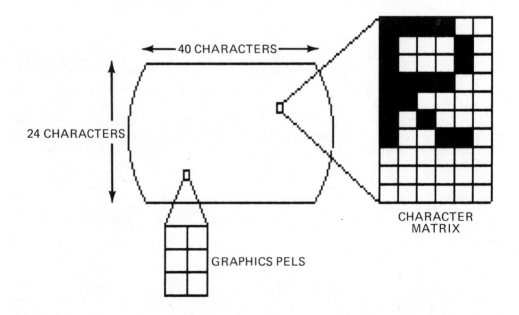

Figure 7–4. Alphamosaic characteristics—PRESTEL videotex.

picture resolution of 80 X 72 picture elements, referred to as *pixels* in graphics terminology. This is clearly a low resolution system, although the alphanumeric characters are well- defined. The PRESTEL standard has a basic display design of 40 character columns by 24 rows. Each character position can be interpreted as an alphanumeric or graphic symbol as shown in Figure 7-4.

In contrast, the alphageometric technique, typified by the Canadian TELIDON technology, allows a much higher resolution—typically as high as 1024 X 1024 pixels. This resolution is achieved by a unique method of image coding: Instead of sending a stream of bits for each pixel on the graphic image (the number of bits depends on the color or other attribute desired for that pixel) as in the PRESTEL system, a picture is broken into its constituent elements such as points, lines, arcs, rectangles, and polygons. Control codes provide information on color selection, color fill, texture, color animation, text size, incremental line drawing, and several other features. An elementary example of how this might be done is shown in Figure 7-5. This particular example, complete with seven colors and some additional text in two sizes, would be completely described within 250–300 bytes. The sequence of picture elements and control codes is termed *Picture Description Instructions (PDIs).* A decoder board on the receiving terminal (adapter card on the IBM PC) interprets the PDIs and displays

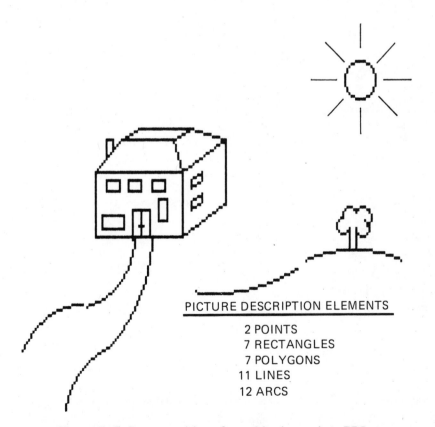

PICTURE DESCRIPTION ELEMENTS

2 POINTS
7 RECTANGLES
7 POLYGONS
11 LINES
12 ARCS

Figure 7–5. Decomposition of graphics image into PDIs.

the image. The resolution of the image would not be determined by the display protocol but by the amount of video RAM available, the decoder board's complexity, and the quality of the display monitor. This alphageometric system is now formalized into a draft standard, the *North American Presentation Level Protocol Syntax (NAPLPS)*, a joint effort of American National Standards Institute (ANSI) and the Canadian Standards Association (CSA).

Alphaphotographic technology allows the transmission of photo quality images and is being developed as a follow-on capability for all VIDEOTEX systems. The Canadian approach to this advanced technique will also employ the PDI method of graphics coding. A viable means of transmitting photo images will require much higher data rates than currently available to home subscribers.

A factor of great importance in graphics transmission systems is the time it takes to send individual frames of data. If the time required is excessive, such capabilities as animation (or at least primitive updating) and true interactivity may not be technically or economically feasible. Table 7-5 lists representative timing data for various technologies of graphics coding—the table compares the time required to transmit the indicated graphics information at both 300 and 1200 baud. In general, the time required to transmit a graphic image can be simply determined if the number of pixels and the number of bits to code each pixel is known. In this case we assume 300 and 1200 baud are equivalent to 300 and 1200 bits/sec, respectively. It should be apparent that 1200 Baud is the minimum acceptable rate for useful graphics transmission applications. The alphageometric method would seem to offer the best combination of reasonable transmission speed and picture quality.

Table 7-5. Graphics transmission speeds.

	Baud Rate: *300/1200*
IBM PC graphics page 16K Color Adapter Buffer Med. resolution, 320 X 200 pixels 4-color, 2-bit coding	427/107 Sec
Alphamosaic page Low resolution, 80 X 72 pixels 16-color, 4-bit coding	77/19 Sec
Alphageometric page 300 byte ASCII PDI file Resolution independent	8/2 Sec
Alphaphotographic image 1/9 of a page British system	240/60 Sec

An interesting software product exists for the IBM PC that, quite by accident, emulates the alphageometric technique. A closer look at this product will allow an insight into the future potential of interactive graphics as well as into alphageometric

VIDEOTEX technology. The product is *PCcrayon*, a graphics generator program distributed by PCSoftware Inc., San Diego, CA. A unique feature of this program is the "capture file" concept—a standard ASCII file is created during the building of a graphics image, or sequence of images. This file records the commands used to create picture drawing, animation, color definition and color changes, text font placement, and standard text entry.

This file is read and interpreted by a BASIC program which results in the display of the original sequence of graphics frames that were generated. A 3-minute, 20-second demonstration scenario on the distribution diskette requires 9950 bytes of file storage—orders of magnitude less than would be required to store several screens of graphics data at 16 + Kbytes apiece. The reader familiar with PC DOS BASIC will recall that to BSAVE a screen of graphics data requires RAM equal to the size of the color adapter card memory, or almost 17K. Any animated sequence or color change would require several pages of graphics data using ordinary representation. At 300 Baud, this 9950 byte demo file would take 4 minutes, 45 seconds to transmit—at 1200 Baud, the file would transmit in 1 minute, 10 seconds. Contrast these figures with the data in Table 7-4, keeping in mind that the values in this table are for a single frame only.

The implications of this example are most interesting—if it takes 70 seconds to transmit a file that runs for 200 seconds, then it only requires appropriate host computer software support to produce effective graphics displays via telephone and modem. The required host software support can be obtained in two ways: first, by the use of a multi-tasking operating system such as Concurrent CP/M-86, wherein one process reads the RS-232-C port and another executes the replay program using data from the communications buffer; or second, the replay program can be rewritten to incorporate the needed communications functions. The former method would necessitate the rewrite of *PCcrayon* in a CP/M-86 compatible language that supports graphics functions. The remaining question is how to create the graphics at the source—either off-line, with the storage of a graphics "data base," or on-line, with the graphics "capture file" being periodically sampled and transmitted. The former appears to be the more practical of the two with the applications and systems software currently available on the PC. A schematic overview of the process on both ends—creation and display—is depicted in Figure 7-6.

As a further illustration of how a "capture file" (or PDIs, in the case of TELIDON) represent graphics images, refer to Figures 7-7 and 7-8—the short capture file in Figure 7-8 will generate the graphics display in Figure 7-7 when interpreted by the appropriate replay software. To BSAVE this picture would require almost 17K of disk storage; the capture file is 128 bytes in length.

In the TELIDON process, the adapter card decodes the PDIs and produces the graphics displays in much the same manner as *PCcrayon*. In the case of TELIDON-based systems, the firmware and memory required to display graphics images are on the adapter card itself. The first TELIDON-based product for the IBM PC is unique in that it does not utilize a decoder board. This product is *TELIgraph*, from Microtaure Inc. in Ontario, Canada. TELIgraph is completely implemented in software. Using a series of utility programs, it is capable of page creation, font definition, PDI interpretation with built-in communications functions, and a "slide show" mode. In the

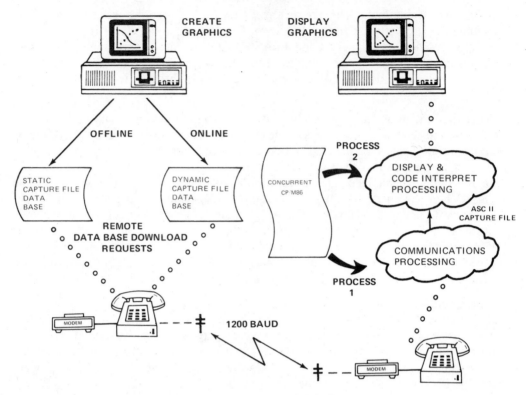

Figure 7–6. Graphics communications processing.

latter, replay is either frame-oriented, as in a normal slide show, or interactive, with logical selection of frame sequences.

TELIgraph has a wide variety of graphics features. It supports eight colors, seven shades of gray, many textures, and macro-definable graphics. This latter capability means the user can create reusable graphics symbols and use them repeatedly in the frame creation process. The full North American Presentation Level Protocol Syntax (NAPLPS-TELIDON) is supported. An average transmission time for one screen is 15 seconds at 300 baud. Graphic files are very compact—300 to 500 screens can be stored on one 320KB double-sided floppy on the PC. Page creation is done with the keyboard—an intelligent graphics tablet will be a future enhancement. The most significant concept of this product and others that are similar is their independence of screen resolution. Screens created with the current IBM PC 320 × 200 medium resolution display will be fully compatible with future display upgrades, such as 512 × 512 or 1024 × 1024 systems.

In the TELIgraph product just described, the PC can be the source of a local VIDEOTEX system. The owner of such a capability can then create and store graphics-oriented data bases for access by local subscribers, much as the community bulletin boards described in Chapter 1 function for alphanumeric data. In the home computer context, graphics can enhance the value of such bulletin boards, particularly in the areas of interactive computer games, computer art, educational material, and personal

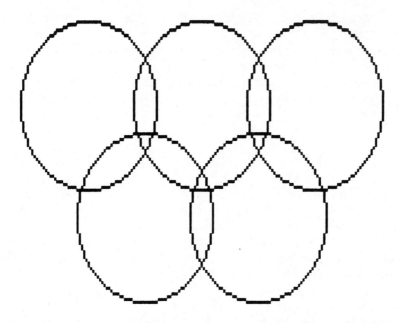

This is the Olympic symbol

Figure 7–7. PCcrayon capture file image.

```
"GTYPE",1                        MEDIUM RESOLUTION
"B",1,1                          BACKGROUND COLOR=BLUE
"K",3                            FOREGROUND COLOR=WHITE
"W",1                            WIDTH=1 (NARROW)
"VFILE","OUTLINE"                USE "OUTLINE" VECTOR FILE
"GFILE","GSYM"                   USE "GSYM" GRAPHICS FILE
"O",90,60,30          ⎫
"O",140,60,30         ⎪
"O",190,60,30         ⎬ CIRCLES (X,Y,RADIUS)
"O",165,100,30        ⎪
"O",115,100,30        ⎭
"X",45,150,"This is the Olympic symbol"   TEXT @ (45,150)
"W",3                            CHANGE WIDTH TO 3
"L",45,156,247,156              LINE FROM 945,156) TO (247,156)
"PAUSE",99                       PAUSE UNTIL USER HITS KEY
```

Figure 7–8. PCcrayon capture file example.

finance. In the business world, such applications as stock market activity, financial planning, sales presentations, business simulations, training, and advertising are appropriate for graphics enhancement. At this juncture, it would be stretching the point to say that graphics communications are essential to the success of distributed processing with personal computers, but there is little doubt that this technology will play an increasing role in the near future.

IV. ELECTRONIC PUBLISHING

With the rapid increase in information-oriented technology and applications, the publishing of ideas is a growing activity. In fact, so much knowledge is becoming available that only the application of the same technology that has spawned this revolution will allow the publishing industry to keep up with the demand. Personal computers have contributed to the more efficient sharing of knowledge through the widespread use of word processing software and hardware. People are motivated to write articles, books, and columns today that they would not have considered just a few years ago because word processing has taken much of the drudgery out of the manuscript writing process. A recent phenomenon is the appearance of computers and data communications in the next level up in the publishing process—the preparation of typeset, camera-ready copy for publication. Not only does professional typesetting offer more efficient text formatting, but it produces that "finished" look that motivates reader and contributor alike.

The first requirement for applying communications technology to this creative activity is to agree on a coding scheme with a selected typesetting service—this will allow you, the author, to directly input codes to control four main variables in the typesetting process: type style, type size, line spacing, and line length. These codes are placed into the manuscript before transmission to the typographer; upon receipt they are interpreted by a computer that interfaces to the typesetting machine. These codes *do not* correspond to the usual text formatting codes found in WordStar, EasyWriter, Volkswriter, or similar word processors; in fact word processor codes should be completely removed prior to the transmission of text to an electronic typesetting service. There are three methods to send manuscripts with typeset codes embedded: direct exchange or conversion of disk media, or telecommunications. Communications generally works out to be the more flexible and cheaper alternative.

If communications is the chosen mode of file transfer, the author must make two decisions: the speed to use for transmission and whether to directly exchange the files using *file transfer protocol*, or an exchange of files using intermediate store-and-forward facilities such as THE SOURCE or CompuServe. The store-and-forward alternative offers a lower error rate due to the ready access to local dial-in points on a packet-switched network. If this method is used, it behooves the author to become familiar with the file handling procedures on THE SOURCE or CompuServe—both services have extensive filing capabilities, with CompuServe having the lower initial cost due to availability of 128K of free disk storage to subscribers. Since time is money, a 1200 baud connection would pay for itself in short time for a busy author, assuming of course that the typographer had 1200 baud available. In addition, the typesetting shop may allow unattended operation, giving the author even more flexibility.

Another variation on the use of personal computer communications for electronic publishing is the direct exchange of compatible word processor files between author and publisher. If the two ends of the file transfer process use the same word processor, significant time savings can result. This is an important consideration for busy editors and for organizational publications that rely largely on volunteer help for production. For example, WordStar files can be exchanged complete with control codes, dot commands, and the special 8-bit coding required to indicate soft margins for on-screen formatting options. Inspection of a WordStar file outside its own environment will reveal strange characters in the last position of each word on a line that does not have a hard carriage return. This reflects the high-order bit (8th bit) set for that character. From a communications standpoint, the significance of this is that an 8-bit data word format must be used when transferring WordStar files without conversion. Even with 8-bit word size the problem may not be over—many terminal communications programs transmit files line-by-line; hard carriage returns are then placed at the end of each line, negating the effect of soft margins. The only solution to this dilemma is to laboriously remove every unwanted carriage return upon receipt of the file. The optimum solution is to locate a communications program that transmits a faithful image of the word processing document bit stream.

Another dimension of electronic publishing merits discussion: the on-line versions of newspapers and other periodicals. THE SOURCE, CompuServe, and Dow Jones offer a wide variety of tailored extracts from such respected sources as the Wall Street Journal, Barron's, the New York Times, and a whole host of newspapers across the country which have published electronic editions. Some of these trial publishing efforts by metropolitan newspapers have been terminated due to economic considerations, but there remain many significant periodicals which can be sampled via data communications. An outgrowth of this form of electronic publishing has been the establishment of what is generally referred to as "user publishing." User publishing can be non-interactive or interactive. In the former, an individual or group maintains an on-line newsletter or similar type of publication. There are many of these publications currently on THE SOURCE, for example.

In the interactive variation, mutual participation by subscribers to the information service is the key characteristic. Electronic "conferencing" has attracted a significant degree of interest on THE SOURCE and is known as *PARTICIPATE.* Conference networking works as follows: A subscriber desires to establish a conference on a particular area of interest. Anyone desiring to join the conference logs in as a member of the group and participates in the ensuing exchange of information. Each member of the group automatically receives all deliberations or publications of the group through access to the information service. There is generally an "organizer," who might be an individual or perhaps an organization anywhere in the public or private sectors. The value of such a service to a business can be considerable. Consider, for example the list of topics in Table 7-6 and the benefit of having a nationwide forum to exchange ideas on these subjects. Furthermore, the system provides a permanent written record of each participant's contributions. Although still an experimental effort in many

Table 7-6. PARTICIPATE conferences on THE SOURCE.

Education of Adults	Responsibility & Crime
CRT Ergonomics	Business on SOURCE
Information Exchange	Aircraft Valuation
IXO Telecomputer	IBM PC
Small Business	Local Area Networks
Computers & Lawyers	Radio Communications
On-Line Retrieval	Multi-Level Marketing
Hazardous Wastes	UNIX
Architecture	Taxes
Helicopters	Boston

respects, PARTICIPATE is destined to become the model for future advances in information exchange.

V. TELESHOPPING SERVICES

The term *teleshopping* is a product of the emergence of data communications as one of the fastest growing segments of the personal computer industry. The term refers collectively to the concepts of shopping at home, the downloading of commercial software for purchase, electronic bartering, and classified advertising. There are sociological factors involved in these concepts as well as the practical factors of technology. It is no secret that ordering products from an inanimate terminal suffers somewhat in comparison to the colorful displays in stores and the ability to put one's hands on the merchandise. On the other hand, traffic jams, frayed nerves, and overcrowded stores make teleshopping a more viable competitor to traditional shopping habits. An additional advantage to teleshopping is the reduction in retail overhead in marketing the product—this often equates to substantial price breaks for the armchair consumer. There is no doubt that this application of communications has potential yet to be realized—for example, the advent of practical VIDEOTEX graphics transmission will bring a new dimension to teleshopping. A review of the shopping services available on THE SOURCE gives a good perspective on the range of goods and services currently offered to VIDEOTEX subscribers:

CSTORE .... Browsing through all categories of the COMP-U-STORE shopping service run by COMP-U-CARD of America Corp.

BEGIN SHOP .... The actual ordering section of COMP-U- STORE. Requires separate membership fee to COMP-U-CARD of America. The buyer's request is transferred to the COMP-U-STORE network through a gateway from THE SOURCE. Comparison shopping and ''bargain basement'' services are also offered. Credit card payment accepted—merchandise shipped direct to buyer. Discount prices on all items.

MUSICSOURCE .... Offers audio and video tapes as well as records. No discounts.

RADIOSOURCE .... Offers classic radio programs and a collection of trivia concerning the old favorites.

PROFESSIONAL BOOK
CENTER .... Offers primarily scientific and technical book titles at no discount. Some fiction and general non-fiction are offered.

POST .... A general classified advertisement bulletin board—both new and used goods as well as services are offered.

BARTER .... A network that offers the exchange of goods and services between participants. No money changes hands in this form of shopping. The bartering of corporate goods and services is prevalent.

Telesoftware, or the downloading of commercial software for sale, has to date only been available on the CompuServe network. At its current stage of development, the products are limited, not only in content, but in availability for a wide range of personal computers. No software of significance was available for the IBM PC as of this writing. Additionally, "name" software products are largely unavailable through this means of shopping. Yet, a well-organized telesoftware operation can offer what few software retail stores offer—an opportunity to try out demonstration versions of the software on the buyer's own equipment. With the maturing of VIDEOTEX technology, many elements of graphics-oriented software packages can be demonstrated on-line. In remote areas that have very few computer stores within easy driving distance, this capability should be exploited. Certainly, telesoftware can offer a more satisfying means of purchasing software than mail order outlets, not to mention less risk if properly managed. The current lack of graphics-oriented products in telesoftware systems does not imply that graphics software cannot be downloaded—it only means that graphics features germane to program operation cannot be demonstrated on-line.

Generally, public domain software offered at no charge to users of local bulletin boards and VIDEOTEX special interest groups is of better quality and more useful than programs found on telesoftware outlets. Some special interest groups (SIGs) charge an annual membership fee; the cost is usually well worth the availability of some excellent software products. Downloading such software from SIG access files is a painless process, especially with the use of software such as CompuServe's VIDTEX which has downloading procedures built in. Although IBM PC software has been primarily available on local bulletin boards, it will undoubtedly be seen on VIDEOTEX services by 1983. Mail-order software, however, has been available from the outset for the PC—this software is heavily advertised on most bulletin boards and on such VIDEOTEX services as THE SOURCE's POST IBM. Prices are generally quite good and ordering is accomplished through the service on which the software is advertised.

Is it conceivable that best-seller software can be economically offered through a telesoftware service with direct download? From a practical standpoint, the answer is no, based on little more evidence than current offerings. Telesoftware does not offer beautifully bound and illustrated user manuals, not does it offer direct contact dealer support. On the other hand, the argument can be made that the next generation software for 16 and 32 bit computers should be so user-friendly that manuals become quasi-obsolete. Indeed there are excellent examples of such software today for the IBM PC. Another drawback to the distribution of serious software by telecommunications has been the lack of binary file transfer capability in many terminal programs that support downloading. This shortcoming is gradually being eliminated from the latest 16-bit communications software—thus the sale of assembly language and compiled software should become feasible through the telesoftware process.

The advantages to the producer of software for download distribution are the minimization of middleman costs to market the products and a wider market penetration; to the buyer, the advantages are "fly-before-buy" and the convenience of this type of transaction. A secondary fallout might be incentive for the development of increasingly user-friendly software. It will be very interesting to watch developments in this field as 16-bit microcomputers mature and software competition becomes sufficiently tough to encourage innovative marketing approaches. The future of this application, tied as it is to economics and a volatile marketplace, would appear to be less certain than others we have discussed.

VI. CASE STUDY—XYZ DISTRIBUTING CORPORATION

To illustrate the many applications of communications in a business environment, a case study is presented next. The case study is hypothetical—more communications features were added to the operation of the business than would normally be encountered in the real world. Not that the technology is not capable; there is more technology available today than the software industry can keep up with. Lack of appropriate applications software and lack of an understanding of the flexibility of data communications both contribute to the limited acceptance of doing business by "remote control." The key to success in this endeavor is the well-designed integration of accounting, inventory, and communications software. The capabilities discussed in this case study are electronic mail, local area networking, inter-warehouse distributed data bases, mainframe access, and remote job entry.

XYZ Distributing Corporation has a three-warehouse operation, with the main business offices co-located at site #1. (Refer to Figure 7-9 for the general characteristics of this multi-plant operation.) XYZ is in the beer and wine distribution business; customers are motels, bars, restaurants, hotels, and retail food stores. Wine is ordered from all the well-known vineyards in California, New York, and Europe (the latter through importers); beer is ordered from the various brewers' home offices and delivered from the nearest breweries by truck. All ordering is done through pre-sales rather than by direct route sales. Each warehouse has an established truck delivery route structure. Salesmen in the field call in pre-orders to the appropriate warehouses; inventories are then adjusted for committed stock, and shipping invoices are made up

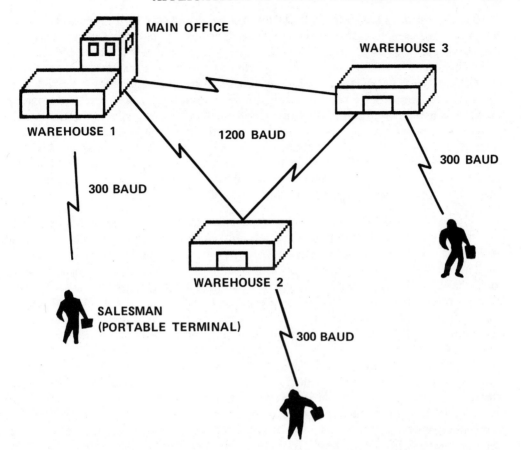

Figure 7–9. Communications system—XYZ Corporation.

for delivery as ordered. Warehouses #2 and #3 report daily inventory and business activity to the home office. The beer and wine distribution industry is very competitive; territorial expansion and market share depend on rapid response to a variety of customers and their needs. Beer and wine have differing requirements for inventory management and marketing.

With this background in the business, let us establish the communications requirements that allow daily activities to move in synchronization with company goals. The central office requires access to mainframe computers operated by their suppliers to query purchase order status and to report sales data. Some shipping companies also operate computer systems that can be queried for the status of rolling stock availability. Subscriptions to THE SOURCE and Dow Jones are maintained for downloading information from the WINE data base and for tracking industry trends. Since XYZ Corporation is in a non-urban area, the surcharges levied for TYMNET and TELENET usage have necessitated a hard look at establishing a company-owned electronic mail system to reduce costs. Currently, the SOURCEMAIL service is utilized for that function.

IBM PCs at the main office are set up in a local area network system. The same holds true for the other two warehouses, more from the standpoint of commonality than from pure capacity needs. The four PCs at the main office are used by the Beer and Wine Sales Managers, the Inventory Manager, and the Bookkeeper. The PCs in the outlying warehouses are used for inventory control and accounting. A fixed asset maintenance system is operated by the main office. Salesmen call in to the appropriate warehouse using portable ASCII terminals, operated in a remote job entry (RJE) mode. Remote job entry is the term used to describe the activity of sending data and processing instructions to a host computer system; in this case, sales data are transmitted to a host in one of the three warehouses where the data are subsequently entered into the master data base. The strategy of distributing data bases in an operation such as this is an interesting topic in itself, but beyond the scope of this book.

Software for the XYZ Corporation is a specially written integrated accounting package. It has the added flexibility of an underlying data base structure that allows custom report writing to meet changing business requirements. The operating system supports multi-level passwords and access locking down to the record level. The package supports the off-line processing of salesman call-ins to create a daily transaction file of pre-orders. This file is then batch-processed into the master data base to update inventories, prepare invoices, and post entries to the general ledger. The main office maintains the historical data base for the entire company which can be accessed by either of the remaining warehouses. Conversely, the main office can initiate transactions or file transfers with the branch warehouses. Communications with vendor computer systems are conducted periodically using asynchronous protocols. The assumption implicit in this example is that this size business would not utilize the more costly Binary Synchronous or SDLC mode of remote communications unless vendor systems were so-equipped. The more likely occurrence is that a 1200 baud asynchronous circuit would be established using the appropriate terminal protocols—VM/370 or MVS/TSO for IBM systems or similar for non-IBM systems. The appropriate files would then be uploaded or downloaded as required from the main office complex.

Table 7-7 lists the hardware and software required for the applications discussed. From the corporate viewpoint, the most important decision made when considering such an architecture is how to structure and integrate the data bases. If each warehouse adopts its own data base scheme, the best communications support in the world will go for naught. Communications must be considered a supporting application that allows the efficient transfer of data within an integrated corporate data base. Integration of communications into the accounting and data base management functions is critical to the success of this operation; such integration is not commonly found in off-the-shelf IBM PC software as of this writing.

The next most important decision is the selection of the proper operating system environment—the chosen DOS must function effectively in a multi-user, multi-tasking environment such as exists in this case study. This does not necessarily mean that it must be a multi-user operating system, although that selection would probably provide the best performance. In this case, the choice would tend to follow what is supported by the desired local area network. The desired operating system must also provide data base protection features such as passwords and record locking. Finally, it should

Table 7-7. Hardware and software required for XYZ Corporation.

Main Office/Warehouse #1
 4 IBM PCs (each with 256K RAM + 1 D/S floppy)
 2 300/1200 baud modems
 1 shared Winchester hard disk—40 MByte
 1 LAN adapter card for each PC
 1 File server (disk server or bare PC)
 1 Modem or communications server
 Appropriate printers
 Multi-user/multi-tasking DOS
 Integrated DBMS/Accounting package
 LAN network management software
 Miscellaneous applications software

Warehouses #2 and #3
 2–3 IBM PCs (same configuration as main office)
 1 300/1200 baud modem
 1 shared Winchester hard disk (20 Mbyte)
 1 LAN adapter card for each PC
 1 File server (disk server or bare PC)
 1 Modem or communications server
 Appropriate printers
 Same software as main office

handle the mixtures of storage media and file sizes required to accommodate corporate date base requirements. The final decision is the selection of the hardware required to carry out the tasks outlined in this case study. The hardware chosen must obviously be capable of handling the software requirements of the application—it should also be chosen on the basis of reliability and service availability. A well-run business can expect to expand; this expansion must be planned for when putting an integrated system such as this together. Current foresight prevents future unpleasant surprises.

This case study does not purport to fulfill the functions of a thorough systems analysis of XYZ Corporation—it is presented to show the versatility of communications applications in a medium size business. It also serves to illustrate the importance of integrating communications into planning for the automation of a business. The overall size of the system and the hardware used is modest in price by today's standards— yet a tremendous amount of distributed processing versatility can be built into a system such as that presented in this brief study. Software costs are a significant portion of the total investment, inasmuch as the availability of off-the-shelf software with the degree of integration required is quite limited. This implies a high degree of customization which in turn drives software costs up rapidly. An approximate cost in the neighborhood of $10,000 would not be unrealistic for a completely customized system; this cost would depend on the language chosen for implementation as much as on the required performance.

VII. SUMMARY

As a conclusion to this chapter, and to the book, a collection of current and future applications is presented in Table 7-8 as food for thought—you may have already thought of equally valid and economical uses of data communications. In this chapter we have explored some of the more challenging opportunities to utilize data communications technology, both in the personal computing and business sectors. The chapter is not a complete compendium of all that is, or will be available. That task is ultimately an exercise in our imagination and creativity to apply the power of electronically communicating ideas and information. It should be clear at this juncture that communications applications are indeed a challenge to the uninitiated; but for those with a pioneering spirit and a vision for more efficient means of doing business, the rewards will be great. We have reviewed and discussed a wide variety of technologies

Table 7-8. Applications for data communications on the IBM PC.

Electronic newspapers	Book reviews
Specialized newsletters	Restaurant reviews
Electronic typesetting	Movie/Play reviews
Manuscript reviews	Interactive games
	Entertainment schedules
Worldwide data base access	
Research reports	Advertising follow-up
	Electronic cataloging
Local bulletin boards	Classified ads
Weather reports	
Group/Coop buying	Bill paying
Emergency services	Bank transactions
Real Estate listings	Investment transactions
Public transportation schedules	Merchandise ordering
Dating/Social services	Ticket purchasing
Specialized services	Travel reservations
Computer assisted instruction	
	Travel planning
Educational material preparation	Flight planning
College entrance assistance	
College loan planning	Electronic mail
	Conferencing
Software development	Mailgrams
Inventory control	TELEX
Remote job entry	Intra-office memos
Financial management	Executive calendars
File storage	Market reports
	SIG BBS
Security monitor	Market research
Energy consumption monitor	Voting
Health monitor	"CB" communications

and applications related to data communications. As in other endeavors, there are no "best" technical or managerial solutions to applying personal computer communications to our business and personal lives. Those who take the time and interest to remain informed and who stay abreast of key policy and technical issues in data communications will reap the greatest benefits from this exciting field.

8
Answers to Frequently Asked Questions

Many communication novices have similar problems. To help the novice get off to a good start with electronic communications, several common questions are answered in this chapter. Since most applications of synchronous communications are in business environments that provide staff assistance to train novice users, the questions answered here are limited to asynchronous and local area network applications. An index is also provided at the end of the book to help users trace key words and phrases used in the answers to these questions.

I. ASYNCHRONOUS COMMUNICATIONS QUESTIONS

1. Q: I have installed all the hardware and software necessary to make my PC communicate using an auto-dial modem, but the modem does not respond to my keyboard commands. How do I get the modem to talk to me?

   A: You should first check to be sure that your RS-232-C cable that connects the modem to the asynchronous adapter has at least pins 1, 2, 3, 4, 5, 6, 7, 8, 20, and 22 connected at both ends. If all the signal wires are connected properly, the modem send indicator light (labeled SD on some modems) should blink when the software is placed in the terminal or conversation mode and keyboard keys are pressed. If the modem send indicator does not blink when keys are pressed, either the cable, the asynchronous adapter, or the modem is not working properly. You should substitute components that do work properly in another communication setup (borrow them from friends or co-workers), identify the component that is not working properly, and have it repaired or replaced.

2. **Q:** I just went through Question 1 and finally got the modem send indicator to blink, but I still cannot get the modem to auto-dial a telephone number or switch from the originate to the answer mode. What do I do now?

   A: First check to be sure that you are using the proper commands contained in the modem manual. If the manual specifies that uppercase letters have to be used in commands, then be sure the commands you use do not contain lowercase letters. Also be sure that all modem switches (including the ones contained inside the cover—if your modem has switches located there) are in the positions specified in your communication software package documentation manual. If your package does not specify switch settings for your particular modem type, then use the switch settings specified in the modem manual. If none of these suggestions solves the problem, then call the software vendor to see if there are software patches or special modem settings required to make the package work with your modem.

3. **Q:** I have a manual-dial modem which does not seem to work with my software package. After I dial the number, get the carrier signal (the high pitch tone), and switch the modem from talk to communicate, the software package locks up. The message "check your modem" comes on my monitor and the PC no longer responds to my keyboard input. How do I get past this hurdle?

   A: First check to be sure that the software is designed to work with manual-dial modems. Some packages will only work with auto-dial modems. If the package is designed to operate with manual modems, try dialing the number and establishing the carrier detect signal (the modem should indicate carrier detect by illuminating an indicator light) before going into the conversation mode with the software. To do this with conversation mode predominant software, you may have to load the software after the carrier detect is established (if the host system will allow you that much time before dropping the carrier signal).

4. **Q:** I have an intelligent modem that does not appear too intelligent. After I dial a number using a special code that makes the modem use touch tone dialing, I cannot get it to switch back to pulse type dialing. How do I get my modem to switch back?

   A: Most intelligent modems have a special command string that can be issued from the PC keyboard that will either change the modem to another dial type or reset the modem to default settings. Before dialing a number, go into the conversation mode and issue that command string from the keyboard. When all else fails, turn the modem off then back on again to reset it to its default, switch-selected parameters.

5. **Q:** I cannot see the characters I input from the keyboard during conversation mode communication with a host system operator. I can see my input displayed while interacting with the host until I page the operator and start conversing from the keyboard. The operator on the host end of the link can

read my input and I can read his, but my own input was not locally displayed. How do I turn on the local display?

A: When you are interacting with a host, you are probably in the full-duplex mode and your input is being echoed back to you from the host. When the host operator comes on line, the host system probably reverts to half-duplex, which does not echo your input back to you. To see your input, you will have to switch your PC to half-duplex (sometimes called local echo).

6. Q: I am having difficulty reading my input when interacting with a host system. Every time I strike a key I get two characters displayed instead of one. How do I turn off the twins generator?

A: The host is probably operating in full-duplex and your PC is operating in half-duplex. The host echoes your input back to you, and your software also displays your input. Change your software setting to full-duplex (sometimes called remote echo or echoplex) to turn off the second character display.

7. Q: I am having even more difficulty than the person asking the last question. I get three of every character I type. Trying the suggestion you gave for question 6 only reduced the number of characters to two. How do I get to one character for every one I type?

A: Your modem is probably set to half-duplex. Besides the character echoed back from a full-duplex host, your modem is also echoing the character back to your display. Change the modem switch setting to the full-duplex mode if it is a manual-dial modem or issue the proper command string to switch the modem to full-duplex if it is an auto-dial modem (full-duplex is normally the default for intelligent modems).

8. Q: I can get my modem to respond properly, but some host systems do not respond after my call to them is completed. After getting the proper carrier detect signal, there is no response to my keyboard input. How do I get the host to talk to me?

A: Check to see that you are using the proper baud rate for the system you are calling. If you are not sure of the host baud rate, try changing your own software setting to different baud rates and return to the conversation mode after each change to see if the host will respond properly.

9. Q: I connect OK with a particular host system, but the response I get is unreadable garbage. The screen just fills with graphic symbols. How do I get back to English?

A: Try changing the number of data bits and parity your software is using. If the software is normally set for eight data bits and no parity, change to seven data bits even parity. If the software is normally set for seven data bits and even or odd parity, try changing to eight data bits and no parity. This change in parameters can be done without breaking the telephone connection with the host with most communications software.

10. Q: I am using seven data bits and even parity, but many characters I receive from a host have been replaced with asterisks. How do I get rid of the asterisks?

     A: Some software packages replace characters that are received with incorrect parity with asterisks. The telephone connection may be too noisy resulting in transmission errors. Log-off the host system and redial the number to try to get a better telephone connection.

11. Q: I have call waiting service on the telephone line that I plan to use for communications. Will that service affect my communications?

     A: Call waiting cannot be used with computer communications. The communications carrier is dropped when the call waiting signal is generated. Communications are terminated by the signal. This could be a costly problem when calling a time sharing service that does not terminate connect charges immediately when a communication session improperly ends.

12. Q: When I try to transmit a file to a host system or try to transmit a prestored message to a bulletin board system, the first few characters of each line are not properly transmitted. When I list the file or message after the transmission is complete, several characters are missing from the beginning of each line. How do I get the lines to upload properly each time?

     A: You are overruning the host system by sending data faster than the host can handle it. To match your PC data transmission speed with the speed at which the host can accept the data, you must use a transmit throttle. The PC software package has to wait a specific period of time, wait for a specific number of prompt characters to return from the host, or wait for a specific character string prompt from the host before sending each line of data. You will have to experiment with these techniques until you achieve proper data transmission.

13. Q: When I am listing bulletin board messages or investment information service reports on my monitor and trying to send them to my printer at the same time, my communication sessions abnormally terminate. I get what appears to be a rerun of data I was receiving and a buffer overflow error message. How do I get copies of this information to go to my printer without killing the whole process?

     A: Many communication software packages will not allow you to simultaneously list and print information received from a host. Your printer may not operate fast enough to keep up with the receipt of data causing a backup of data in the communication link. If you can increase the size of your communication receive buffer or install a print spooler, you may be able to list and print simultaneously. Otherwise, you will have to download the information to a disk file, then print that file after the communication session is completed.

II. LOCAL AREA NETWORK QUESTIONS

14. Q: How difficult is it to install a local area network?

A: The most difficult part of the installation will probably be placement of the main bus cable. Depending on the complexity of the office or building layout, it may be necessary or desirable to have an electrical contractor install the coaxial or twisted wire. This phase of installation must be planned carefully to allow for future growth. The bus cable should go through every space that might conceivably be equipped with a work station on the network, even if not currently envisioned. The added cost of wire to do this is negligible compared to later installation changes that might be required. Keep in mind the various ways that work stations or servers connect to the bus: Some are direct connections to the adapter card, and others use branch lines off the main bus.

15. Q: How much of my communications needs will be satisfied with a local area network as opposed to long-distance communications?

A: This is a hard question to answer, but a generally accepted rule of thumb is that 80% of organizational communications are conducted within local environments. There are obvious applications where this does not apply, but it appears to be a good starting point for planning purposes.

16. Q: Since local area networks are designed to be accessed by many users simultaneously, aren't there problems with collisions and subsequent delays in service?

A: Such problems occur a surprisingly small percentage of the time. In tests using an experimental 3 megabit/sec Ethernet with over a hundred nodes, collisions occurred only *0.03%* of the time! In most practical installations, the occurrence of collisions will be transparent to the user. Disk read delays will contribute far more to perceived waiting time for service.

17. Q: I am confused by the use of the terms Omninet and CONSTELLATION II when referring to the local area network sold by Corvus. Don't they refer to the same thing?

A: Omninet is the communications portion of the local area network offered by Corvus. It consists of the transporter cards (adapter cards on the IBM PC), server(s), and the twisted-wire bus cable. CONSTELLATION II is the software and firmware that allows multiple DOS/multiple user access to the shared hard disk drive(s). It also includes various access management utilities. CONSTELLATION II is the third generation of Corvus disk sharing software—the original product, CONSTELLATION, was used on a star network, the Corvus Multiplexer. The two parts of this local area network are essentially independent: In theory, Omninet could support other shared access schemes, and CONSTELLATION II could run on other network architectures.

18. Q: Are there any limitations to the operation of the "remote" command in the PCnet local area network?

    A: Yes, there is one major limitation: The command executed by the "remote" feature of PCnet must return to the operating system level, otherwise the network will hang up. In other words, any command sent to another PC must execute and return to the PC DOS prompt "A>". It is possible to modify some programs so that they return to the DOS level.

19. Q: Does the user see any noticeable differences when operating on a local area network compared to normal single-user operation?

    A: Hopefully not. Except in those cases where someone is responsible for configuring or managing a local area network, the existence of the network should be virtually unknown to an operator at a work station. The only concern of the operator should be to whom an inter-office memo should be sent or on what drive designator a particular file can be found. A well-designed application program will even hide the dependency between files and where they are located.

20. Q: Why are all the current IBM PC local area networks designed for single-user operating systems? Wouldn't it be better to operate a network under a multi-user or multi-tasking operating system?

    A: Yes, it would make concurrent access a lot more sophisticated than currently possible. The practical reason that current offerings are single-user only is that PC DOS has such an overwhelming market share of all IBM PC installations and applications software is equally weighted toward PC DOS. This situation is not likely to persist indefinitely—a number of excellent multi-user or multi-tasking DOSs are becoming, or soon will become, available. It is natural that local area networks would want to take advantage of the built-in concurrency of these operating systems. For example, UNIX has an excellent capability to run in a local area network environment with built-in commands. Presumably its look-alikes will also have that capability when they become available for the IBM PC.

21. Q: Digital Research has a networking system in the CP/M-80 world called CP/NET. Is this system available for the IBM PC and if so, how does it compare to the three networks reviewed in this book?

    A: CP/NET is not available for the IBM PC as of the first half of 1983, but it is expected to become available by the end of 1983. Presumably it will run with both Concurrent CP/M-86 and MP/M-86 as well as CP/M-86 itself. CP/NET does not provide the physical structure of a local area network such as the network adapter cards or main bus cable. It is actually a software product that works in conjunction with a host operating system to establish a local area network application. It supports all three topologies described in Chapter 6. In order to implement a network with CP/NET, an organization would have to find a compatible hardware product that would provide the required network connections and communications protocol. CP/NET does not deal with the physical world of network communications, but instead manages the logical world of shared resources. One typical hardware installation that is compatible with CP/NET is an RS 232-to-network protocol adapter that makes use of existing asynchronous communications hardware in a microcomputer. Such a system is manufactured by Orange CompuCo in Orange, California and is called ULCnet. The data path for this system is provided by ordinary telephone wire.

Appendix A

ASCII Character Set

The following table contains the standard 7-bit ASCII character set (decimal values 0–127) and the IBM Personal Computer special 8-bit ASCII character set (decimal values 128–255). The Control Character designations for ASCII decimal values 0–31 are also shown.

ASCII Value	Hex Value	Character		Control Character
000	00	(null)		NUL
001	01	☺		SOH
002	02	☻		STX
003	03	♥		ETX
004	04	♦		EOT
005	05	♣		ENQ
006	06	♠		ACK
007	07	•	(beep)	BEL
008	08	▨	(backspace)	BS
009	09	○	(tab)	HT
010	0A	◉	(line feed)	LF
011	0B	♂	(home)	VT
012	0C	♀	(form feed)	FF
013	0D	♪	(carriage return)	CR
014	0E	♫		SO
015	0F	☼		SI
016	10	►		DLE
017	11	◄		DC1
018	12	↕		DC2
019	13	‼		DC3
020	14	¶		DC4
021	15	§		NAK
022	16	▬		SYN
023	17	↨		ETB
024	18	↑		CAN
025	19	↓		EM
026	1A	→		SUB
027	1B	←		ESC
028	1C	∟	(cursor right)	FS
029	1D	↔	(cursor left)	GS
030	1E	▲	(cursor up)	RS
031	1F	▼	(cursor down)	US

ASCII Value	Hex Value	Character	ASCII Value	Hex Value	Character
032	20	(space)	064	40	@
033	21		065	41	A
034	22	"	066	42	B
035	23	#	067	43	C
036	24	$	068	44	D
037	25	%	069	45	E
038	26	&	070	46	F
039	27	'	071	47	G
040	28	(	072	48	H
041	29	)	073	49	I
042	2A	*	074	4A	J
043	2B	+	075	4B	K
044	2C	,	076	4C	L
045	2D	—	077	4D	M
046	2E	.	078	4E	N
047	2F	/	079	4F	O
048	30	0	080	50	P
049	31	1	081	51	Q
050	32	2	082	52	R
051	33	3	083	53	S
052	34	4	084	54	T
053	35	5	085	55	U
054	36	6	086	56	V
055	37	7	087	57	W
056	38	8	088	58	X
057	39	9	089	59	Y
058	3A	:	090	5A	Z
059	3B	;	091	5B	[
060	3C	<	092	5C	\
061	3D	=	093	5D	]
062	3E	>	094	5E	∧
063	3F	?	095	5F	—

ASCII Value	Hex Value	Character	ASCII Value	Hex Value	Character
096	60	'	128	80	Ç
097	61	a	129	81	ü
098	62	b	130	82	é
099	63	c	131	83	à
100	64	d	132	84	ä
101	65	e	133	85	à
102	66	f	134	86	å
103	67	g	135	87	ç
104	68	h	136	88	ê
105	69	i	137	89	ë
106	6A	j	138	8A	è
107	6B	k	139	8B	ï
108	6C	l	140	8C	î
109	6D	m	141	8D	ì
110	6E	n	142	8E	Ä
111	6F	o	143	8F	Å
112	70	p	144	90	É
113	71	q	145	91	æ
114	72	r	146	92	Æ
115	73	s	147	93	ô
116	74	t	148	94	ö
117	75	u	149	95	ò
118	76	v	150	96	û
119	77	w	151	97	ù
120	78	x	152	98	ÿ
121	79	y	153	99	Ö
122	7A	z	154	9A	Ü
123	7B	{	155	9B	¢
124	7C	¦	156	9C	£
125	7D	}	157	9D	¥
126	7E	~	158	9E	Pt
127	7F	△	159	9F	ƒ

ASCII Value	Hex Value	Character	ASCII Value	Hex Value	Character
160	A0	á	192	C0	└
161	A1	í	193	C1	┴
162	A2	ó	194	C2	┬
163	A3	ú	195	C3	├
164	A4	ñ	196	C4	─
165	A5	Ñ	197	C5	┼
166	A6	ª	198	C6	╞
167	A7	º	199	C7	╟
168	A8	¿	200	C8	╚
169	A9	⌐	201	C9	╔
170	AA	¬	202	CA	╩
171	AB	½	203	CB	╦
172	AC	¼	204	CC	╠
173	AD	¡	205	CD	═
174	AE	«	206	CE	╬
175	AF	»	207	CF	╧
176	B0	░	208	D0	╨
177	B1	▒	209	D1	╤
178	B2	▓	210	D2	╥
179	B3	│	211	D3	╙
180	B4	┤	212	D4	╘
181	B5	╡	213	D5	╒
182	B6	╢	214	D6	╓
183	B7	╖	215	D7	╫
184	B8	╕	216	D8	╪
185	B9	╣	217	D9	┘
186	BA	║	218	DA	┌
187	BB	╗	219	DB	█
188	BC	╝	220	DC	▄
189	BD	╜	221	DD	▌
190	BE	╛	222	DE	▐
191	BF	┐	223	DF	▀

ASCII Value	Hex Value	Character
224	E0	∝
225	E1	β
226	E2	Γ
227	E3	π
228	E4	Σ
229	E5	σ
230	E6	μ
231	E7	τ
232	E8	Φ
233	E9	Θ
234	EA	Ω
235	EB	δ
236	EC	∞
237	ED	Ø
238	EE	ε
239	EF	∩
240	F0	≡
241	F1	±
242	F2	≥
243	F3	≤
244	F4	⌠
245	F5	⌡
246	F6	÷
247	F7	≈
248	F8	°
249	F9	•
250	FA	·
251	FB	√
252	FC	ⁿ
253	FD	²
254	FE	■
255	FF	(blank 'FF')

Appendix

Line Feed Addition Program

The following is a listing of an IBM Personal Computer BASIC program that will add line feeds after each carriage return contained in an ASCII file that is not already followed by a line feed. A file that does not have a line feed after each carriage return cannot be properly listed using the DOS TYPE command and cannot be edited using the EDLIN single line editor.

```
5    'Public domain program to add linefeeds to downloaded files.
7    'Written by Don Withrow, 1982
8    ,
10   CLS:LOCATE 10,1,1
20   INPUT"FILENAME that needs linefeeds (without drive)";FILEONE$
30   PRINT
35   INPUT"Drive file is on (without colon)";DRIVE$:DRIVE$=DRIVE$+":"
40   OPEN DRIVE$+FILEONE$ FOR INPUT AS #1
50   OPEN DRIVE$+"temp" FOR OUTPUT AS #2
60   IF EOF(1) THEN 90 ELSE LINE INPUT #1, THELIN$
70   PRINT #2, THELIN$
80   GOTO 60
90   CLOSE
91   KILL DRIVE$+FILEONE$
92   NAME DRIVE$+"temp" AS DRIVE$+FILEONE$
95   PRINT
97   PRINT"File ";FILEONE$;" now has linefeeds after carriage returns."
98   PRINT:PRINT
100  END
```

Appendix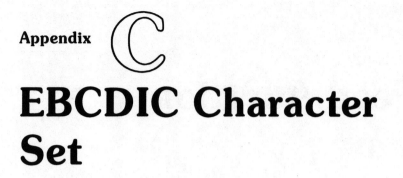

EBCDIC Character Set

ASCII Binary Code	EBCDIC Binary Code	Character
1 0 0 0 0 0 0	0 1 1 1 1 1 0 0	@
1 0 0 0 0 0 1	1 1 0 0 0 0 0 1	A
1 0 0 0 0 1 0	1 1 0 0 0 0 1 0	B
1 0 0 0 0 1 1	1 1 0 0 0 0 1 1	C
1 0 0 0 1 0 0	1 1 0 0 0 1 0 0	D
1 0 0 0 1 0 1	1 1 0 0 0 1 0 1	E
1 0 0 0 1 1 0	1 1 0 0 0 1 1 0	F
1 0 0 0 1 1 1	1 1 0 0 0 1 1 1	G
1 0 0 1 0 0 0	1 1 0 0 1 0 0 0	H
1 0 0 1 0 0 1	1 1 0 0 1 0 0 1	I
1 0 0 1 0 1 0	1 1 0 1 0 0 0 1	J
1 0 0 1 0 1 1	1 1 0 1 0 0 1 0	K
1 0 0 1 1 0 0	1 1 0 1 0 0 1 1	L
1 0 0 1 1 0 1	1 1 0 1 0 1 0 0	M
1 0 0 1 1 1 0	1 1 0 1 0 1 0 1	N
1 0 0 1 1 1 1	1 1 0 1 0 1 1 0	O
1 0 1 0 0 0 0	1 1 0 1 1 0 0 0	P
1 0 1 0 0 0 1	1 1 0 1 1 0 0 1	Q
1 0 1 0 0 1 0	1 1 0 1 1 0 0 1	R
1 1 0 0 1 0 1	1 1 1 0 0 0 1 0	S
1 0 1 0 1 0 0	1 1 1 0 0 0 1 1	T
1 0 1 0 1 0 1	1 1 1 0 0 1 0 0	U
1 0 1 0 1 1 0	1 1 1 0 0 1 0 1	V
1 0 1 0 1 1 1	1 1 1 0 0 1 1 0	W
1 0 1 1 0 0 0	1 1 1 0 0 1 1 1	X
1 0 1 1 0 0 1	1 1 0 1 1 0 0 0	Y
1 0 1 1 0 1 0	1 1 0 1 1 0 0 1	Z
1 0 1 1 0 1 1		[(left bracket)
1 0 1 1 1 0 0		/ (left slash)
1 0 1 1 1 0 1		] (right bracket)
1 0 1 1 1 1 0		∧(caret or up arrow)
1 0 1 1 1 1 1	0 1 1 0 1 1 0 1	____
1 1 0 0 0 0 0	0 1 1 1 1 1 0 1	'
1 1 0 0 0 0 1	1 0 0 0 0 0 0 1	a
1 1 0 0 0 1 0	1 0 0 0 0 0 1 0	b
1 1 0 0 0 1 1	1 0 0 0 0 0 1 1	c
1 1 0 0 1 0 0	1 0 0 0 0 1 0 0	d
1 1 0 0 1 0 1	1 0 0 0 0 1 0 1	e
1 1 0 0 1 1 0	1 0 0 0 0 1 1 0	f
1 1 0 0 1 1 1	1 0 0 0 0 1 1 1	g
1 1 0 1 0 0 0	1 0 0 0 1 0 0 0	h
1 1 0 1 0 0 1	1 0 0 0 1 0 0 1	i
1 1 0 1 0 1 0	1 0 0 1 0 0 0 1	j
1 1 0 1 0 1 1	1 0 0 1 0 0 1 0	k
1 1 0 1 1 0 0	1 0 0 1 0 0 1 1	l
1 1 0 1 1 0 1	1 0 0 1 0 1 0 0	m
1 1 0 1 1 1 0	1 0 0 1 0 1 0 1	n
1 1 0 1 1 1 1	1 0 0 1 0 1 1 0	o
1 1 1 0 0 0 0	1 0 0 1 0 1 1 1	p
1 1 1 0 0 0 1	1 0 0 1 1 0 0 0	q
1 1 1 0 0 1 1	1 0 0 1 1 0 0 1	r
1 1 1 0 0 1 1	1 0 1 0 0 0 1 0	s
1 1 1 0 1 0 0	1 0 1 0 0 0 1 1	t
1 1 1 0 1 0 1	1 0 1 0 0 1 0 0	u
1 1 1 0 1 1 0	1 0 1 0 0 1 0 1	v
1 1 1 0 1 1 1	1 0 1 0 0 1 1 0	w
1 1 1 1 0 0 0	1 0 1 0 0 1 1 1	x
1 1 1 1 0 0 1	1 0 1 0 1 0 0 0	y
1 1 1 1 0 1 0	1 0 1 0 1 0 0 1	z
1 1 1 1 0 1 1		{
1 1 1 1 1 0 0	0 1 1 0 1 0 1 0	}
1 1 1 1 1 0 1		}
1 1 1 1 1 1 0		~
1 1 1 1 1 1 1		DEL

ASCII Binary Code	EBCDIC Binary Code	Character
0 0 0 0 0 0 0	0 0 0 0 0 0 0 0	NUL
0 0 0 0 0 0 1	0 0 0 0 0 0 0 1	SOH
0 0 0 0 0 1 0	0 0 0 0 0 0 1 0	STX
0 0 0 0 0 1 1	0 0 0 0 0 0 1 1	ETX
0 0 0 0 1 0 0		EOT
0 0 0 0 1 0 1	0 0 1 0 1 1 0 1	ENQ
0 0 0 0 1 1 0		ACK
0 0 0 0 1 1 1		BEL
0 0 0 1 0 0 0		BS
0 0 0 1 0 0 1		HT
0 0 0 1 0 1 0		LF
0 0 0 1 0 1 1		VT
0 0 0 1 1 0 0	0 0 0 0 1 1 0 0	FF
0 0 0 1 1 0 1		CR
0 0 0 1 1 1 0		SO
0 0 0 1 1 1 1		SI
0 0 1 0 0 0 0		DLE
0 0 1 0 0 0 1		DC1
0 0 1 0 0 1 0		DC2
0 0 1 0 0 1 1		DC3
0 0 1 0 1 0 0		DC4
0 0 1 0 1 0 1		NAK
0 0 1 0 1 1 0	0 0 1 1 0 0 1 0	SYN
0 0 1 0 1 1 1	0 0 1 0 0 1 1 0	ETB
0 0 1 1 0 0 0		CAN
0 0 1 1 0 0 1	0 0 0 1 1 0 0 1	EM
0 0 1 1 0 0 1	0 0 1 1 1 1 1 1	SUB
0 0 1 1 0 1 1	0 0 0 1 0 1 1 1	ESC
0 0 1 1 1 0 0		FS
0 0 1 1 1 0 1		GS
0 0 1 1 1 1 0		RS
0 0 1 1 1 1 1		US
0 1 0 0 0 0 0	0 1 0 0 0 0 0 0	SP
0 1 0 0 0 0 1	0 1 0 1 1 0 1 0	!
0 1 0 0 0 1 0	0 1 1 1 1 1 1 1	"
0 1 0 0 0 1 1		#
0 1 0 0 1 0 0	0 1 0 1 1 0 1 1	$
0 1 0 0 1 0 1	0 1 1 0 1 1 0 0	%
0 1 0 0 1 1 0	0 1 0 1 0 0 0 0	&
0 1 0 0 1 1 1	0 1 1 1 1 1 0 1	'
0 1 0 1 0 0 0	0 1 0 0 1 1 0 1	(
0 1 0 1 0 0 1	0 1 0 1 1 1 0 1	)
0 1 0 1 0 1 0		*
0 1 0 1 0 1 1	0 1 0 0 1 1 1 0	+
0 1 0 1 1 0 0	0 1 1 0 1 0 1 1	'
0 1 0 1 1 0 1	0 1 1 0 0 0 0 0	-
0 1 0 1 1 1 0	0 0 1 0 0 1 0 0	.
0 1 0 1 1 1 1	0 1 1 0 0 0 0 1	/
0 1 1 0 0 0 0	1 1 1 1 0 0 0 0	0
0 1 1 0 0 0 1	1 1 1 1 0 0 0 1	1
0 1 1 0 0 1 0	1 1 1 1 0 0 1 0	2
0 1 1 1 1 0 0	1 1 1 1 0 0 1 1	3
0 1 1 0 1 0 0	1 1 1 1 0 1 0 0	4
0 1 1 0 1 0 1	1 1 1 1 0 1 0 1	5
0 1 1 0 1 1 0	1 1 1 1 0 1 1 0	6
0 1 1 0 1 1 1	1 1 1 1 0 1 1 1	7
0 1 1 1 0 0 0	1 1 1 1 1 0 0 0	8
0 1 1 1 0 0 1	1 1 1 1 1 0 0 1	9
0 1 1 1 0 1 0	0 1 1 1 1 0 1 0	:
0 1 1 1 0 1 1	0 1 0 1 1 1 1 0	;
0 1 1 1 1 0 0	0 1 0 0 1 1 0 0	<
0 1 1 1 1 0 1	0 1 1 1 1 0 1 1	=
0 1 1 1 1 1 0	0 1 1 0 1 1 1 0	>
0 1 1 1 1 1 1	0 1 1 0 1 1 1 1	?

D

Baudot Character Set

Baudot Code	Lowercase	Uppercase
1 1 0 0 0	A	-
1 0 0 1 1	B	?
0 1 1 1 0	C	:
1 0 0 1 0	D	$
1 0 0 0 0	E	3
1 0 1 1 0	F	'
0 1 0 1 1	G	&
0 0 1 0 1	H	British Pound
0 1 1 0 0	I	8
1 1 0 1 0	J	'
1 1 1 1 0	K	(
0 1 0 0 1	L	)
0 0 1 1 1	M	
0 0 1 1 0	N	
0 0 0 1 1	O	9
0 1 1 0 1	P	0
1 1 1 0 1	Q	1
0 1 0 1 0	R	.
1 0 1 0 0	S	Bell
0 0 0 0 1	T	5
1 1 1 0 0	U	7
0 1 1 1 1	V	;
1 1 0 0 1	W	2
1 0 1 1 1	X	/
1 0 1 0 1	Y	6
1 0 0 0 1	Z	"
1 1 1 1 1	LETTERS (Shift to Lowercase)	
1 1 0 1 1	FIGURES (Shift to Uppercase)	
0 0 1 0 0	SPACE	
0 0 0 1 0	CARRIAGE RETURN	
0 1 0 0 0	LINE FEED	
0 0 0 0 0	BLANK	

Appendix E

PC-SPEAK.BAS Communications Program

Contained in this appendix is the listing of a simple BASIC communications program called PC-SPEAK. This listing is provided to illustrate the techniques used to transfer data from an IBM PC keyboard to a communications link. It also illustrates simple techniques for transferring data received from a communications link to the IBM PC display, printer, and disk drive. The flow chart for this program is provided in Appendix F.

```
10 'PC-SPEAK.BAS by Larry E. Jordan, 1982
20 '
30 'This program should only be run after
40 'initializing into BASICA using DOS
50 'command  BASICA PC-SPEAK/S:512/C:4096
60 '
70 'Store auto-log-on for later use with BBS....
80 AUTOLOGON$="First Name;Last Name;City,State"
90 'Close all files and define all variables as integers...
100 CLOSE: DEFINT A-Z
110 'Define default communication parameters....
120 SPEED$="300":PARITY$="N":BITS$="8":STP$="1"
130 'Get the screen ready for communications......
140 KEY OFF: SCREEN 0,0: WIDTH 80: COLOR 7,0: CLS
160 FOR I=1 TO 10:KEY I,"":NEXT
170 'Initialize flag values to be used......
180 FALSE=0:TRUE=NOT FALSE
190 DISKFLAG=0:PRINTFLAG=0:SCREENFLAG=0
200 'Define the XOFF and XON characters for speed-matching...
210 XOFF$=CHR$(19): XON$=CHR$(17)
220 'Define default duplex as full (no local echo)...
230 ECH$="N"
240 'Cause all errors to print error messages....
250 ON ERROR GOTO 0
320 'Clear screen (used on return from BASIC)......
330 CLS
360 'Assign function keys to tasks located in subroutines....
370 KEY(1) ON:KEY(2) ON:KEY(3) ON:KEY(4) ON
380 ON KEY(1) GOSUB 2350:ON KEY(2) GOSUB 2360:ON KEY(3) GOSUB 2370
390 ON KEY(4) GOSUB 2460
400 'Finally...Print the menu so we can get going....
410 LOCATE 2: PRINT TAB(10) "COMMUNICATIONS MENU"
420 LOCATE 6,3: PRINT "Choose one of the following:"
430 LOCATE 9,10: PRINT "1 Description of program"
440 PRINT TAB(10) "2 Dow Jones/News Retrieval"
450 PRINT TAB(10) "3 IBM Personal Computer"
460 PRINT TAB(10) "4 Bulletin Board (Full-Duplex)"
470 PRINT TAB(10) "5 The SOURCE or CompuServe"
480 PRINT TAB(10) "6 User Defined Link"
490 PRINT TAB(10) "7 Reconnect Defined Link (6)"
500 PRINT TAB(10) "8 Back to Basic
510 LOCATE 18,10,1: PRINT "Choice ?";
520 'Input choice from keyboard as INKEY$......
530 A$=INKEY$:IF A$="" THEN 530
550 IF LEN(A$)=1 THEN LT=VAL(A$) ELSE 740
650 'Branch to selected menu item......
660 IF LT<>8 THEN 680
670 CLS:PRINT TAB(10)"== Enter CONT to resume ==": STOP
680 IF (LT=2 OR LT=3 OR LT=4 OR LT=5) THEN 950
690 IF LT=1 THEN GOSUB 1850:GOTO 140
700 IF LT=6 THEN 770
710 IF LT=7 GOTO 890
720 IF LT=8 GOTO 330
```

```
730 'Selection less than 1 or greater than 8 error trap.....
740 LOCATE 18: PRINT TAB(3) "Invalid choice, try again"
750 FOR I=1 TO 2500: NEXT: LOCATE 19: PRINT SPACE$(40):GOTO 510
760 'The user wants to define a communication parameter set....
770 CLS: LOCATE 1,10: PRINT "USER DEFINED LINK"
780 LOCATE 4,3,1:INPUT "BAUD RATE ";SPEED$
790 LOCATE 5,3,1:INPUT "PARITY ";PARITY$
800 LOCATE 6,3,1:PRINT "NUMBER OF DATA BITS PER CHARACTER ";
810 INPUT BITS$
820 LOCATE 7,3,1:INPUT "NUMBER OF STOP BITS ";STP$
830 LOCATE 10,3,1:PRINT "CHARACTERS ECHOED TO SCREEN (Y/N) ";
840 INPUT ECH$
850 LOCATE 12,3,1: PRINT "Data entered correctly (Y/N) ";
860 INPUT ANSWER$
870 'Go to start of input if data incorrect...
880 IF ANSWER$="N" OR ANSWER$="n" THEN 770
890 ' Setup communication link as file #1.......
900 NM$="Selected User Protocol"
910 COMFIL$="COM1:"+SPEED$+","+PARITY$+","+BITS$+","+STP$
920 OPEN COMFIL$ AS #1
930 GOTO 1080
940 'The following are predefined parameter sets for specific Hosts..
950 IF LT<>4 THEN 980
960 NM$="Bulletin Board"
970 OPEN "com1:300,e,7,1" AS #1:ECH$="N":GOTO 1080
980 IF LT<>3 THEN 1010
990 NM$="IBM Personal Computer"
1000 OPEN "com1:300,e,7,1" AS #1:ECH$="Y":GOTO 1080
1010 IF LT<>2 THEN 1040
1020 NM$="Dow Jones News/Retrieval"
1030 OPEN "com1:300,N,8,1" AS #1:ECH$="N":GOTO 1080
1040 IF LT<>5 THEN 330
1050 NM$="The SOURCE or CompuServe"
1060 OPEN "com1:300,N,8,1" AS #1:ECH$="N"
1070 'Print modem connect message.......
1080 GOSUB 1750
1090 'Set up the parallel printer as file #2....
1100 OPEN "LPT1:" FOR OUTPUT AS #2
1105 'All housekeeping is done. Get ready to communicate...
1110 LOCATE 25,1:COLOR 0,7
1120 PRINT"F1=PRT  F2=PRT-OFF  F3=DWNLD  F4=LD-OFF";
1130 COLOR 7,0
1140 LOCATE 21,1,1
1150 PAUSE=FALSE
1160 'Redefine error trap to go to specific error messages...
1170 ON ERROR GOTO 1490
1180 '***** START COMMUNICATIONS INPUT POLLING LOOP ***********
1190 'Comment statements in this loop will slow communications
1200 'down and could cause receive buffer overflows.......
1210 B$=INKEY$:IF B$="" THEN 1290
1230 IF LEN(B$)>1 THEN IF ASC(MID$(B$,2,1))=68 THEN 1480 ELSE 1290
1240 IF B$<>CHR$(8) THEN 1270
1250 IF (ECH$<>"Y" OR ECH$<>"y") THEN 1270
1260 IF POS(0)>1 THEN LOCATE ,POS(0)-1,1:PRINT " ";:LOCATE ,POS(0)-1,1
1270 PRINT #1,B$;
```

```
1280 IF B$<>CHR$(8) AND (ECH$="Y" OR ECH$="y") THEN PRINT B$;
1290 IF EOF(1) THEN 1210
1300 IF LOC(1)>128 THEN PAUSE=TRUE:PRINT #1,XOFF$;
1310 A$=INPUT$(LOC(1),#1)
1320 IF DISKFLAG=1 THEN PRINT #3,A$;
1330 FOR I=1 TO LEN(A$)
1340 DT$=MID$(A$,I,1)
1350 IF DT$<>CHR$(8) THEN 1375
1360 IF POS(0)=1 THEN 1430
1370 LOCATE ,POS(0)-1:PRINT " ";:LOCATE ,POS(0)-1:GOTO 1430
1375 IF DT$=CHR$(7) THEN BEEP:GOTO 1430
1380 IF DT$=CHR$(5) THEN PRINT #1,AUTOLOGON$:GOTO 1430
1390 IF (ASC(DT$)<31 AND DT$<>CHR$(13)) THEN 1430
1400 IF DT$=CHR$(127) THEN 1430
1410 PRINT DT$;
1420 IF PRINTFLAG=1 THEN PRINT #2,DT$;
1430 NEXT I
1440 IF LOC(1)>0 THEN 1210
1450 IF PAUSE THEN PAUSE=FALSE:PRINT #1,XON$;
1460 GOTO 1210
1470 'F10 SOFT KEY, ASCII value 68, return to menu ***************
1480 CLOSE: ON ERROR GOTO 0: GOTO 140
1490 'Error Routines *****************************************
1495 IF ERR=57 THEN RESUME
1500 IF ERR<>24 THEN 1560
1510 PRINT:BEEP:PRINT:BEEP
1520 PRINT "A DEVICE TIMEOUT ERROR HAS OCCURRED."
1530 PRINT "MAKE SURE THE HARDWARE IS CORRECTLY."
1540 PRINT "SET UP THEN PRESS ENTER TO RESUME."
1550 FOR JJ=1 TO 5000:NEXT JJ:RESUME
1560 IF ERR<>68 THEN 1610
1570 CLS: LOCATE 12,8:BEEP:BEEP
1580 PRINT "THIS PROGRAM REQUIRES THE"
1590 PRINT TAB(3) "ASYNCHRONOUS COMMUNICATIONS ADAPTER.": END
1600 'If the error is not one of the above, tell me what it is...
1610 ON ERROR GOTO 0
1740 'COMMUNICATION CHANNEL NAME DISPLAY ************************
1750 CLS: LOCATE 3,1: PRINT NM$+" Channel Open":PRINT:BEEP
1760 'MODEM CONNECT INSTRUCTIONS ******************************
1770 PRINT:PRINT:PRINT TAB(3) "- You are now linked to your modem."
1780 PRINT TAB(3) "  You should proceed with dialing the"
1790 PRINT TAB(3) "  host you wish to connect with. For"
1800 PRINT TAB(3) "  use with the SMARTMODEM input the"
1810 PRINT TAB(3) "  command ATDnumber <RETURN>.":PRINT :PRINT
1820 PRINT TAB(3) "- PRESS F10 TO GO TO MENU":PRINT
1830 RETURN
1840 'PROGRAM DESCRIPTION ***********************************
1850 CLS: LOCATE 1,15: PRINT "DESCRIPTION"
1860 LOCATE 4,3: PRINT "An asynchronous communication link"
1870 PRINT TAB(3) "will be established between the"
1880 PRINT TAB(3) "selected service and the"
1890 PRINT TAB(3) "IBM PERSONAL COMPUTER, as follows:"
1900 LOCATE 9,3: PRINT "Baud rate";TAB(13)"300"
1910 PRINT TAB(3) "Parity";TAB(14)"Even"
1920 PRINT TAB(3) "Data bits";TAB(14);"7"
```

```
1930 PRINT TAB(3) "Stop bits";TAB(14);"1"
1940 LOCATE 15,3: PRINT "Options 6 and 7 allow for the above"
1950 PRINT TAB(3) "characteristics to be supplied by"
1960 PRINT TAB(3) "the user to define a communication"
1970 PRINT TAB(3) "link to other services or computers."
2020 LOCATE 24,3: PRINT "PRESS SPACE BAR TO CONTINUE";
2030 CR$=INKEY$:IF CR$<>" " THEN 2030
2040 CLS:LOCATE 1,10:PRINT "PRINT AND DOWNLOAD"
2050 LOCATE 4,3:PRINT "The following soft function keys"
2060 PRINT TAB(3) "contol printing and downloading"
2070 PRINT TAB(3) "while connected to a host or"
2080 PRINT TAB(3) "bulletin board:"
2090 PRINT :PRINT TAB(3) "F1 = Printer On   F2 = Printer Off"
2100 PRINT :PRINT TAB(3) "F3 = Download On  F4 = Download Off"
2110 PRINT :PRINT TAB(3) "Downloaded files will have names in"
2120 PRINT TAB(3) "the form DWNLDx.TXT. The number x "
2130 PRINT TAB(3) "will begin with 1 and increment by 1"
2140 PRINT TAB(3) "with each download. Be sure and"
2150 PRINT TAB(3) "rename each file after a download run"
2160 PRINT TAB(3) "to keep later runs from erasing files."
2170 LOCATE 24,3: PRINT "PRESS SPACE BAR TO CONTINUE";
2180 CR$=INKEY$:IF CR$<>" " THEN 2180
2190 CLS:LOCATE 1,10:PRINT "OPERATING TIPS"
2200 LOCATE 4,3:PRINT "The following tips will make "
2210 PRINT TAB(3) "operation of this program easier:"
2220 PRINT :PRINT TAB(3) "1. Use DOS command:"
2225 PRINT TAB(3) "    BASICA PC-SPEAK/S:512/C:4096"
2230 PRINT TAB(3) "to load BASICA and run this program."
2240 PRINT TAB(3) "This will give you a 4096 character"
2250 PRINT TAB(3) "communication receive buffer to keep"
2260 PRINT TAB(3) "data from being lost during printing."
2270 PRINT :PRINT TAB(3) "2. Edit line 20 of this program"
2280 PRINT TAB(3) "to put your own log-on name and"
2290 PRINT TAB(3) "address in before running. This"
2300 PRINT TAB(3) "saves you time when you call"
2310 PRINT TAB(3) "bulletin boards that have auto-log-on."
2320 PRINT :LOCATE 23,3:PRINT "PRESS ANY KEY TO RETURN TO MENU";
2330 CR$=INKEY$:IF CR$="" THEN 2330 ELSE RETURN
2340 'Printer turn on subroutine ****************************
2350 BEEP:PRINTFLAG=1:DF$="*PRINTER ON*":GOSUB 2600:RETURN
2360 BEEP:PRINTFLAG=0:DF$="             ":GOSUB 2600:RETURN
2370 'Start download routine *****************************************
2380 FILENUMBER=FILENUMBER +1:X$=STR$(FILENUMBER)
2390 X$=RIGHT$(X$,LEN(X$)-1)
2400 FILENAME$="A:DWNLD"+X$+".TXT"
2410 OPEN "O",#3,FILENAME$
2420 DISKFLAG=1:BEEP
2430 DF$="*DOWNLOADING*"
2440 GOSUB 2490
2450 RETURN
2460 'Stop downloading routine ***********************************
2470 BEEP:CLOSE #3:DISKFLAG=0:DF$="             ":GOSUB 2490
2480 RETURN
2490 'Put "Downloading" message on screen ***********************
2510 'Record current cursor line position....
```

```
2520 RC=CSRLIN
2530 'Record current cursor column position....
2540 CC=POS(0)
2550 LOCATE 25,68
2560 PRINT DF$
2570 'Restore cursor to prior position...
2580 LOCATE RC,CC
2590 RETURN
2600 'Put "Printer on" message on screen ***************************
2620 RC=CSRLIN
2630 CC=POS(0)
2640 LOCATE 25,56
2650 PRINT DF$
2660 LOCATE RC,CC
2670 RETURN
9999 'The end of PC-SPEAK.BAS
```

Appendix

PC-SPEAK.BAS
Flow Chart

Contained in this appendix is the flow chart for the simple BASIC communications program PC-SPEAK listed in Appendix E.

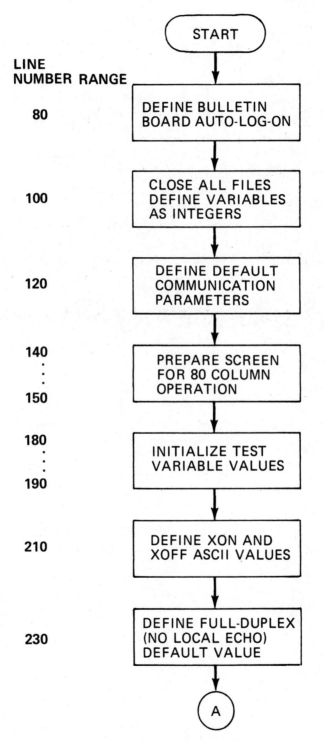

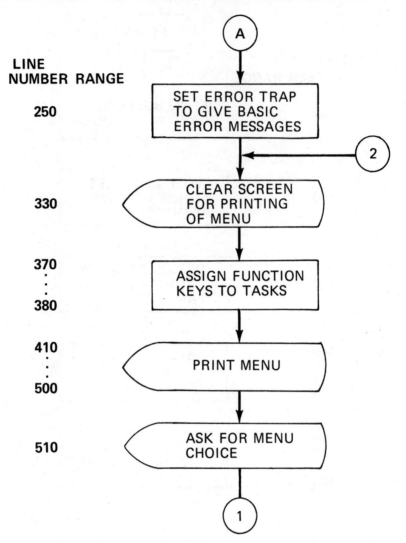

LINE
NUMBER RANGE

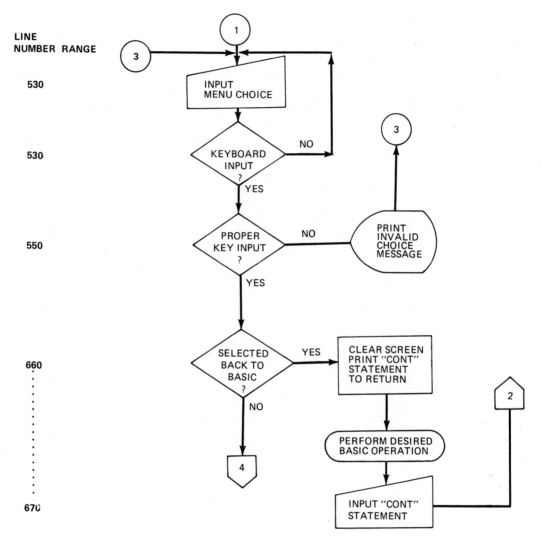

530

530

550

660

670

**LINE
NUMBER RANGE**

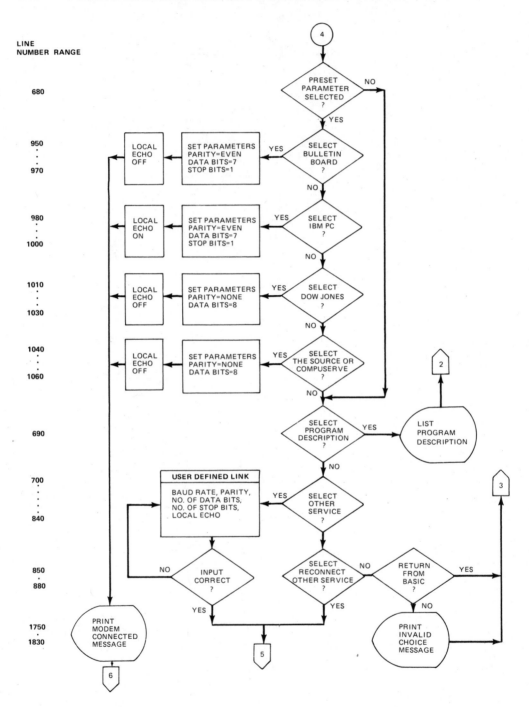

**LINE
NUMBER RANGE**

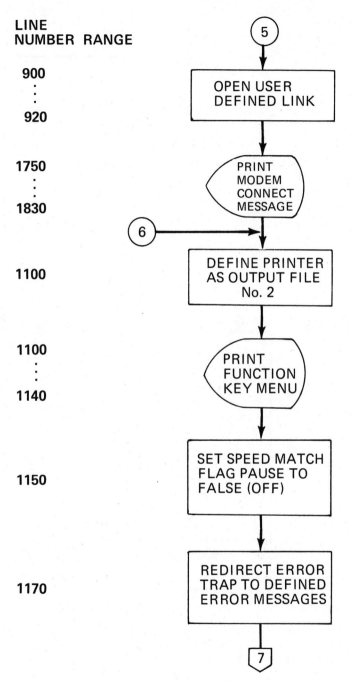

900
.
.
920

1750
.
.
1830

1100

1100
.
.
1140

1150

1170

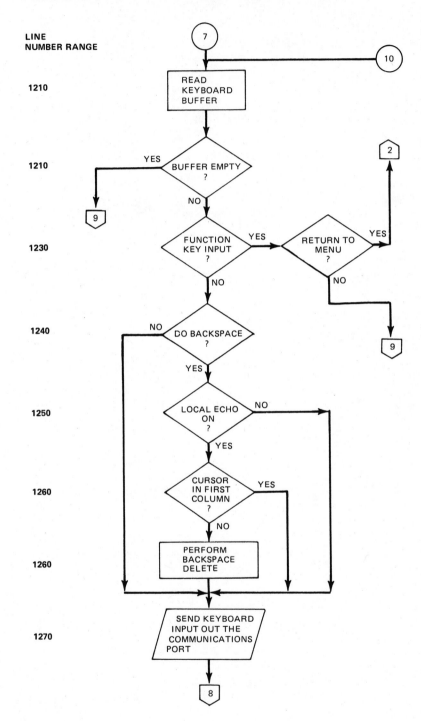

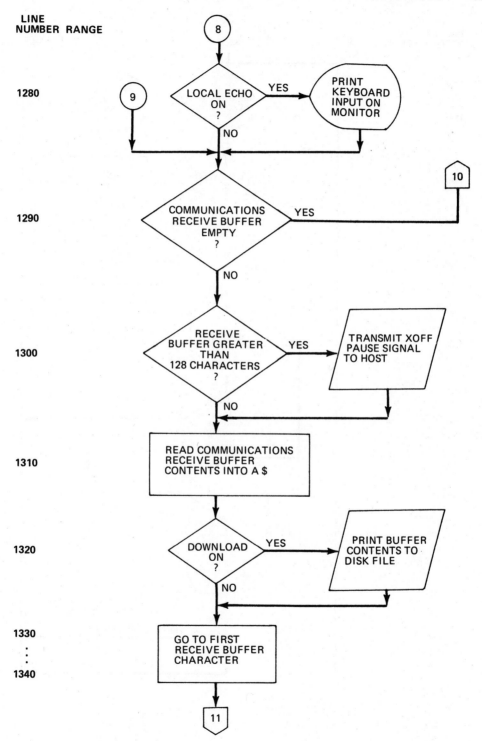

LINE
NUMBER RANGE

8

1280　　LOCAL ECHO ON ?　YES → PRINT KEYBOARD INPUT ON MONITOR

9

NO

10

1290　　COMMUNICATIONS RECEIVE BUFFER EMPTY ?　YES

NO

1300　　RECEIVE BUFFER GREATER THAN 128 CHARACTERS ?　YES → TRANSMIT XOFF PAUSE SIGNAL TO HOST

NO

1310　　READ COMMUNICATIONS RECEIVE BUFFER CONTENTS INTO A $

1320　　DOWNLOAD ON ?　YES → PRINT BUFFER CONTENTS TO DISK FILE

NO

1330
⋮
1340　　GO TO FIRST RECEIVE BUFFER CHARACTER

11

LINE
NUMBER RANGE

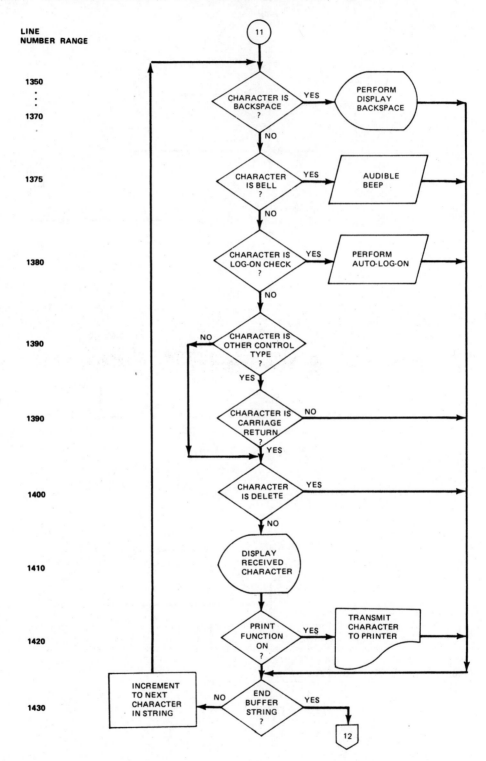

**LINE
NUMBER RANGE**

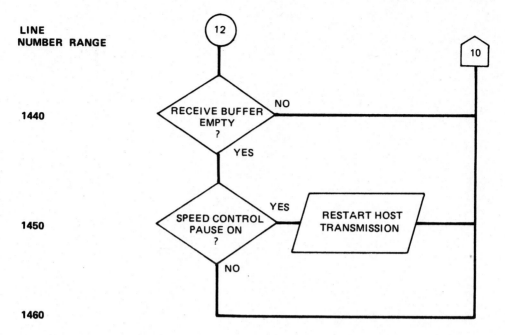

1440

1450

1460

Index